IMAGES
of America

CAPITAL REGION MOTORCYCLING

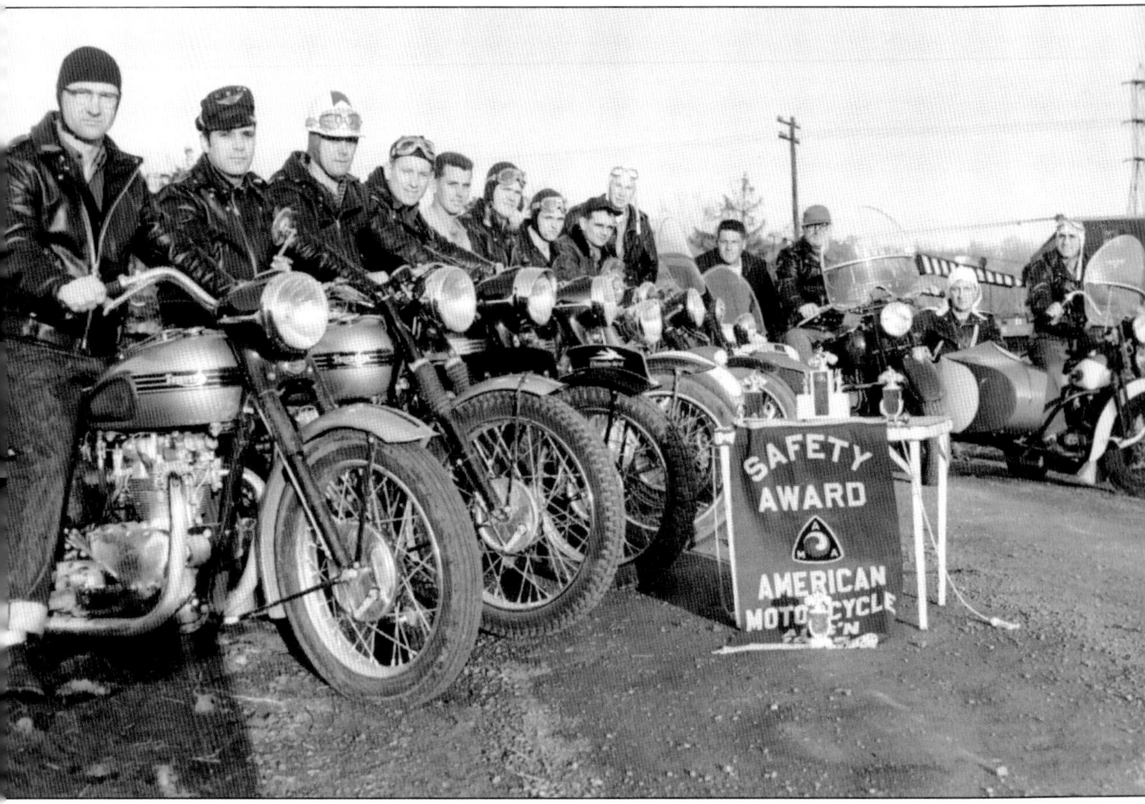

Electric City Riders receive the American Motorcycle Association Safe Rider Award for 1957. The award was given to clubs that had a safe riding record in the previous year. The riders are, from the left to right, Joe Debie, Bob Newell, Howard Newell, Kenny Finch, Conrad Rapant, Dick Debie, Wayne Hovey, George Friskey, Clint Weast, unidentified, Fred Goodrow, unidentified, and Larry Dagostino. (Larry Dagostino Jr. collection.)

On the Cover: The Schenectady Motorcycle Club lines up on State Street in front of the Citizens Trust bank. As motorcycles became more popular, clubs were formed that were more brand specific, such as the Indian Riders Club and the Harley-Davidson Enthusiasts. (The Effner collection.)

IMAGES
of America

CAPITAL REGION MOTORCYCLING

Mark A. Supley
Foreword by Ron Hedger

ARCADIA
PUBLISHING

ISBN 978-1-4671-2222-1

Published by Arcadia Publishing
Charleston, South Carolina

Printed in the United States of America

Library of Congress Control Number: 2014932360

For all general information, please contact Arcadia Publishing:
Telephone 843-853-2070
Fax 843-853-0044
E-mail sales@arcadiapublishing.com
For customer service and orders:
Toll-Free 1-888-313-2665

Visit us on the Internet at www.arcadiapublishing.com

To my motorcycling companion and wife, Paula, and to all the early riders who made this book possible

Contents

FOREWORD

I met Mark Supley through his father, Bob, who always attends my wildly popular Lost Speedways programs at the Saratoga Automobile Museum.

The Supleys are both ardent racing fans and knew me through my writing for *National Speed Sport News*, *Stock Car*, *Open Wheel*, and *Speedway Illustrated* magazines and the *Schenectady Gazette*. As I came to know them, it became apparent that while Mark liked auto racing, his primary reason for living is motorcycle racing in all its shapes and forms.

From there, becoming my resident expert on all things motorcycle was a quick and, for my audience, providential jump. Each summer, fans and racers at the region's speedways bombard me with questions about the upcoming Lost Speedways, and the number one question is always some variation of "What's that crazy motorcycle guy going to talk about this year?"

Mark has raced scrambles, competed on area short tracks and on the region's frozen lakes with both racing bikes and a sidecar, has done sand drags, hill climbs, and has even tried observed trials, so he knows what he speaks of when he talks motorcycle racing.

A restoration expert as well, he has used skills honed as an assembler at the huge General Electric facility in Schenectady to restore his 1926 Harley-Davidson to a level that earned him the Antique Motorcycle Club of America's national Best Restored Antique Award, with the gorgeous Harley currently on display at the Motorcyclepedia Museum in Newburgh, New York. Mark's other restorations include a 1975 Kawasaki 250cc Short Tracker and a 1976 Honda 550 Super Sport.

There is no reason to believe that his first book will be any less impressive than his other motorcycle-related accomplishments, because he has lived the stories. Let's get started.

— Ron Hedger

ACKNOWLEDGEMENTS

When I set out to write this book, I thought I had a good Idea of local motorcycle history. As I interviewed more people, everyone had a story to tell. The more the word got out of what I was doing, the more people were willing to share their photographs and memories. I was surprised to hear how the idea of me writing about this topic brought a smile to so many people's faces. Without the following people's assistance and patience, most of these images would not be possible: the Newell family, especially Tim, who shares the same passion for saving local motorcycle history; Mary and Sandy Debie; Jim Romeo; Greg Rickes; the Kvinlaug family, especially Marty for lending his album; Bob "Sprocket" Eckardt, for sharing his collection of race memorabilia, especially of the Saratoga motorcycle races; George "Ricky" Richtmeyer, for loaning me his photographs and bench racing.

Thanks also to Ernie Belanger for his photographs of motorcycle polo; to Marjorie Corbett for donating her late husband Joe's negatives; the Effner History Center in the city hall of Schenectady, New York, especially Cynthia Seacord, the managing archivist, for her patience in finding and reproducing the glass negatives we found.

A special thanks to Larry Dagostino Jr. for allowing me to scan photographs from his father's collection and Randi Hebert, the daughter of Chuck Hebert, one of the top riders of his era, for lending me the family album.

Thanks also to Erv and Dean Splittgerber, the sons of John Splittgerber from Spitzies Harley-Davidson fame.

I greatly appreciate Bob Clough for spending hours scanning hundreds of black-and-white negatives onto CDs to be used in this book.

Finally, thank you to Remy Thurston and Arcadia Publishing for encouraging me on this project. If not for their creative suggestions, I may have been unable to complete this book. A special thank you to my editor, Rebekah Collinsworth, who talked me into continuing when I thought I had taken on more than I had planned.

Introduction

New York and the Capital Region were hotbeds of motorcycle activity at the beginning of the 20th century. With a large industrial base stretching from Albany to Buffalo, New York was home to a large portion of the nation's motorcycle inventors and manufacturers. Many motorized bicycles and motorcycles were built in New York. E.R. Thomas Motor Company of Buffalo started making motorized bicycles in 1901.

Many early designs were innovative and useful, resulting in the production of thousands of New York–built motorcycles.

The Capital Region played a large part in getting riders into the sport. Albany and Schenectady were well-populated cities with decent roads, making motorcycles an attractive option for transportation. Easy day rides to Saratoga and other rural areas made good arguments for owning a motorcycle.

The early motorcycle was priced within reach of the common man, allowing for many young men to explore outlying areas that they could not access before.

Since the invention of the motorcycle, one brand would try to outdo the other to improve sales. Also, one man would try to outperform the other to show who was the best rider.

The motorcycle never took hold the way its supporters had hoped. In part, this is because the motorcycle demanded interaction from its rider. Early machines needed assistance from their riders by pedaling up inclines that were too steep for the underpowered engines. A certain type of person took to the motorcycle, one that was not discouraged by the dust and oil thrown up by the unimproved roads of the time.

With the invention of Ford's Model T in 1910, the motorcycle became a seasonal recreational vehicle. Fortunately for the motorcycle industry, people still enjoy the thrill of riding a motorcycle on or off the road.

Initially, companionship was the reason to get together with the same interest in mind. Clubs were formed to encourage others to ride or compete.

This book highlights some of the many activities that went on during the 20th century involving the motorcycle and its many characters. In essence, *Capital Region Motorcycling* is a snapshot of the sport at its height of popularity. Hopefully the various images prove to be useful and entertaining and, most importantly, lead to an appreciation for the rich history of the motorcycle hobby.

One

The Early Days

The sport of motorcycling got its start in the early part of the 20th century. The popularity grew each year with the introduction of bigger and better machines. This was a time of much experimentation as to where to mount the engine, what kind of valve train was needed, and what kind of suspension would be best. Many of the features commonly found on today's motorcycles were conceived in the early 1900s but were not used due to cost or availability of quality materials.

From the beginning, the motorcycle was used not only for transportation but for racing and sport as well. The interest in racing drove the companies to not only design bigger and faster machines but to also make them more reliable. By 1912, all the larger motorcycle companies, like Indian, Reading Standard, Flying Merkel, Emblem, Excelsior, and Cyclone, were fielding racing bikes, on both dirt and board tracks. Prior to World War I in 1914, there were over 200 companies manufacturing motorcycles in the United States.

The first group to organize riders was the Federation of American Motorcyclists (FAM) in 1917. It disbanded in 1919 and was replaced by the Motorcycle and Allied Trades Association (M&ATA). The American Motorcycle Association was formed in 1924 and continues today to organize both road and competition activities.

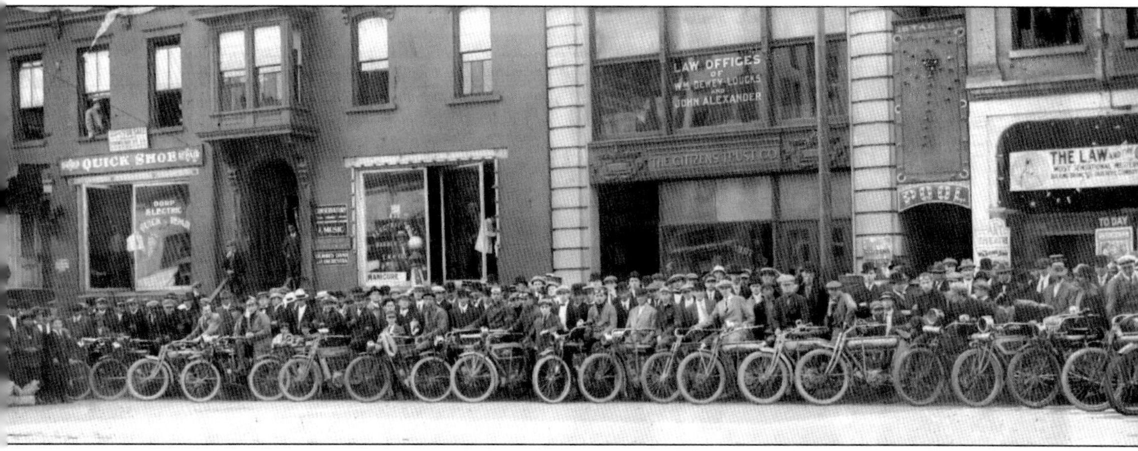

The Schenectady Motorcycle Club is lined up in front of the Art Theater on State Street in 1913 for a showing of *The Wartime Siren*. The coming attraction is *The Law and the Outlaw*, starring Tom Mix and billed as "the most sensational western ever produced." Notice the large crowd of onlookers meeting the riders. (The Effner collection.)

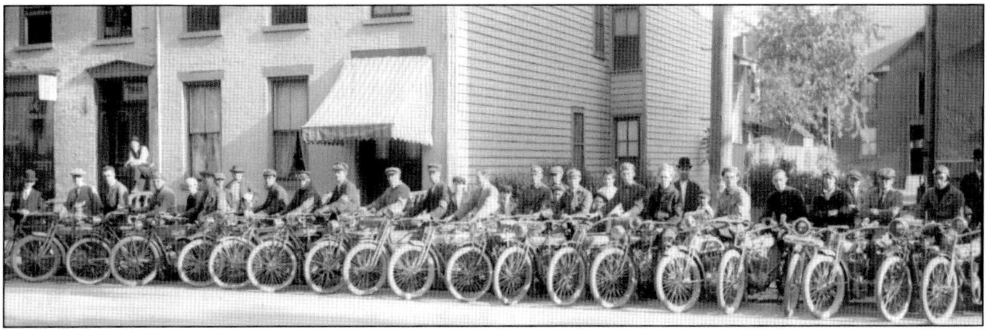

The Schenectady Motorcycle Club poses on Erie Boulevard in front of the Schenectady Motorcycle and Bicycle Repair store. The store sold Eagle and M+M brand motorcycles, as well as Warren automobiles. The club consisted of motorcycles from Eagle, Indian, Harley-Davidson, Thor, and Yale. (The Effner collection.)

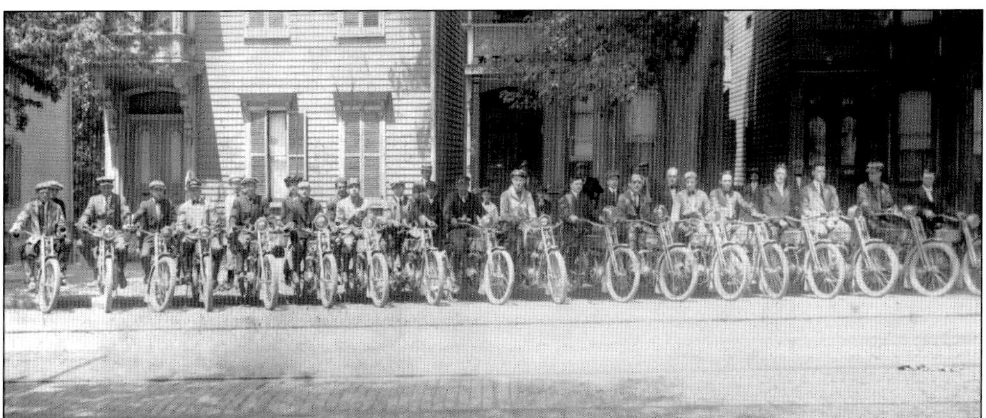

The Harley-Davidson Club of Schenectady lines up with their bikes on Union Street alongside the trolley tracks. After a run of 80 years, the trolleys were overtaken by buses and cars. They were discontinued in 1946. (The Effner collection.)

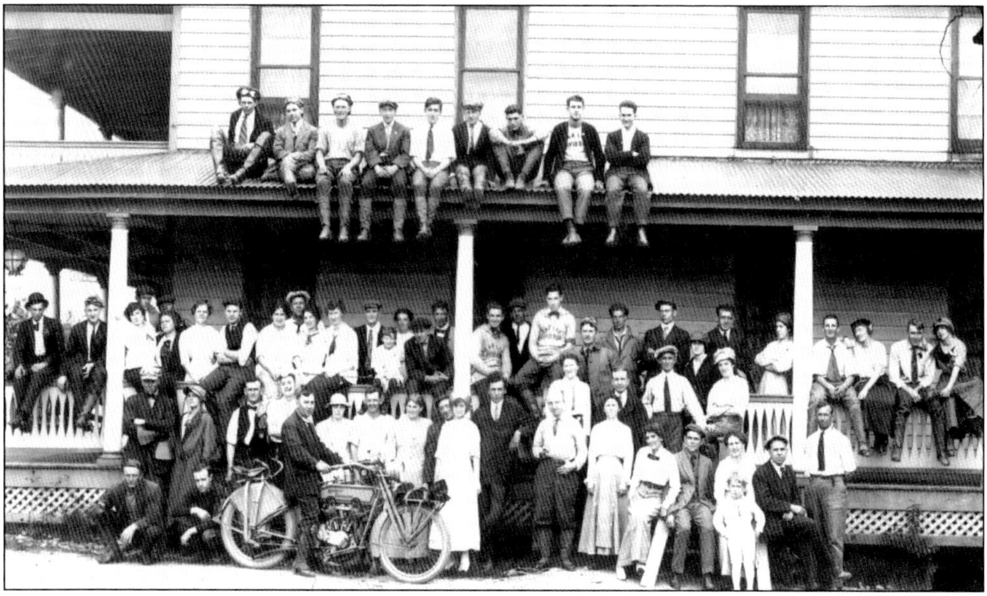

The Harley-Davidson Club poses for a photograph at an undisclosed hotel. The club was family oriented. Notice the passenger seat on this 1915 Harley-Davidson motorcycle; it must have been an uncomfortable ride. (The Effner collection.)

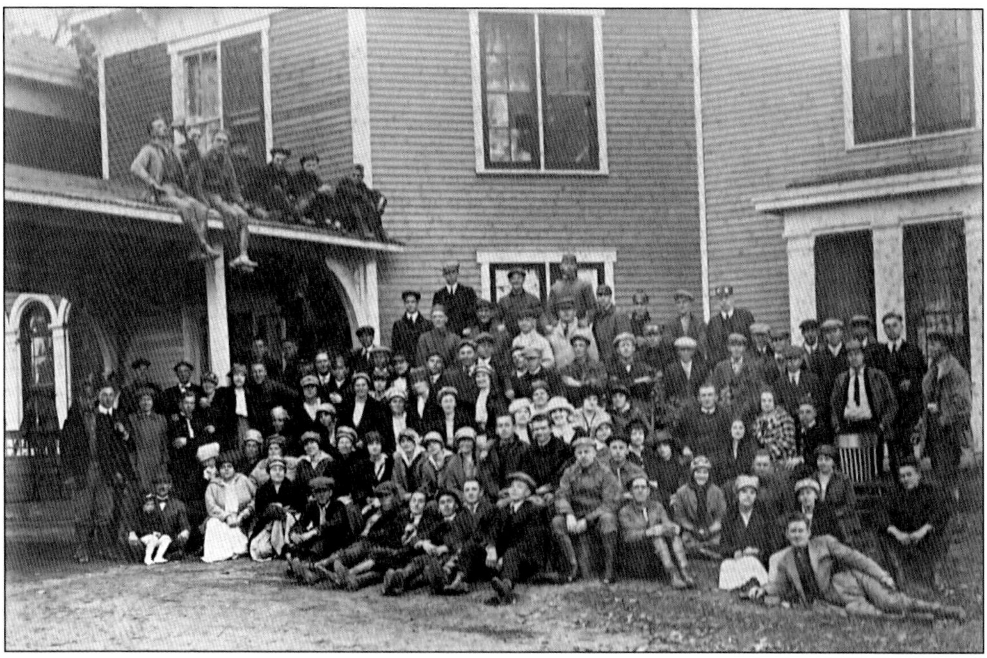

A group of Harley-Davidson riders meets for the annual Harley Grin event on September 24, 1916. The location is believed to be in Saratoga. The man on the roof is getting a head start on the festivities. (Bob Eckardt collection.)

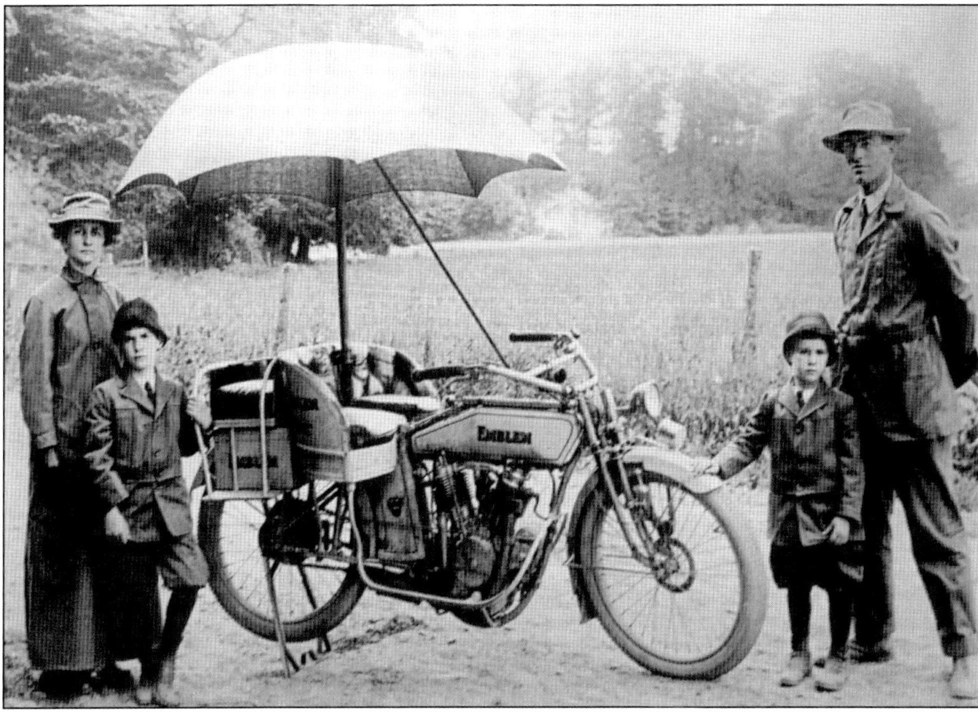

Maurice Gale became known for tackling long-distance rides by himself and at times with his wife, Mattie, and his kids all aboard specially modified machines that he used to promote the Emblem Manufacturing Company. In 1913, Gale braved January cold and snow on a 500-mile ride through Schenectady to New York City to display his machine in the New York Motorcycle Show. The trip through rain, sleet, and snow took four days. (New York State Museum.)

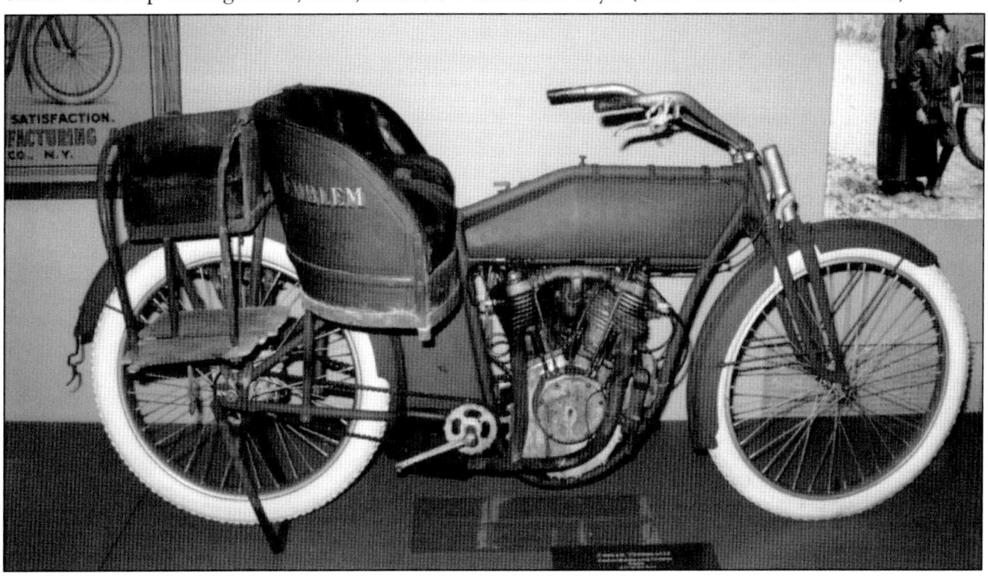

In 1914, one of the Gales' four-up journeys took the family to Saratoga, New York, for a Federation of American Motorcyclists (FAM) meeting. Out of 1,150 motorcyclists in attendance, the Gales were the most remarkable. This meeting corresponded with the motorcycle races held at the Saratoga horse track. (Photograph by the author.)

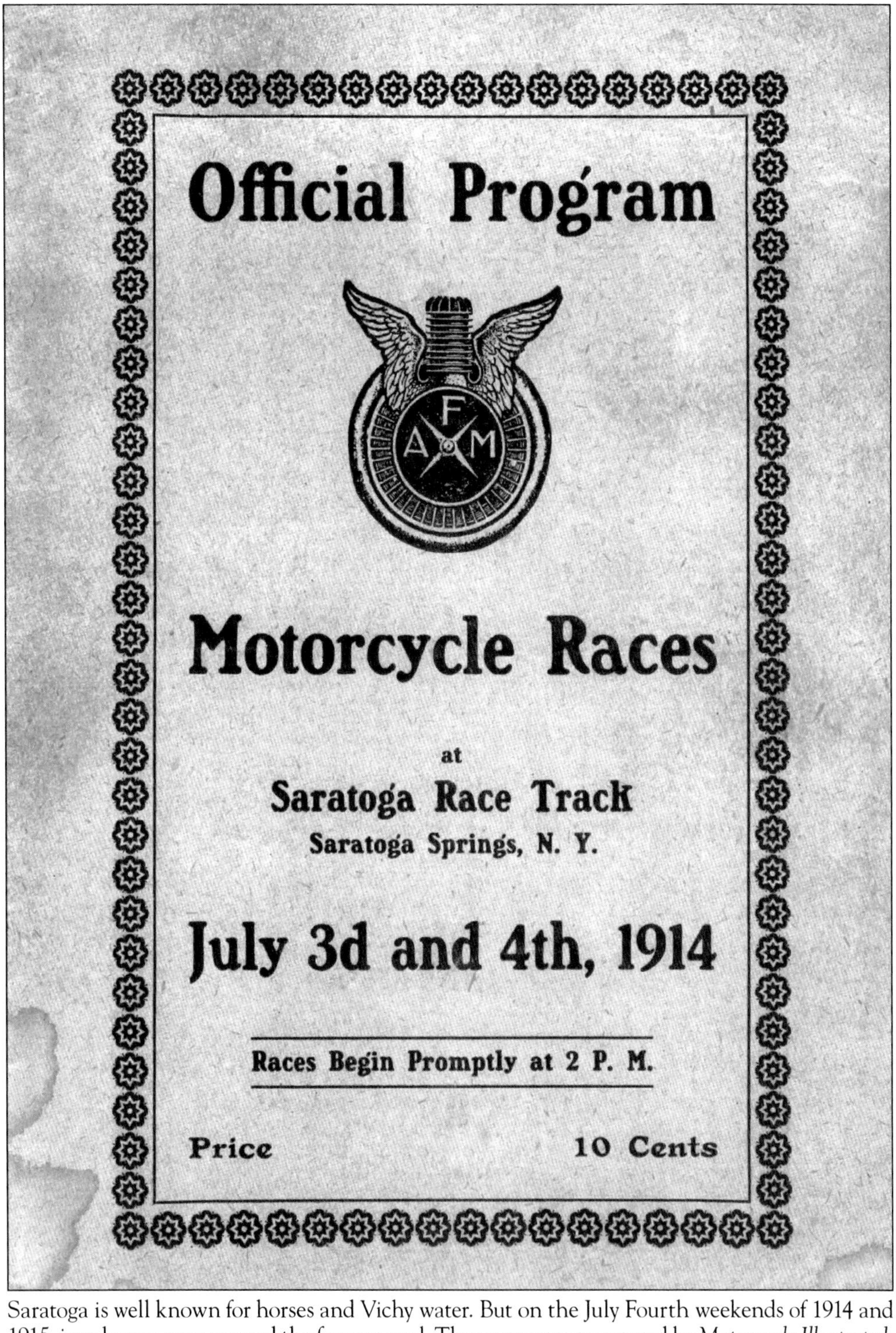

Saratoga is well known for horses and Vichy water. But on the July Fourth weekends of 1914 and 1915, iron horses spun around the famous oval. The races were sponsored by *Motorcycle Illustrated*, who paid the Saratoga Racing Association one half of the take from the gate for the privilege of using the track. (Bob Eckardt collection.)

A medal was given to every rider attending the 1914 races by *Motorcyclist Illustrated* magazine. These medals and other memorabilia are highly sought after today. (Bob Eckardt collection.)

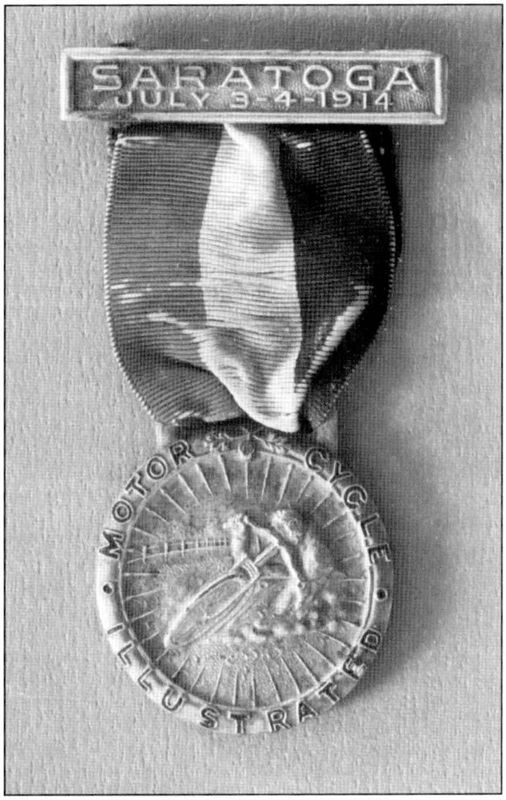

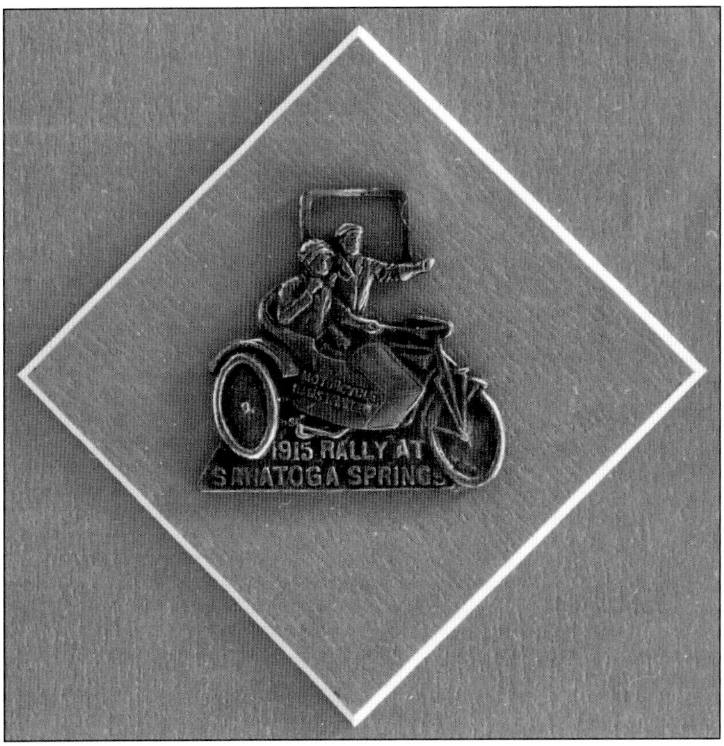

In 1915, each rider received a key fob. The publisher of *Motorcycle Illustrated*, J.L. Sauer, was impressed with the overwhelming success of the venue. He said the meet "demanded not only a repetition but institution as an annual affair." But it was not to be; the outbreak of World War I put an end to the races. (Bob Eckardt collection.)

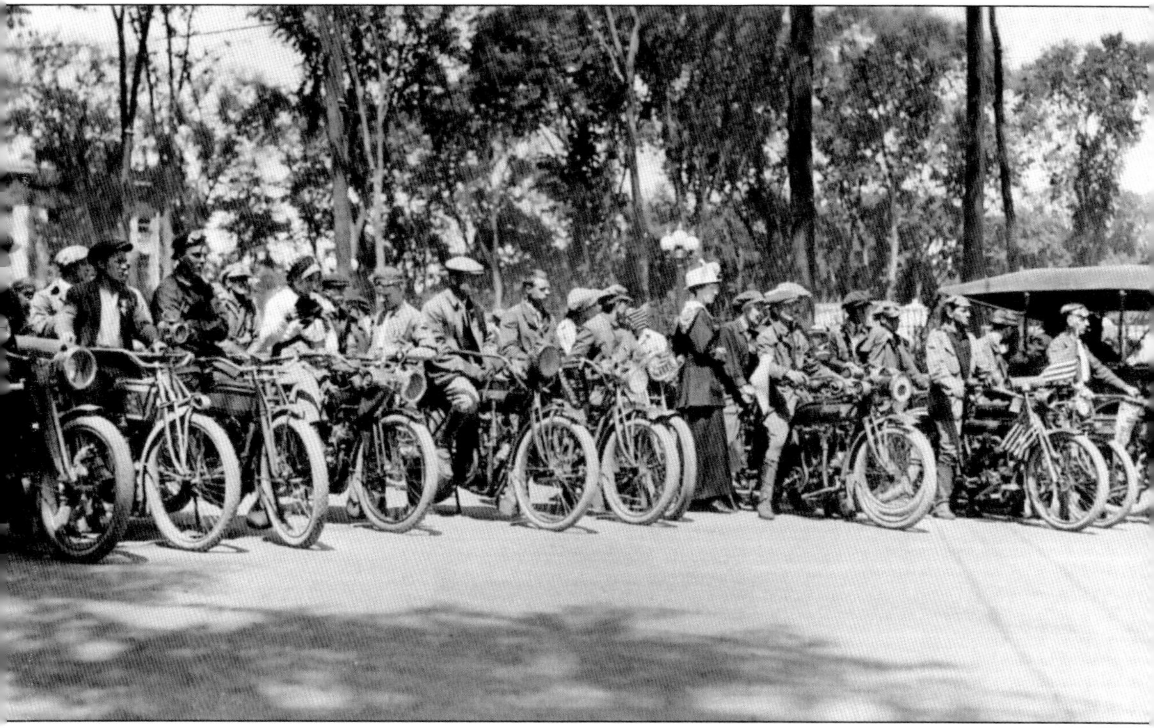

On both Friday and Saturday during the race meet, held on Independence weekend, Broadway was filled with motorcyclists in motor garb. The visitors were, for the most part, young people and did not hesitate to let loose their holiday excitement. (Courtesy of Michael Noonan.)

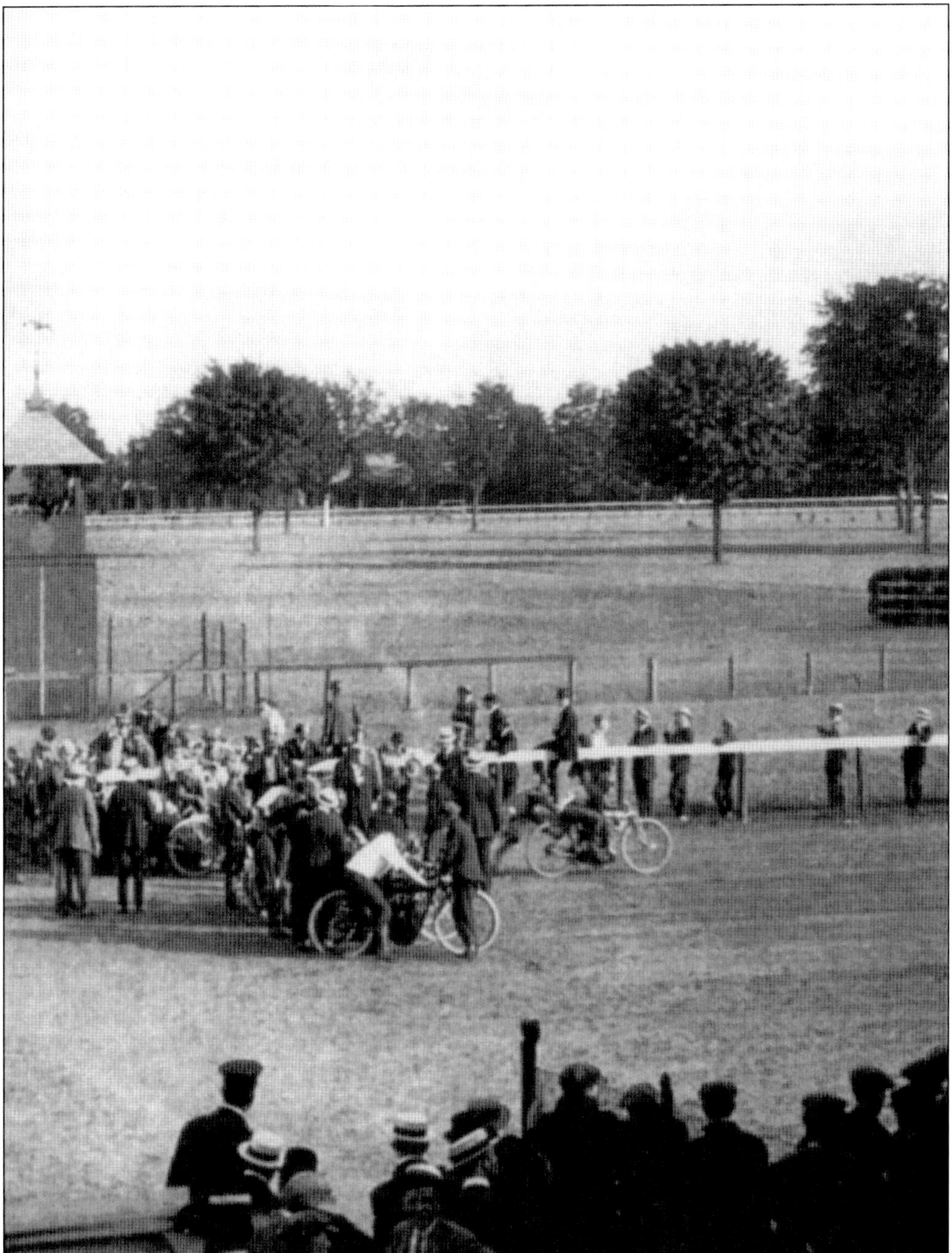

Riders prepare for the start of one of the races at the Saratoga Race Course. The bikes had to be pushed to start back then. The riders would be riding side by side when the starter waved the flag; this was called a flying start. (Bob Eckardt collection.)

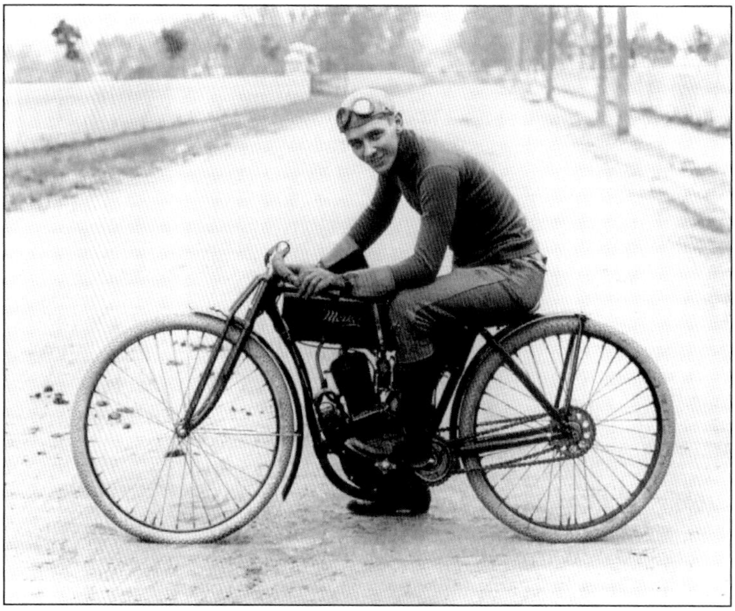

One of the amateur riders is preparing to compete on his Flying Merkel machine. These machines had total-loss oil systems, meaning the oil went through the engine and onto the ground. Also, there were no mufflers or brakes. They were built for speed. (Bob Eckhardt collection.)

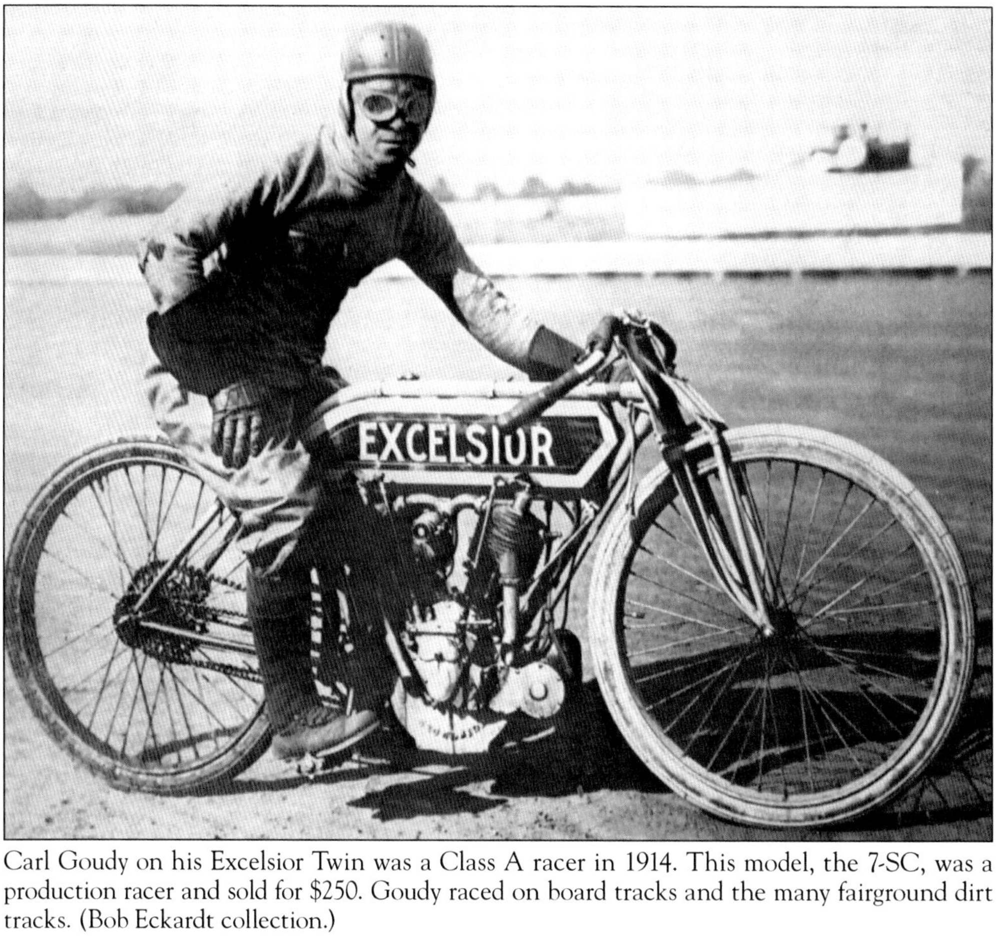

Carl Goudy on his Excelsior Twin was a Class A racer in 1914. This model, the 7-SC, was a production racer and sold for $250. Goudy raced on board tracks and the many fairground dirt tracks. (Bob Eckardt collection.)

Jim Davis was a Harley-Davidson–sponsored rider. He won the 1915 Professional Race at Saratoga on the "oldest race track in America." Davis went on to have a long and successful career and became a starter at many events. Davis was one of the few racers to survive this tumultuous era; he lived to be 100 years old. (Courtesy of the Harley-Davidson Company.)

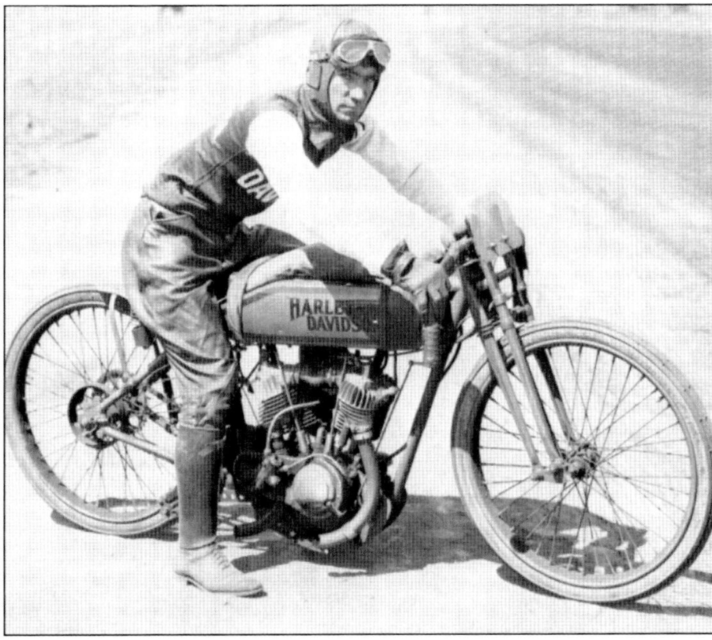

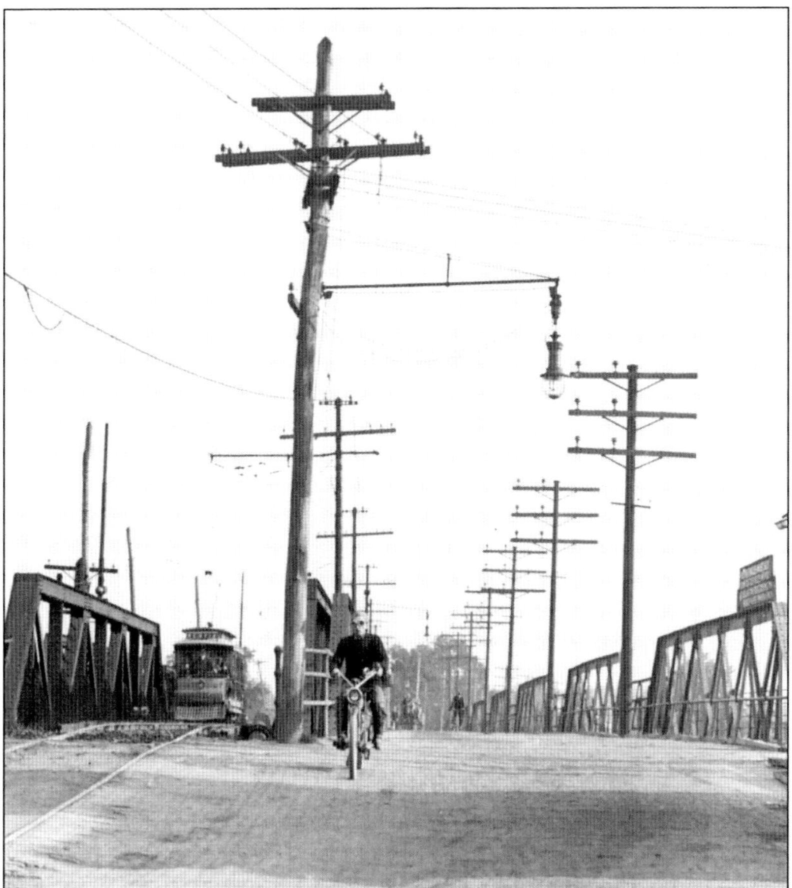

A trolley and motorcycle cross the Scotia iron bridge from the Schenectady end of Washington Avenue. This bridge was replaced by the Western Gateway Bridge in 1926. The old bridge abutments are still visible today. (Photograph by John Papp.)

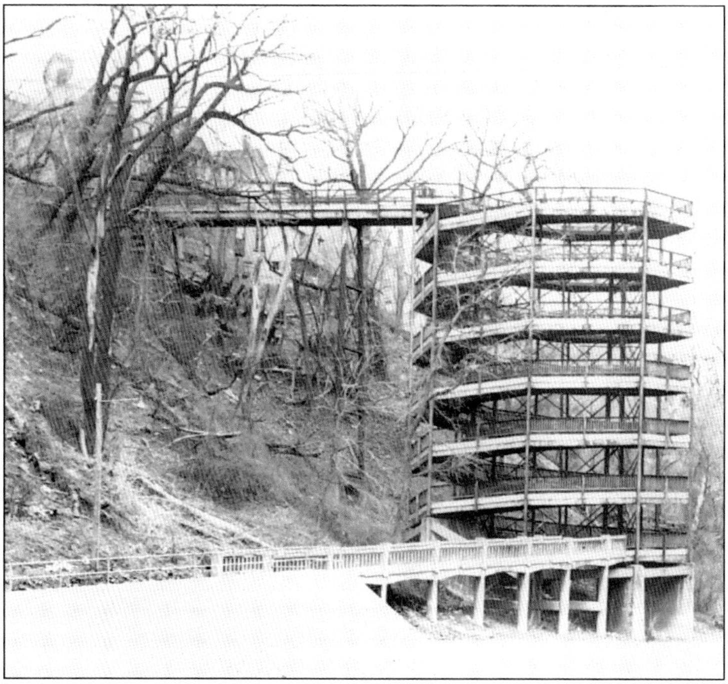

The Seven Heavens was a spiral pedestrian ramp built in the mid-1930s to accommodate the General Electric employees going to work. It was so cold in the winter that it was called "the Klondike." With the winds howling through the valley, people said it was like being in Alaska's Klondike region. Remains of the lower ramp are still visible along I-890 near Broadway. (Effner Collection.)

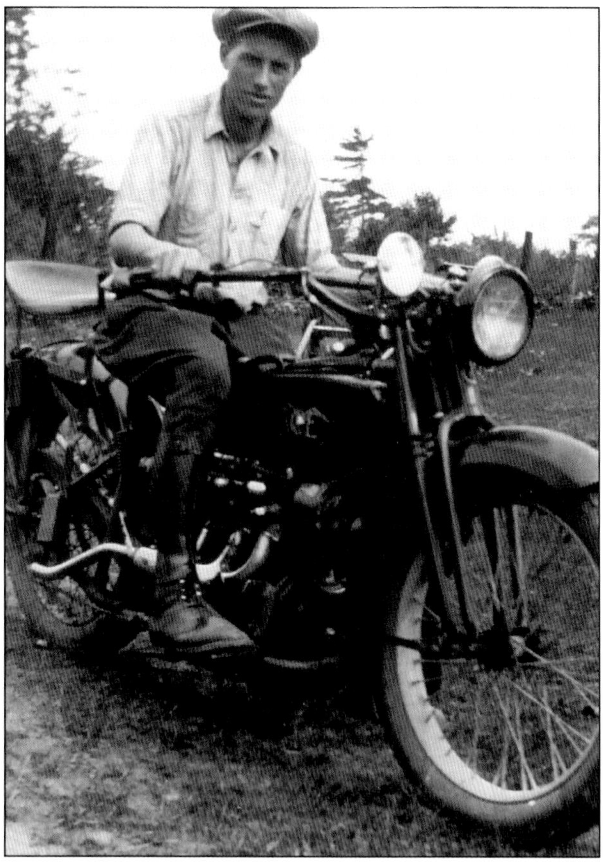

Albert Ellis grew up in the Hungry Hill section of Schenectady. His claim to fame was that he rode his motorcycle three abreast down the Seven Heavens pedestrian ramp. Albert's motorcycle is a four-cylinder Ace. The Ace Company existed from 1919 to 1924, when the Indian Motorcycle Company purchased it. (Ellis family collection.)

Two

Motorcycle Polo

Motorcycle polo got its start in the 1920s. It was played like soccer, except with motorcycles. The term "polo" was used to elevate the status of the game, because polo was considered the "sport of kings." Teams were formed in numerous cities on the East Coast, like Trenton and Atlantic City, New Jersey, and Philadelphia and Reading, Pennsylvania. Closer to home, there were clubs in Albany, Schenectady, and Amsterdam. The clubs belonged to the Eastern Motopolo League and traveled to different cities to compete.

While motorcycle polo faded out by the 1950s in the United States, it remained popular in Europe, where it is still played today.

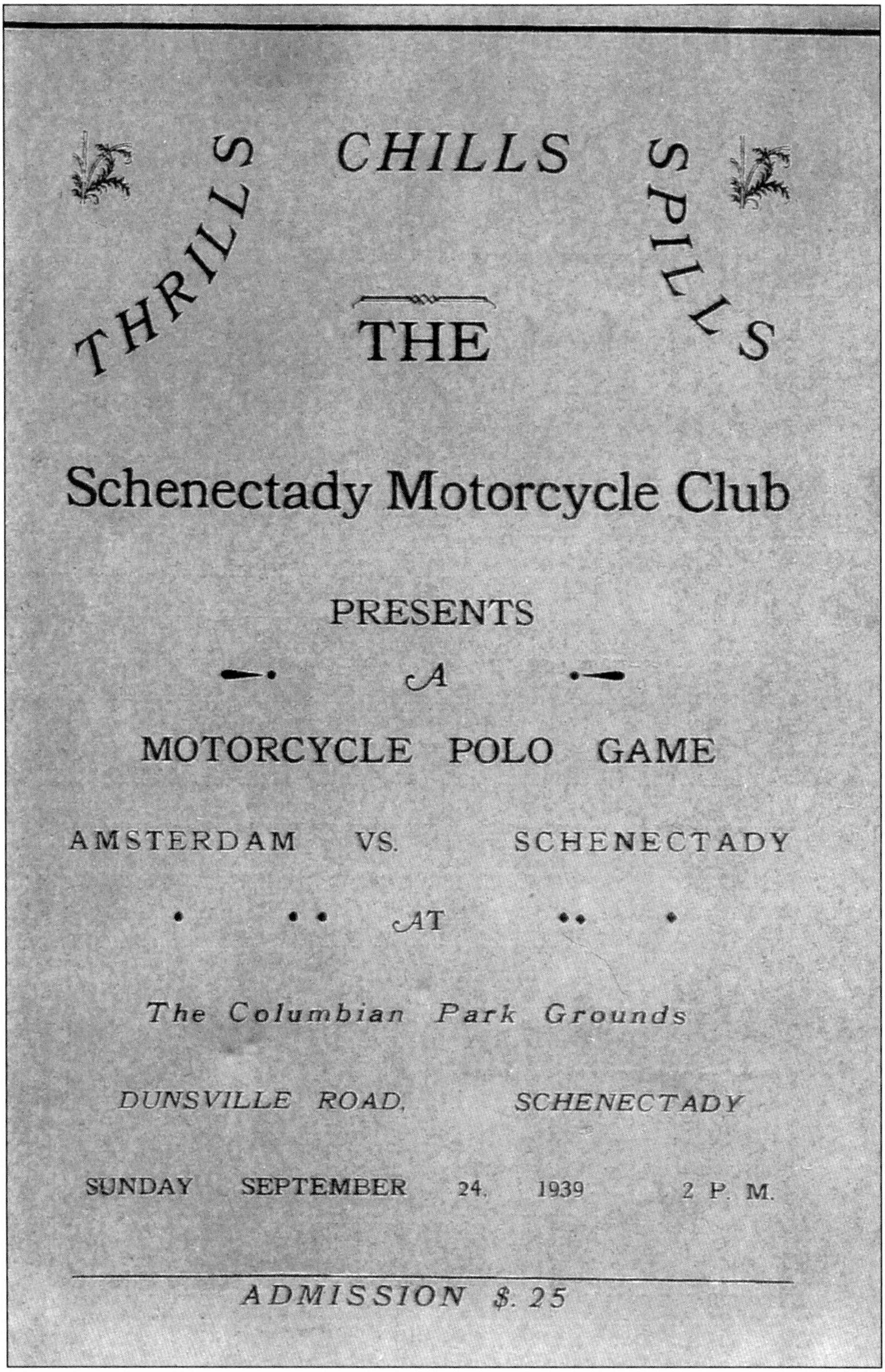

The Schenectady Motorcycle Club presented a motorcycle polo game in 1939. Motorcycle polo was really like playing soccer, as no clubs were used to move the ball. The polo grounds where this event was held are now a park, located on Dunsville Road before the thruway overpass. (Larry Dagostino Jr. collection.)

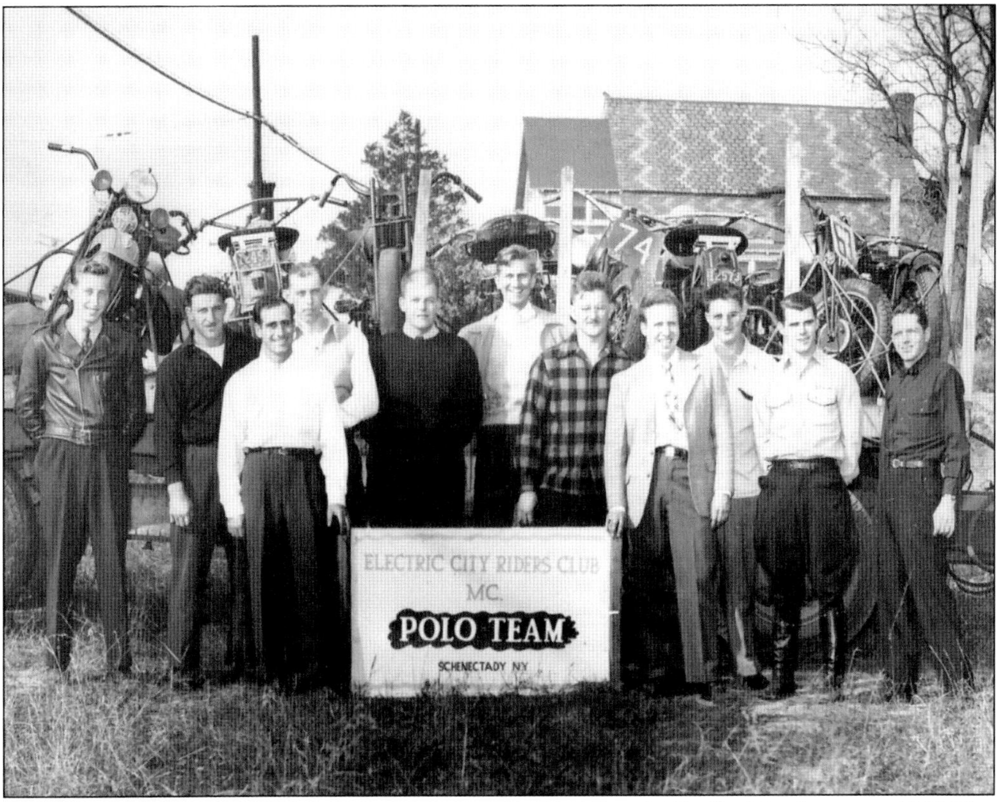

The Electric City Riders polo team prepares for competition in Millville, New Jersey, in 1947. The Electric City Riders formed in 1943. Their main purpose was to act as a civil defense messenger service, on standby to deliver messages during wartime. Initially, the club only promoted organized road-riding tours. From left to right, the members are Glen Brust, the unidentified truck driver, Larry Dagostino, Clint Weast, Charlie Smith, George Herold, Ed Krunis, Bob Jetter, Chet Van Atten, Howard Newell, and Bob Pudvah. (Larry Dagostino Jr. collection.)

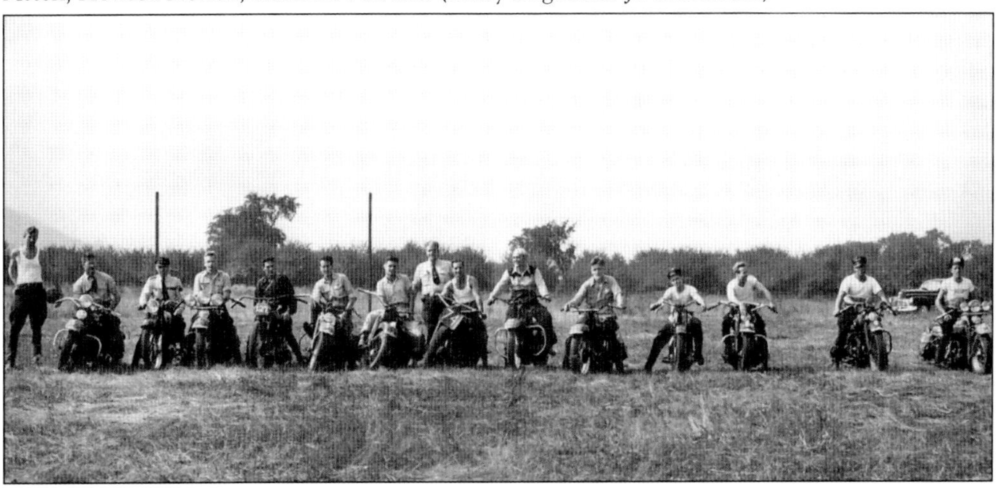

The Electric City Riders polo team lines up prior to a game at the Columbian Park polo grounds on Dunsville Road in Rotterdam. The Electric City Riders became New York State champions in 1947. (Photograph by Ernie Belanger.)

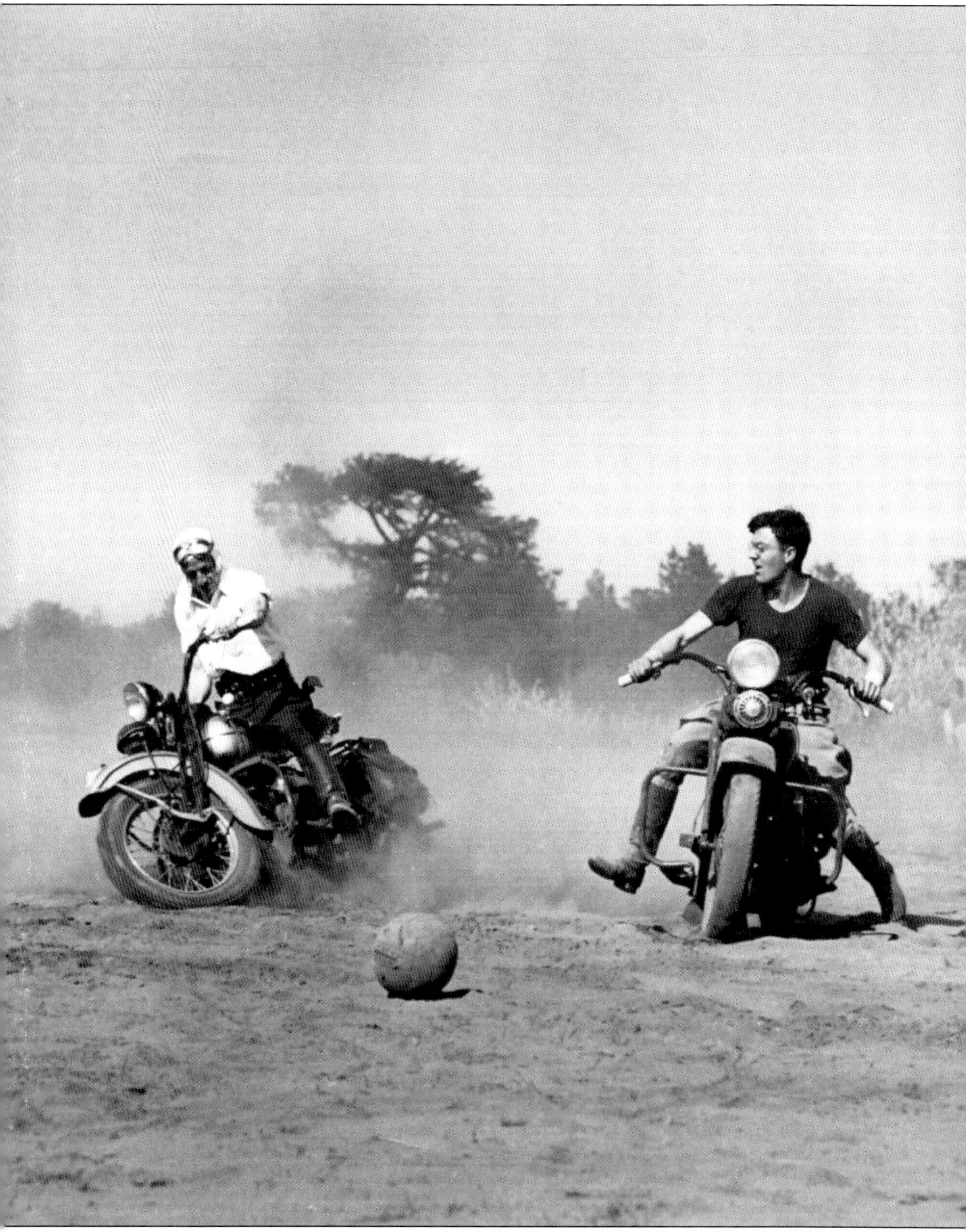

Two contestants battle for the ball in this image. Notice that the motorcycles are basically road bikes, headlights and saddlebags still attached. The rider on the right is Ed Schoonmaker. (Photograph by Ernie Belanger.)

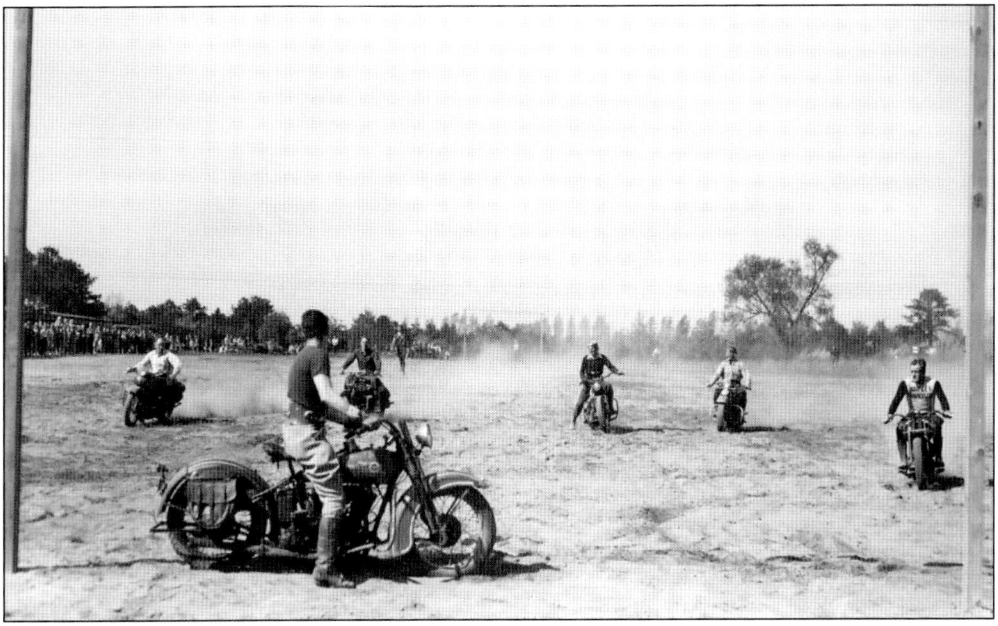

The goalie, Ed Schoonmaker, is ready as the riders prepare for a shot. John Splittgerber is on the right, trying to help block the shot from the opposing team. (Photograph by Ernie Belanger.)

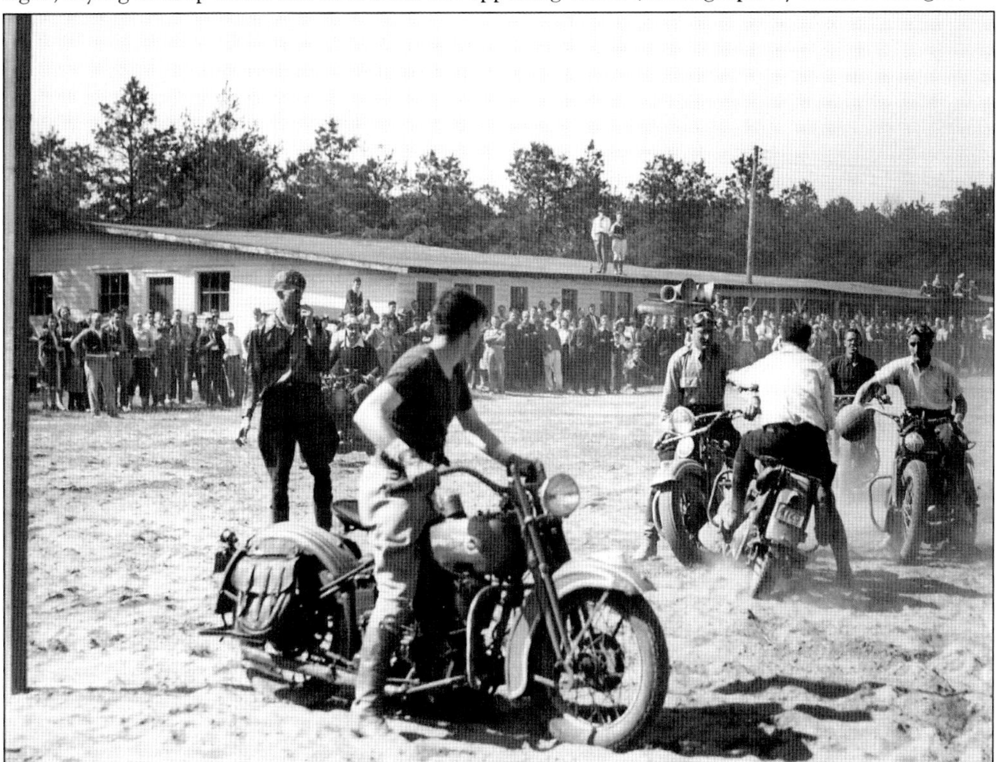

With the ball in midair, four riders are jammed and the referee prepares to whistle for a toss-up. With the ball so near, the goalie is on edge. A large crowd was on hand at the Columbian Park grounds to witness the excitement. (Photograph by Ernie Belanger.)

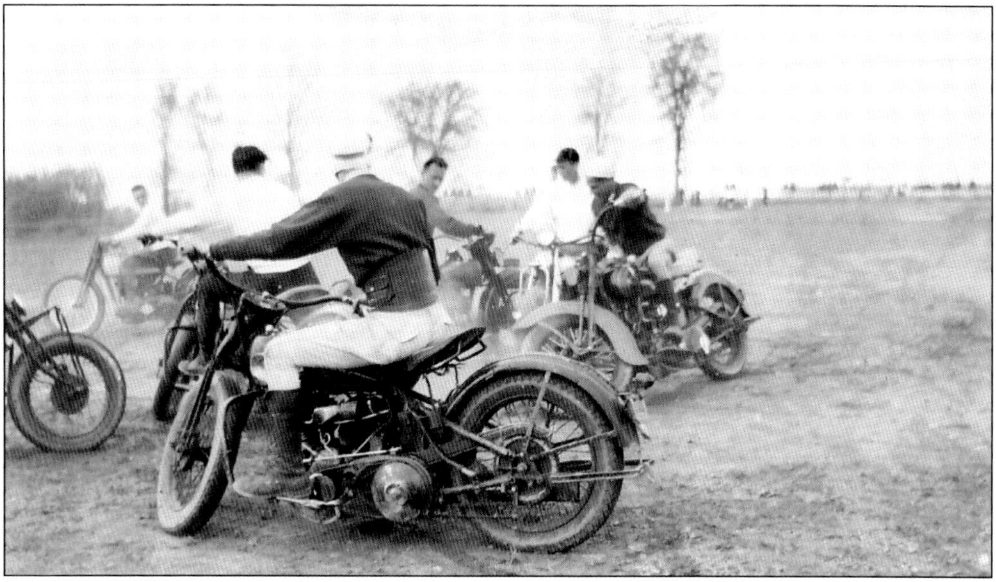

A group of riders converges on the ball at Patricks Field on Guy Park Avenue in Amsterdam. The Amsterdam Motorcycle Club, which later became the Mohawk Valley Riders, also fielded a polo team. (Erv Splittgerber collection.)

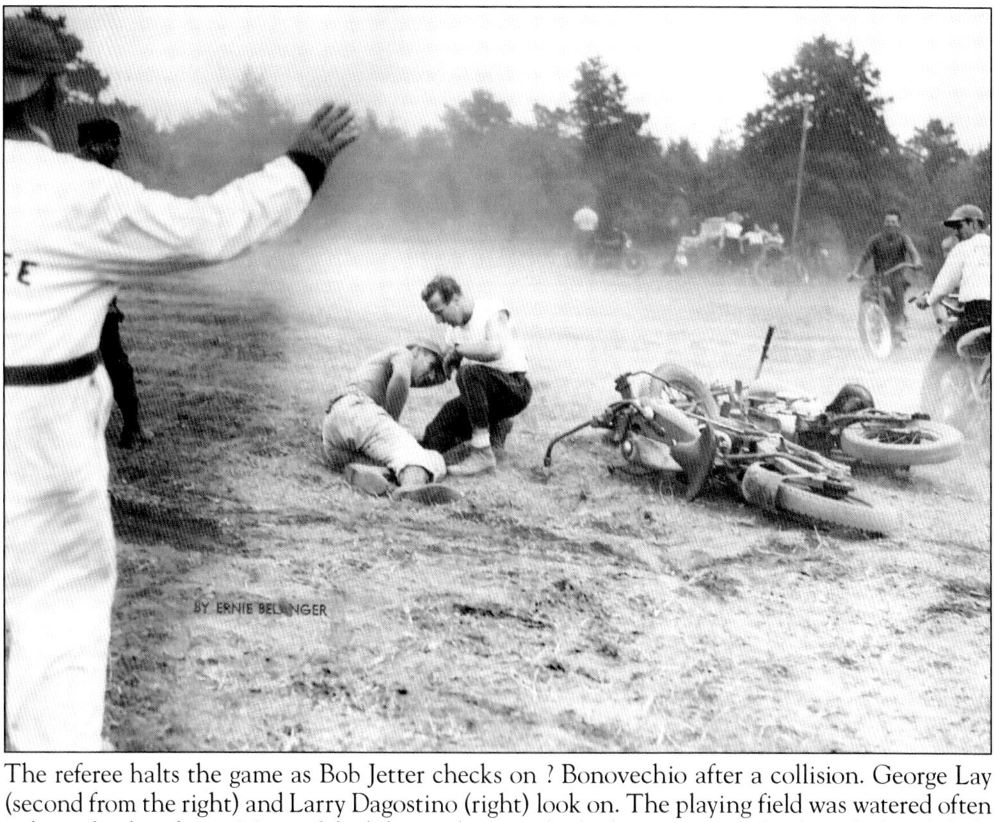

The referee halts the game as Bob Jetter checks on ? Bonovechio after a collision. George Lay (second from the right) and Larry Dagostino (right) look on. The playing field was watered often to keep the dust down. Many of the bikes at this time had a foot-operated clutch and a hand shift, making it difficult to maneuver. (Photograph by Ernie Belanger.)

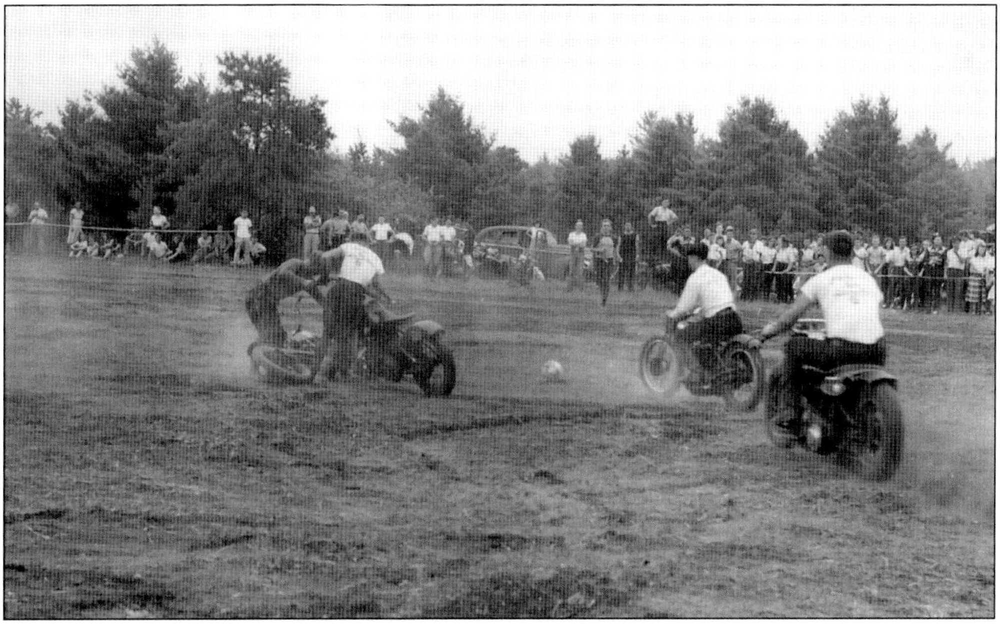

Tangles were commonplace, but injuries were minor as the speeds were low. Polo demanded good slow-speed bike handling. Road-riding clubs would ride out to the event to enjoy the day with other riders. (Photograph by Ernie Belanger.)

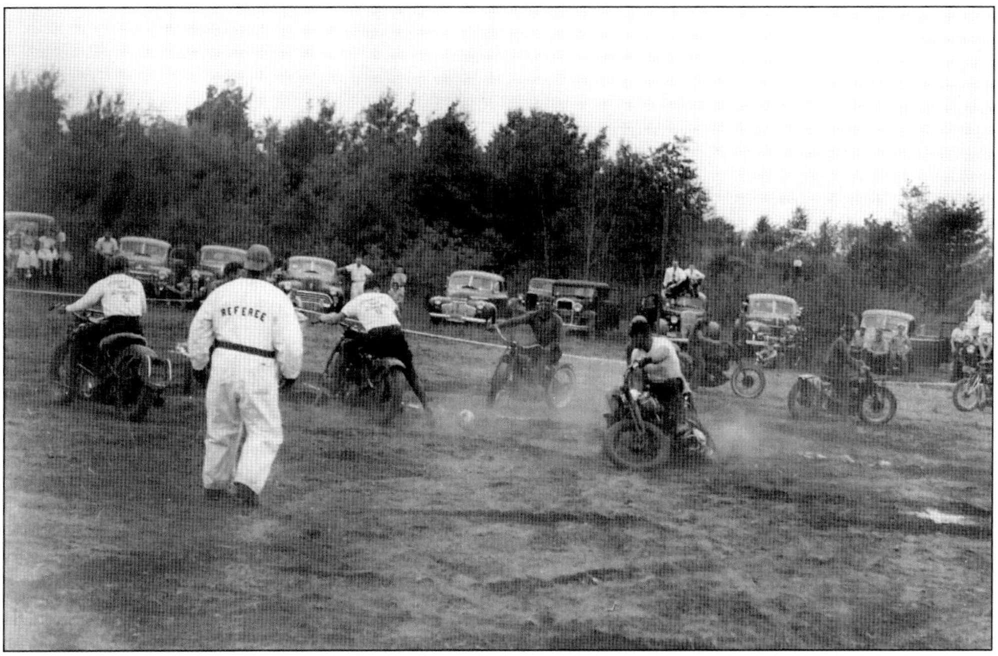

Other polo fields in the area were at Empire Speedway in Menands and on Route 50 in Glenville, at the site of the current Price Chopper. There was also a field at McNearney's Stadium, which was the home of the Schenectady Blue Jays baseball team until 1957; it is now the location of the Stadium Golf Club. The year 1954 saw the demise of area polo because of blue laws that restricted any paying events on Sunday. The last local event was held at the Empire Speedway in Menands. (Photograph by Ernie Belanger.)

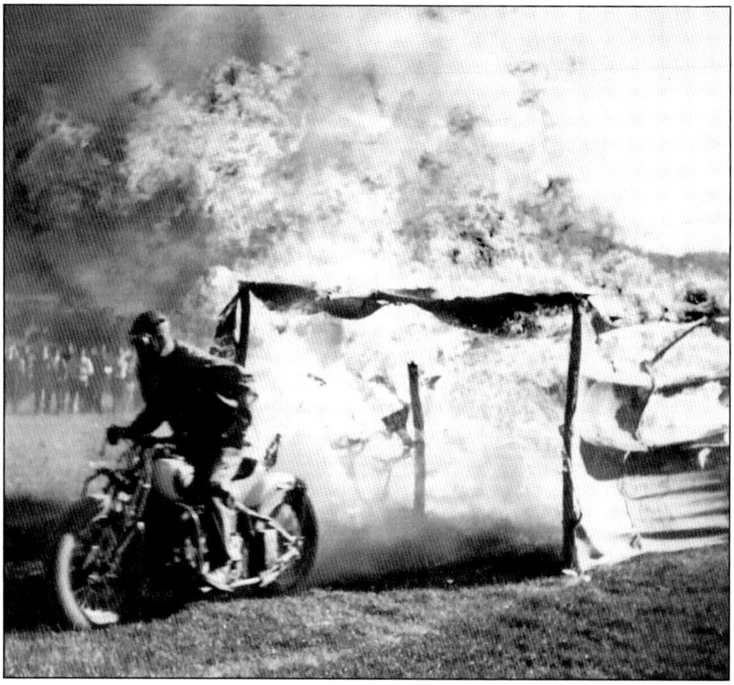

During an intermission at one of the polo events, an unidentified rider goes through the tunnel of fire on an Indian motorcycle. He would also ride through a glass wall. During World War II, the club painted the glass with a portrait of Hitler and wrote "To Hell with Hitler." The crowd cheered loudly as the rider crashed through it. (Larry Dagostino Jr. collection.)

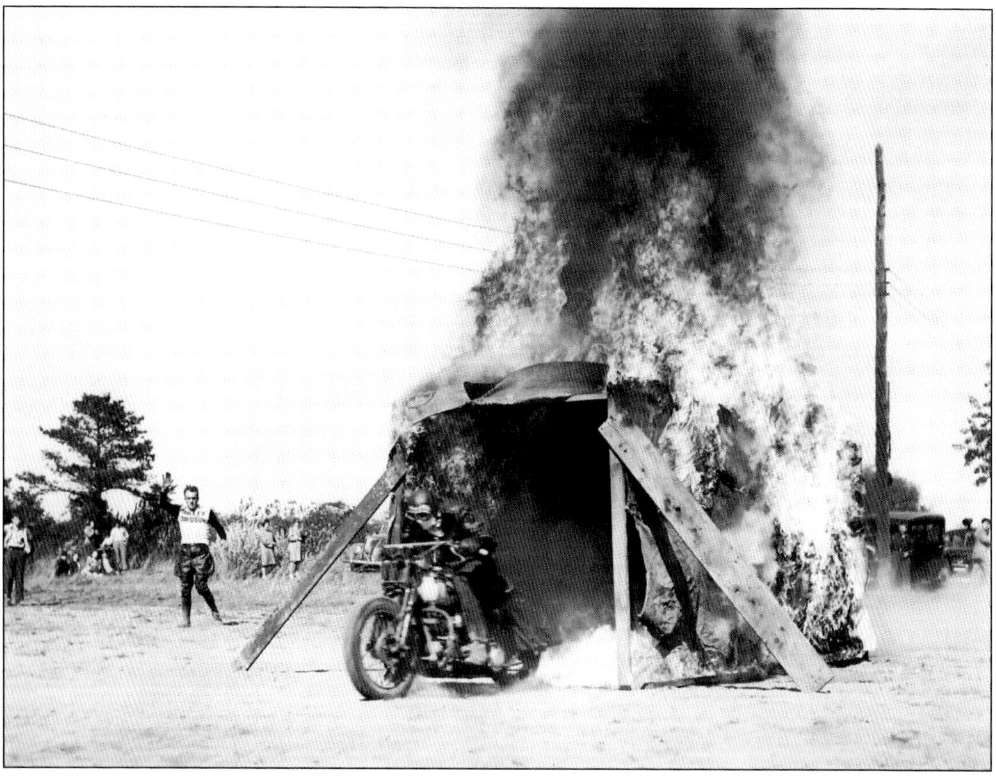

Ed Schoonmaker goes through the tunnel of fire as John Splittgerber looks on. Riders would jump through hoops of fire and crash through a wooden wall of fire to entertain the crowd. (Julie Debie collection.)

Three

Hill Climbing

Hill climbing has been a popular form of motorcycle competition for over 75 years. The golden era was from 1920 to 1940, when the factories entered specially built machines ridden by the top riders, who were under contract to represent their respective brand of motorcycles. Winning a hill climb would allow the companies to advertise the quality of their machines.

Locally, hill climbs were held for the amateurs as well as the professionals. Large crowds would gather to watch both man and machine take on the steep grade, with varying results. A hill climb is still held at Royal Mountain every summer, promoted by the Northeast Hill Climb Association.

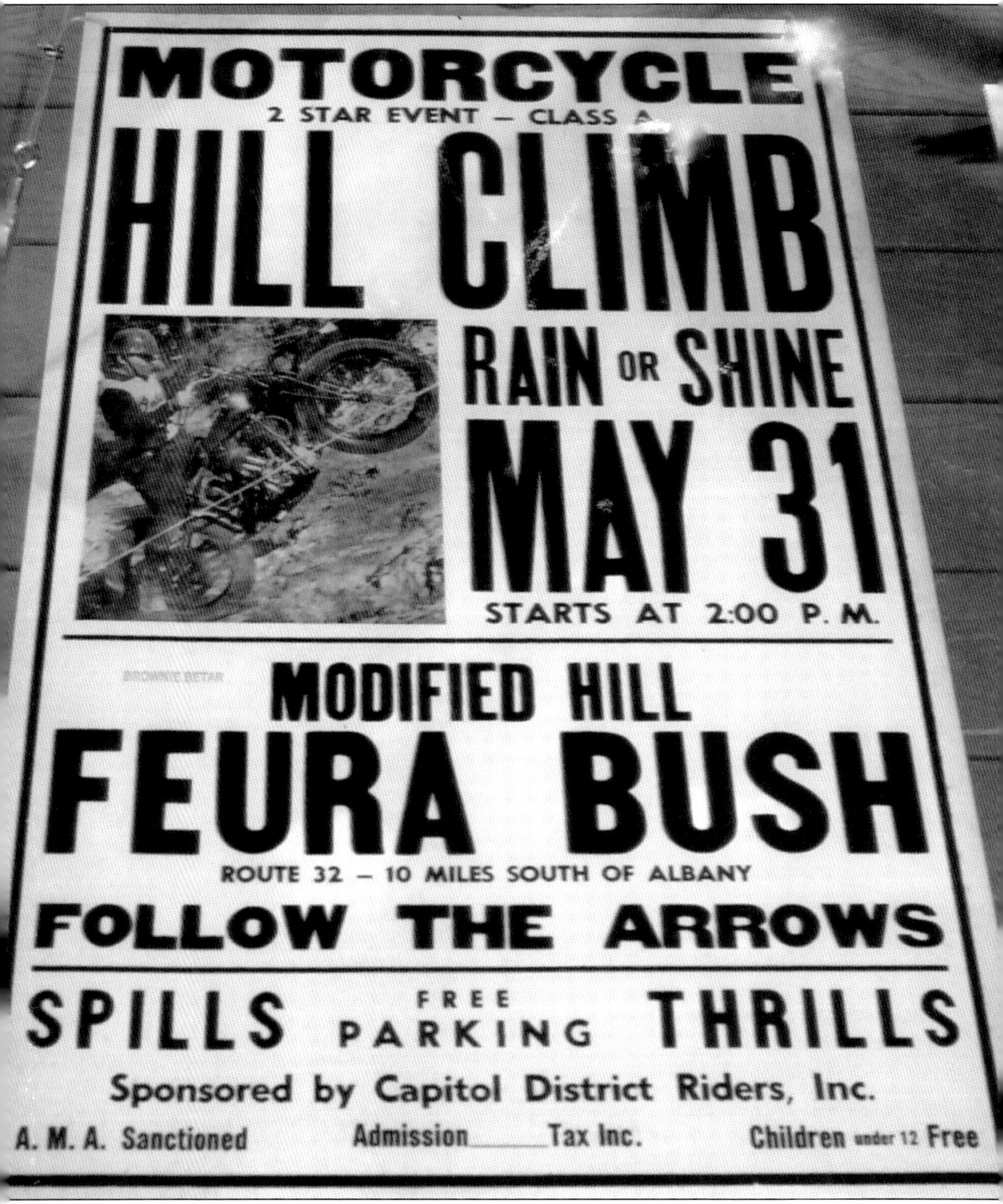

Motorcycle hill climbs were a popular sport for both contestant and spectator. The goal was to see who could go the farthest or the fastest depending on the steepness of the hill. Hill climb events were held for both amateur and expert classes. There were also classes for professional hill climbers that ran at separate events. Feura Bush Hill was south of Albany and was a challenging climb. (Chuck Myles collection.)

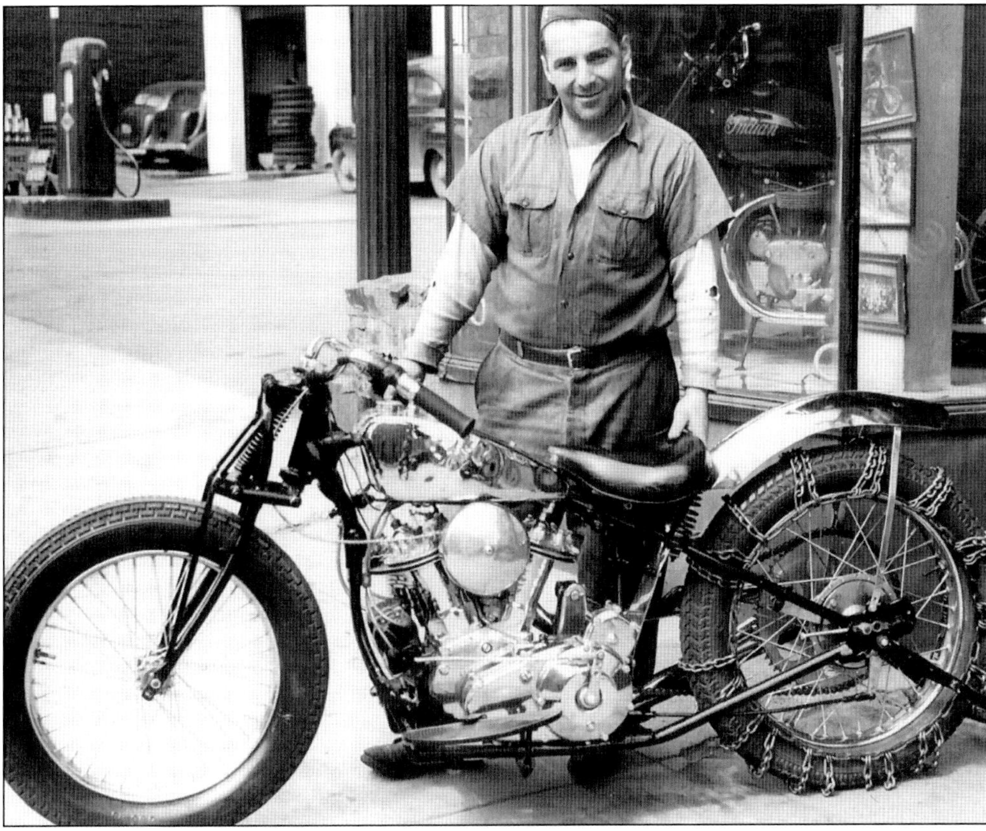

Abraham "Brownie" Betar's career began in 1925, when he became a mechanic for William "Slim" Nelson, the premier Indian motorcycle dealer in upstate New York. Nelson introduced Betar to hill climbing, in which he went on to become the Class C champ, Class B champ, then finally a Class A expert. Brownie took over the shop in 1950 but was displaced in 1965 when the Empire State Plaza was built in Albany. (Bob Eckhardt collection.)

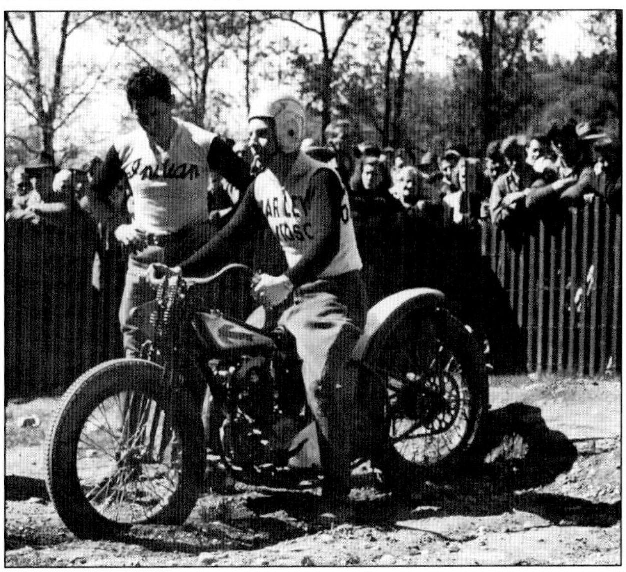

John Ciccarelli, who owned the Indian dealership in Utica, looks at his competition. Harley-Davidson–mounted Harold "Hap" Seamons prepares to conquer the Feura Bush Hill. Seamons became the 1937 80ci Class B national champion. (Erv Splittgerber collection.)

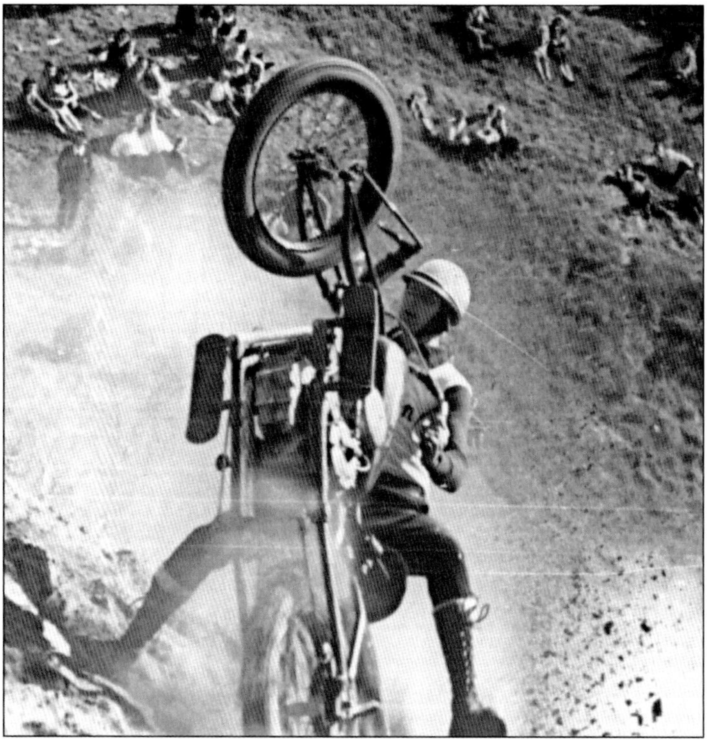

Professional riders rode highly modified machines, with chains wrapped around the rear wheels to increase traction. Most runs on the Feura Bush Hill in the 1940s took about four seconds. The Capital Area Riders, based out of Brownie's shop, hosted the events to raise money for the club. (Larry Dagostino Jr. collection.)

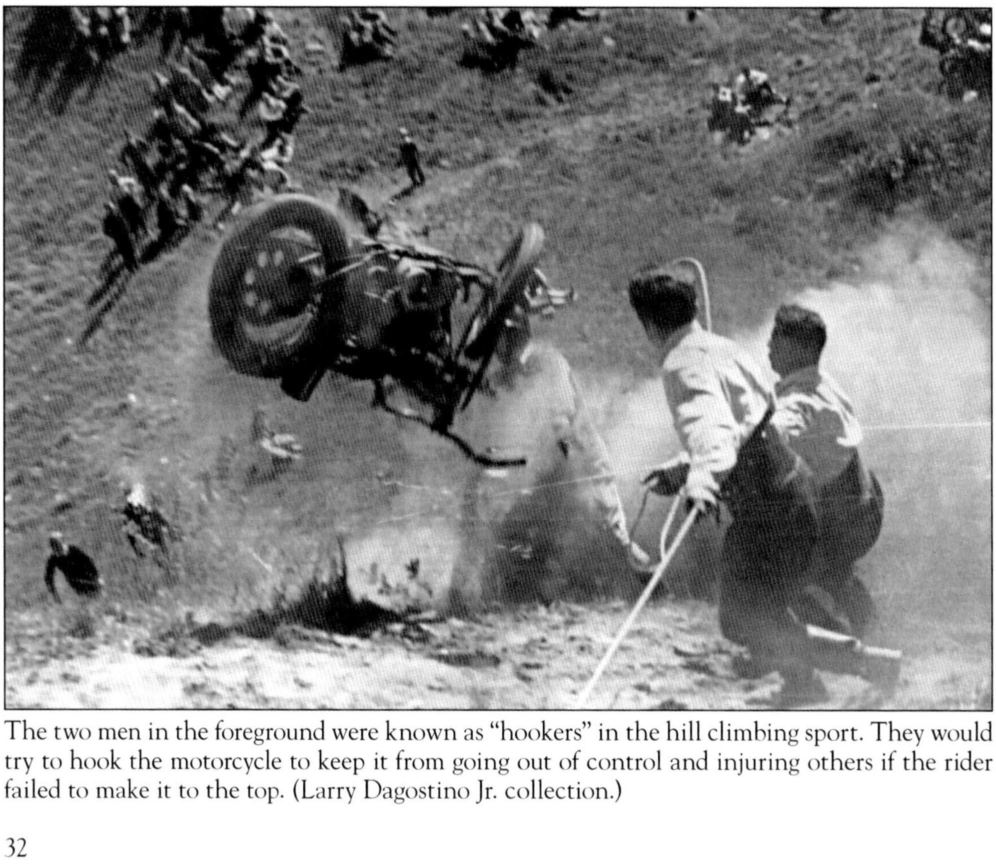

The two men in the foreground were known as "hookers" in the hill climbing sport. They would try to hook the motorcycle to keep it from going out of control and injuring others if the rider failed to make it to the top. (Larry Dagostino Jr. collection.)

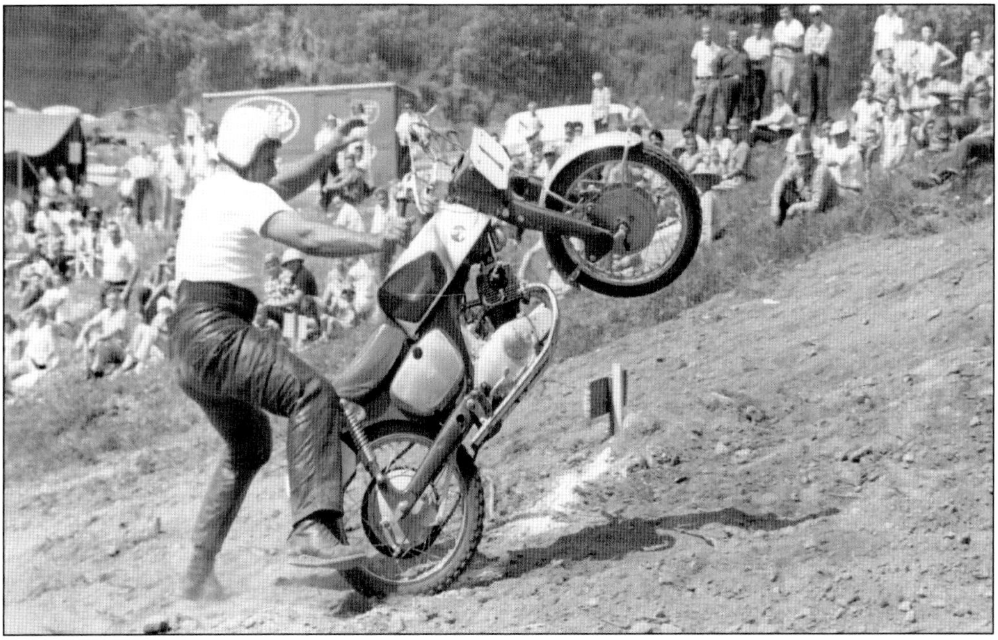

Bob Newell loses control of his 125cc Honda at the hill climb at Royal Mountain near Caroga Lake. The event was sponsored by the Central New York Harley Dealers Association as part of the American Motorcycle Association Gypsy Tour. Gypsy tours began as one-day events around the country where riders would travel to a specific site and enjoy the company of other riders. (Bob Newell collection.)

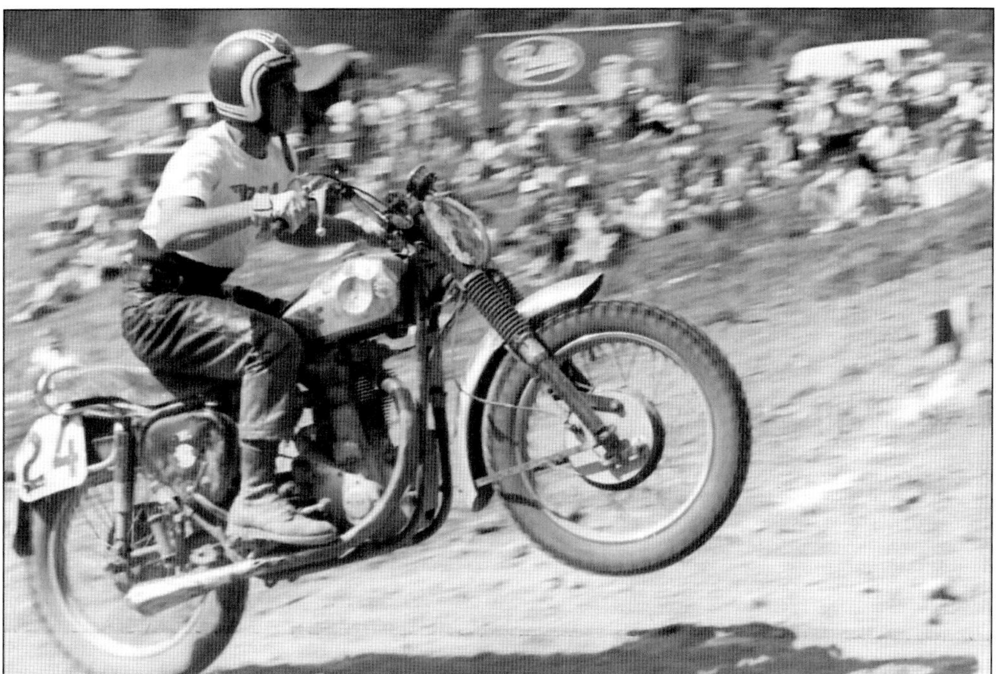

Chuck Hebert from Schenectady shows good form while riding Owen Christman's BSA (Birmingham Small Arms) up the hill at Royal Mountain in 1962. Hebert was a championship rider in scramble events at this time. (Chuck Hebert collection.)

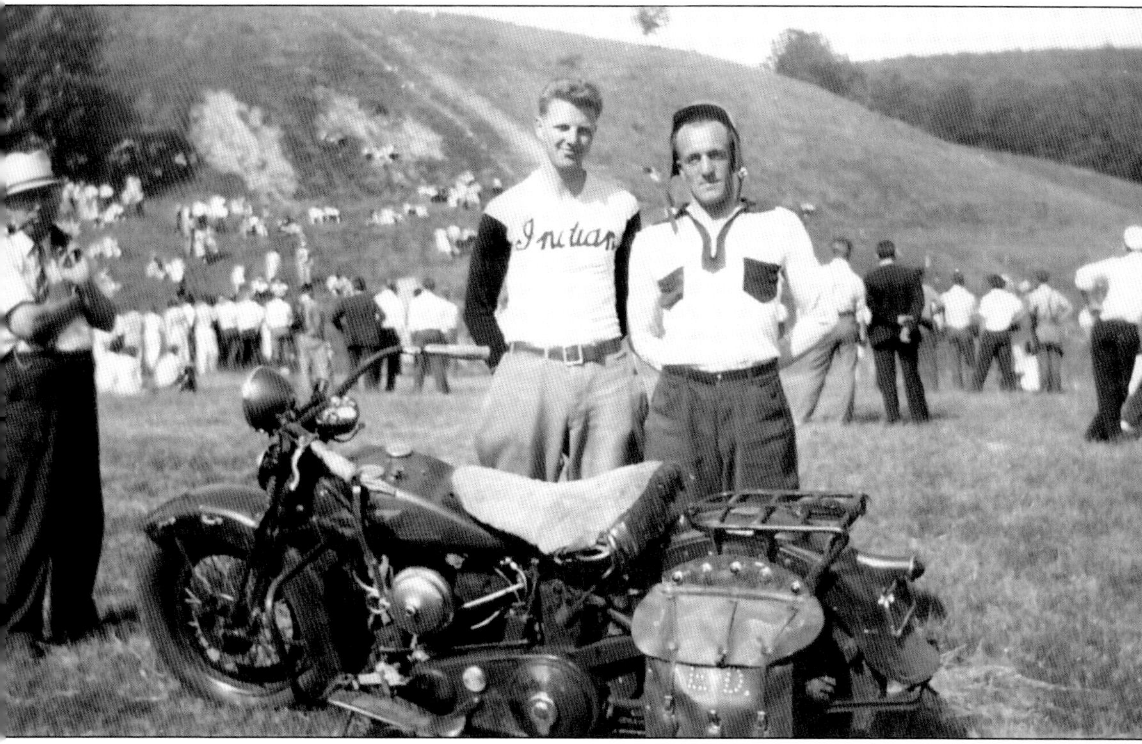

Professional Indian rider Bob Fonda stands with John Splittgerber in front of the Hoffmans Hill. This climb was located on Route 5 in Hoffmans behind the current business called Aunt Katie's Attic. This was a sportsman hill climb for mainly street bikes. Fonda ran an Indian motorcycle shop and sold bicycles in the area. (Dean Splittgerber collection.)

Four

Club Activities and Field Meets

Local clubs like the Electric City Riders, Spitzies Roamers, and Amsterdam Motorcycle Club would put on field meets. Sometimes, the event was an inner-club affair; other times, the competition would be with other clubs. Events such as a barrel race, broad jump, slalom course, and slow race would be run. It was a friendly competition, ending with a picnic and trophies for the winners.

Other club activities included road rides, fashion shows, daredevil exhibitions, and community service.

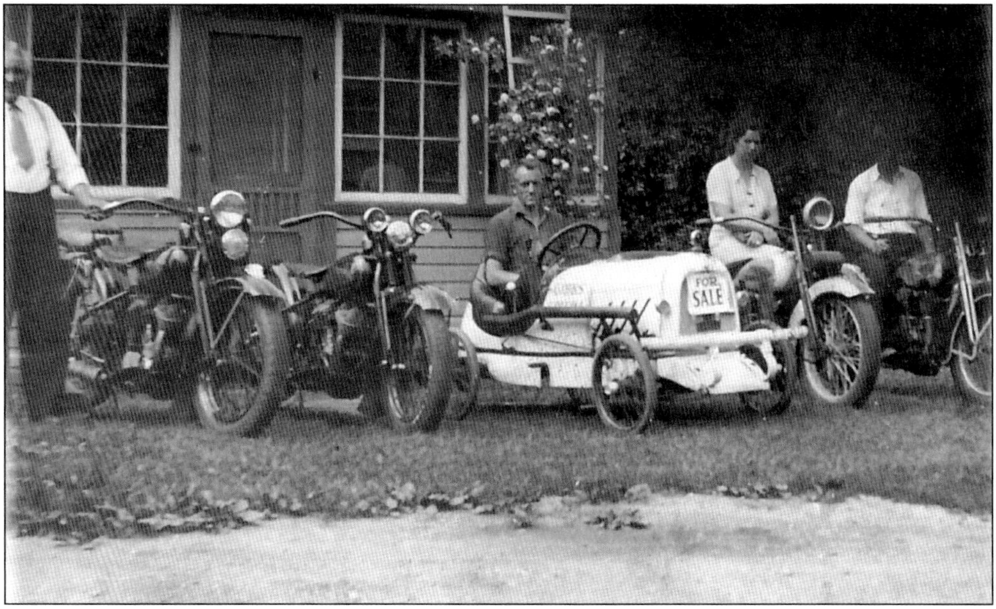

John Splittgerber sits in a midget race car in front of the Snowden residence on Route 5. The Splittgerbers rented the property at this time. This is where John got his start in the motorcycle business. He went on to form Spitzies Motorcycle Sales. The Snowdens' was located next to the Hoffmans garage; both were removed when Route 5 was widened to four lanes in the 1950s. (Dean Splittgerber collection.)

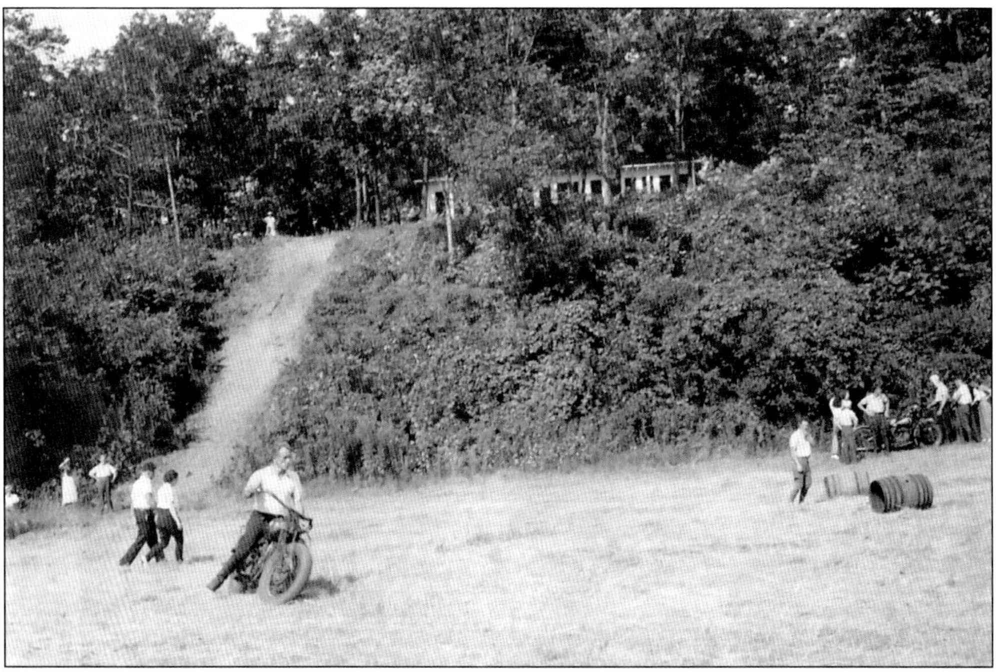

John Splittgerber heads for the start of the barrel race. Riders would head to wooden barrels laid on the ground, drop their bikes, and crawl through a barrel. They would then remount their bikes and head for the finish line. The rider with the fastest time would win. In the background is a hill climb for street bikes. (Erv Splittgerber collection.)

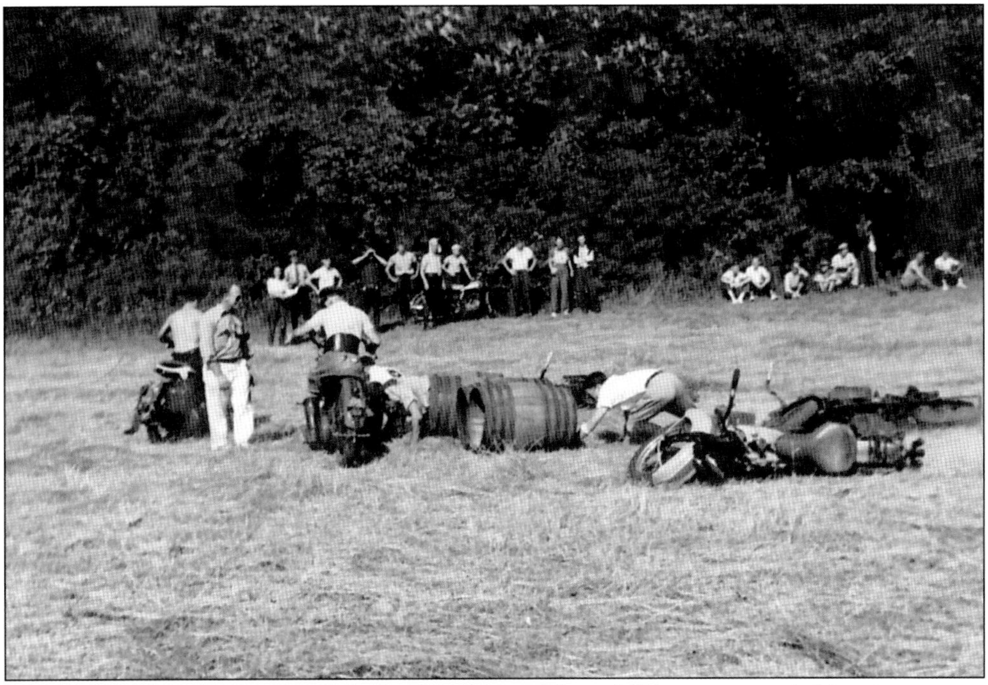

Riders crawl through the barrels in the barrel race. These field events were held at the current location of the Arrowhead Marina in Scotia, also known as the Scotia Flats, in 1938. (Erv Splittgerber collection.)

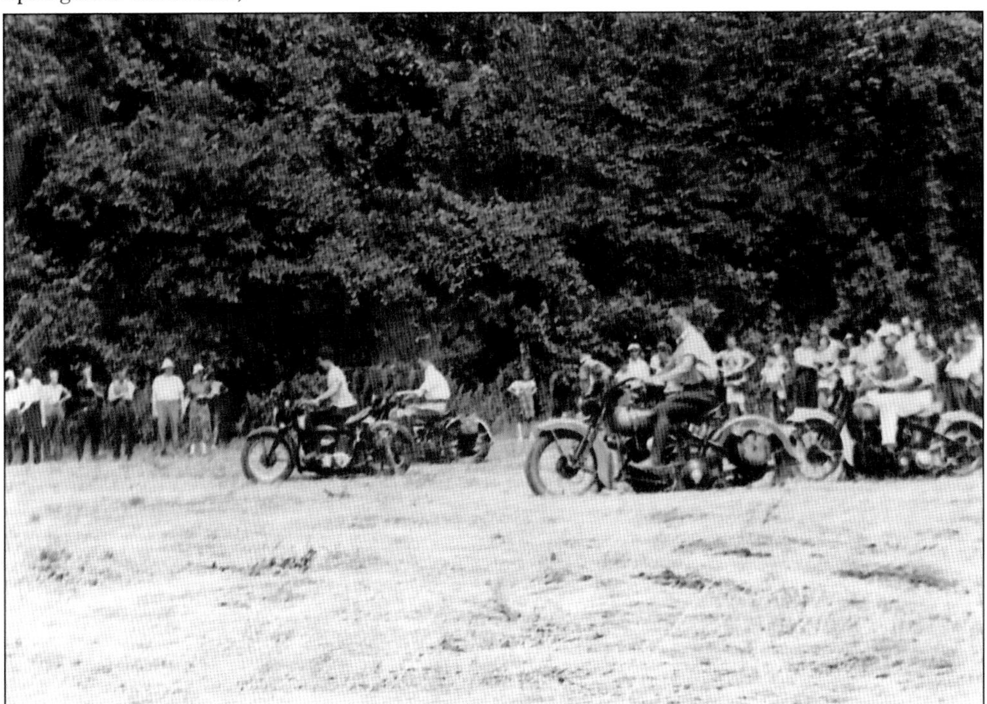

Riders compete in the slow race alongside the Mohawk River west of Scotia. Riders who went the slowest without putting their feet down were the winners. (Erv Splittgerber collection.)

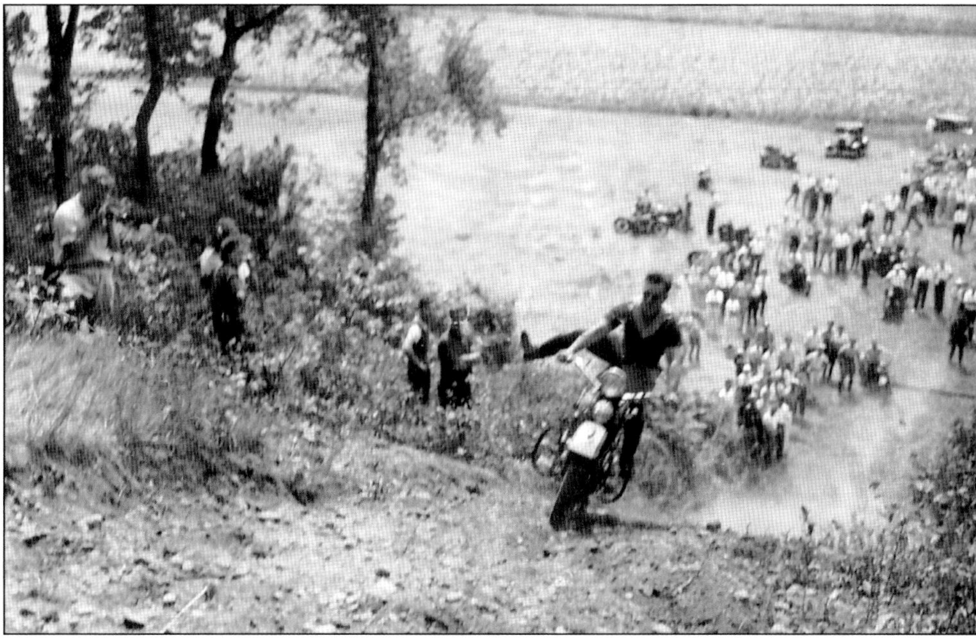

Erv Splittgerber clears the top of the hill climb in style. Notice that the machine he is riding is a street bike with headlight and spill bars attached. The Spitzies Roamers Motorcycle Club put on this event, as well many others through out the season. (Erv Splittgerber collection.)

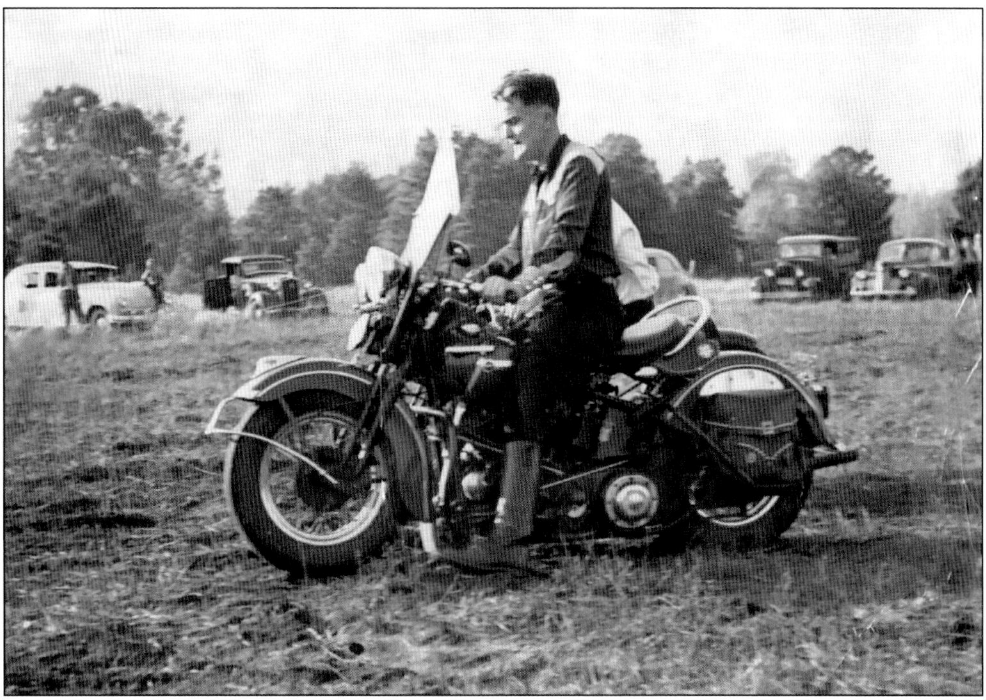

Another game at a field meet was called the Australian Pursuit. Riders would line up equally spaced around a circle track; they would then all start at the same time. If a rider got passed he was eliminated. The last rider on the track was the winner. Erv Splittgerber passes a rider just before his bike quit due to dirt in the carburetor. (Erv Splittgerber collection.)

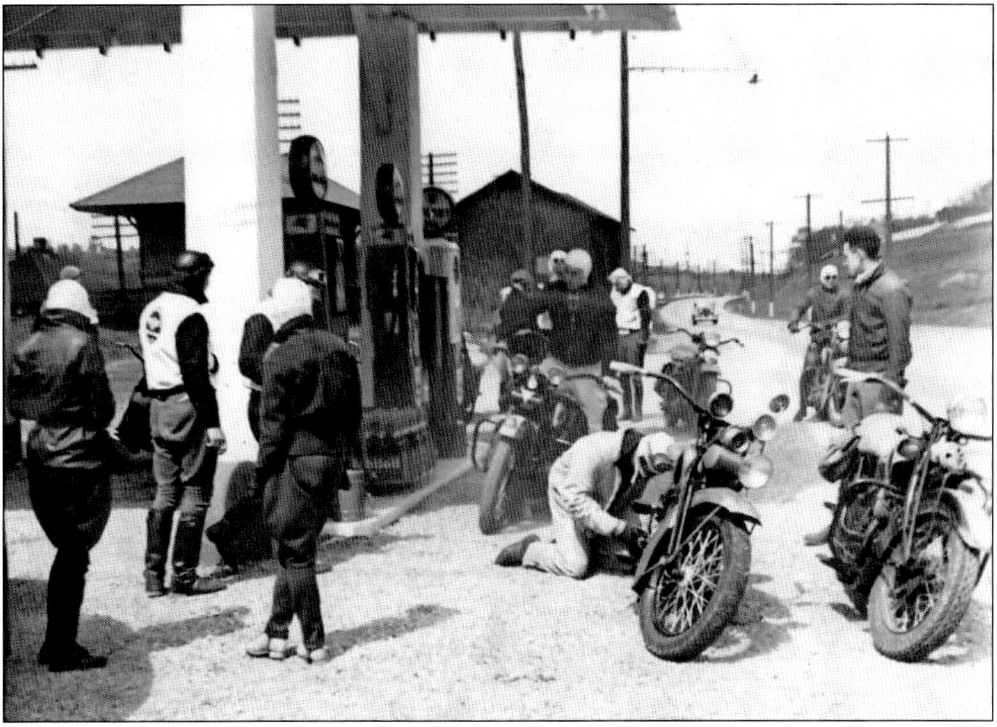

Riders fill up with Mobil gas at the Hoffmans garage on Route 5. The road was known as "Suicide Highway" at the time because it was a three-lane road that allowed cars to pass in either direction. This caused many head-on collisions. The road was widened in the 1950s, eliminating the location of the Hoffmans hill climb. The old Hoffmans train station is in the background. (Erv Splittgerber collection.)

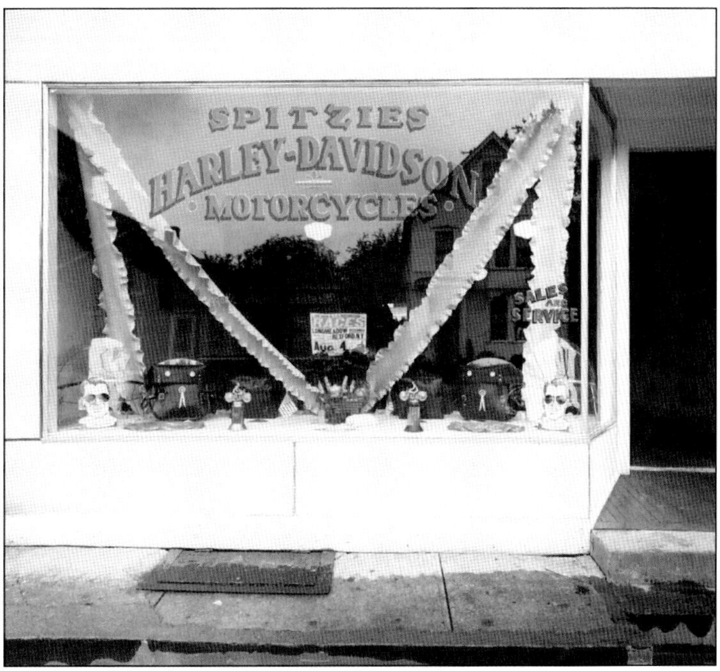

John Splittgerber opened his first Harley-Davidson dealership in Scotia in 1946. The building stood next to the current Dragon Garden restaurant on Mohawk Avenue. In the window is a poster for motorcycle races at the new Longmeadow Speedway in Rexford. (Bob Eckardt collection.)

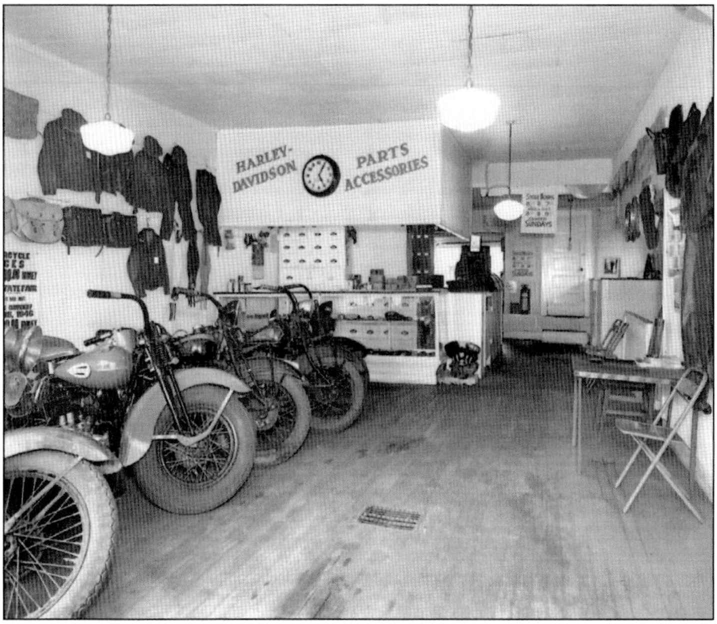

The front showroom and the parts counter of the new Spitzies are shown here. On display are two 1936 VL Harley-Davidsons, two Indian Chiefs, and one 45-cubic-inch Harley. Notice the bikes do not have any chrome parts. As this was just after World War II, chrome was not available. (Erv Splittgerber collection.)

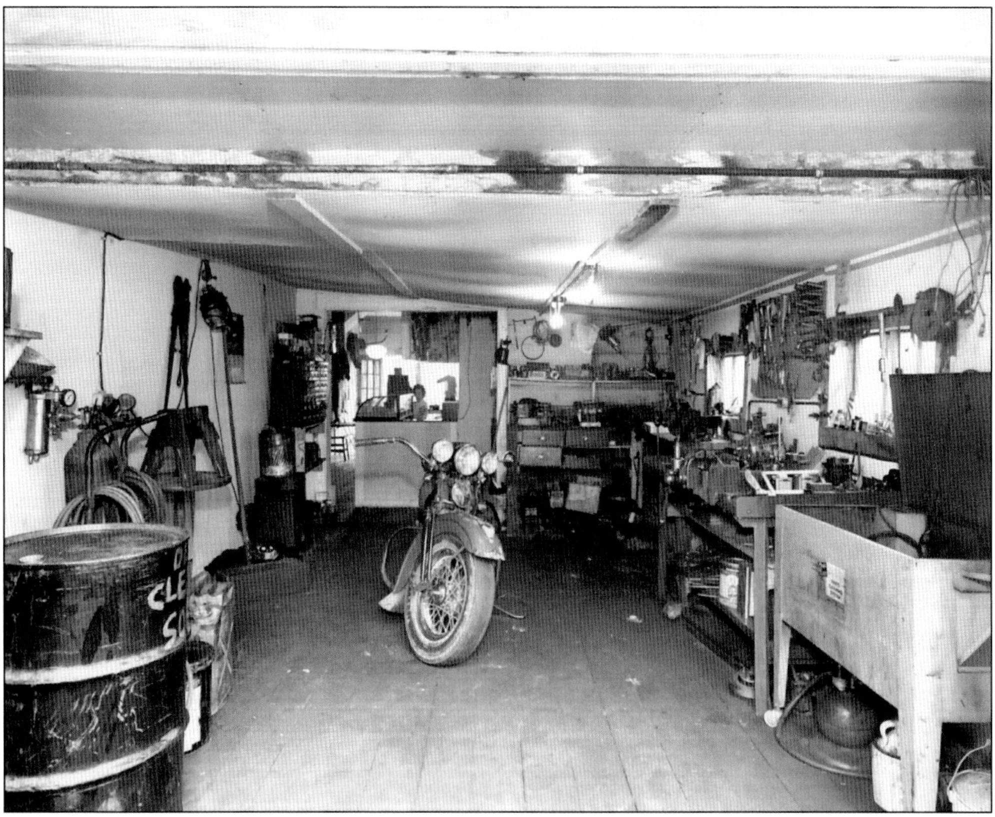

Seen here is the inside of the Spitzies workshop on Mohawk Avenue in Scotia in 1946. John's wife, Joyce, tends the front counter as a bike awaits a tire change. (Erv Splittgerber collection.)

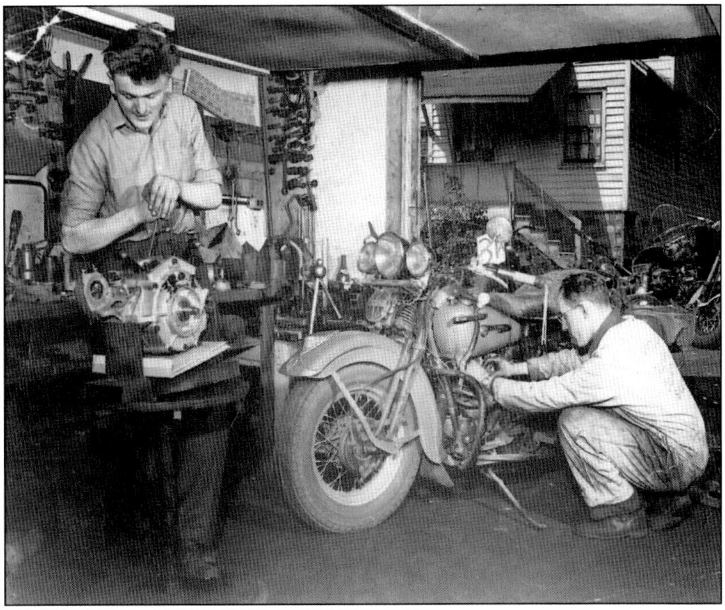

Erv Splittgerber, on the left, and Chuck Wiedman work on a Harley-Davidson in the workshop behind Spitzies. Erv was a Harley-Davidson mechanic for 50 years, retiring in 1990. (Erv Splittgerber collection.)

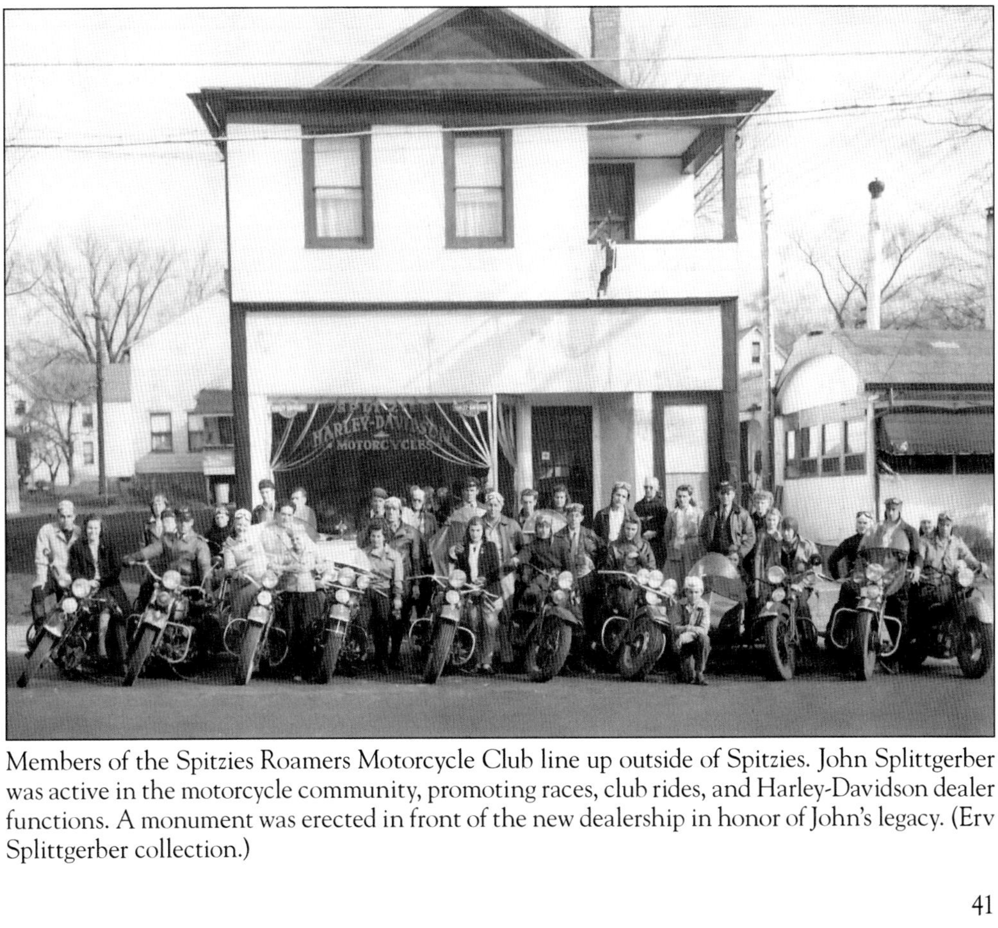

Members of the Spitzies Roamers Motorcycle Club line up outside of Spitzies. John Splittgerber was active in the motorcycle community, promoting races, club rides, and Harley-Davidson dealer functions. A monument was erected in front of the new dealership in honor of John's legacy. (Erv Splittgerber collection.)

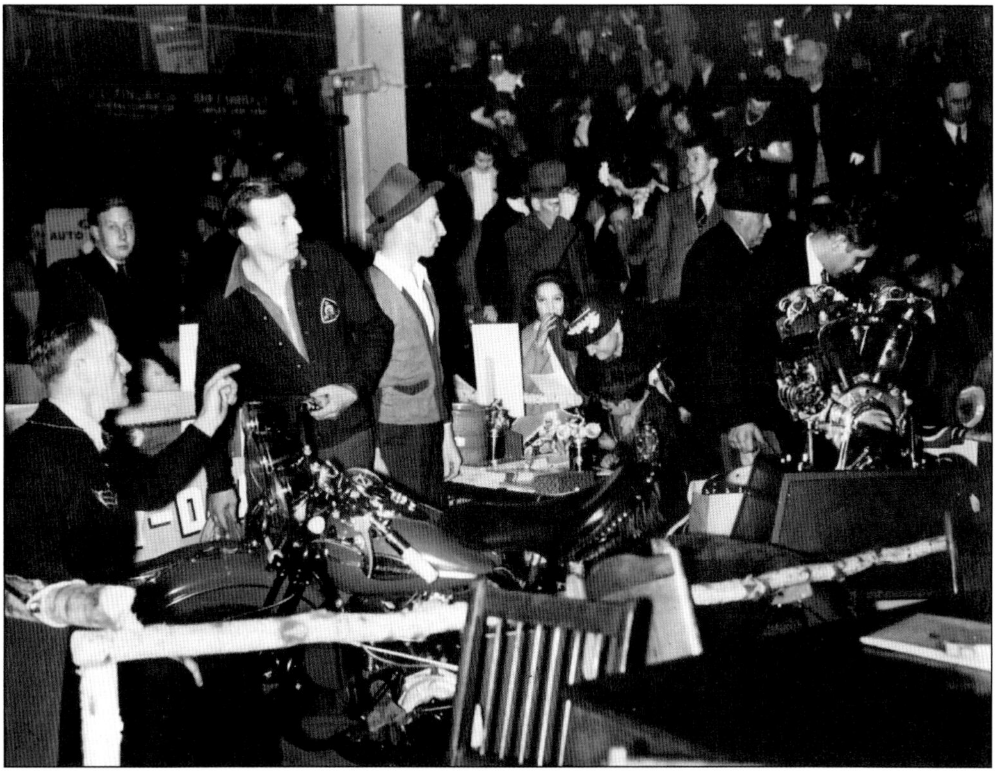

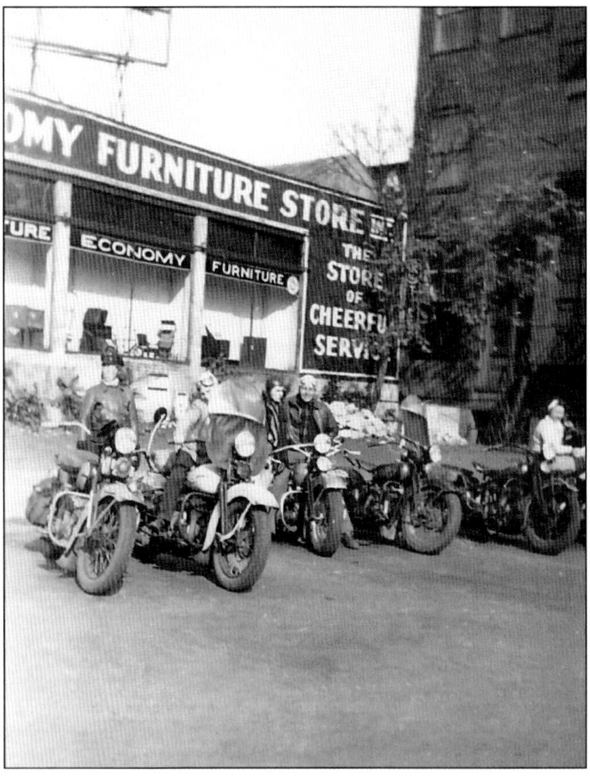

John Splittgerber, on the left, points out the cut-away motor on display at the 1941 Sportsman Show on Guy Park Avenue in Amsterdam. The motor was turned with an electric motor to show the inner workings of the new engine. John's son, Erv, remembers the motor attracting a lot of attention; it began squealing after it ran awhile due to the lack of any lubricant. (Erv Splittgerber collection.)

The Spitzies Roamers meet behind Economy Furniture Store, which was part of the Union Fern Furniture building on State Street. Later, this building became Olender Furniture, which is slated for demolition in 2014. (Erv Splittgerber collection.)

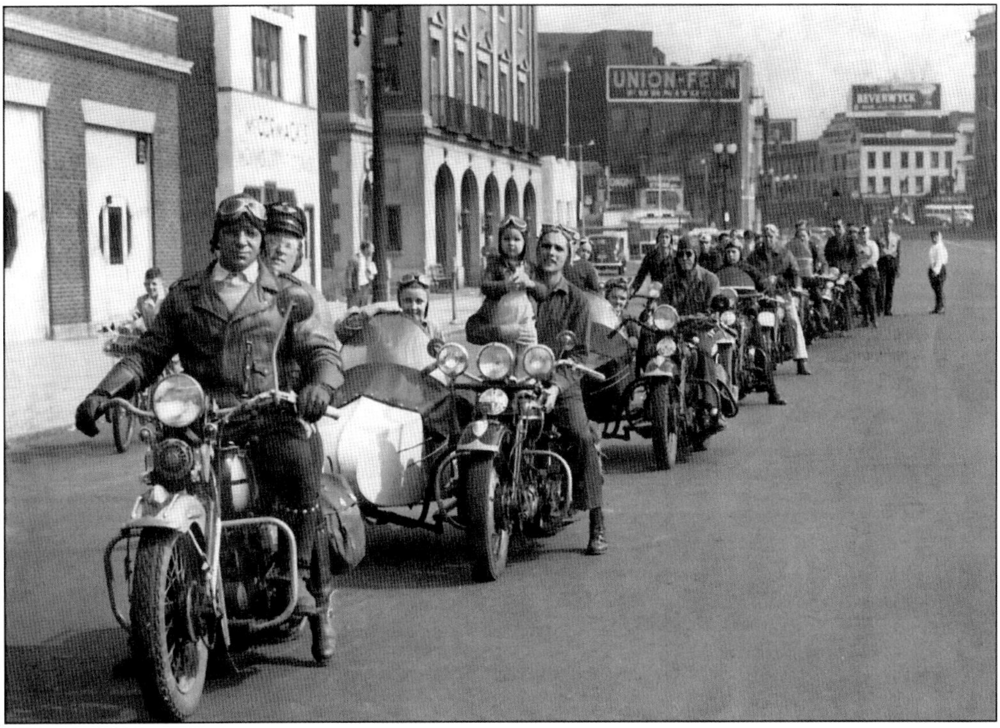

On Sunday, September 29, 1946, the Spitzies Roamers assemble in front of McCormack's Real Estate and the old Schenectady Fire Department on Erie Boulevard. The club was heading out on a scenic road ride. Sidecars were a popular option for riders with children. (Erv Splittgerber collection.)

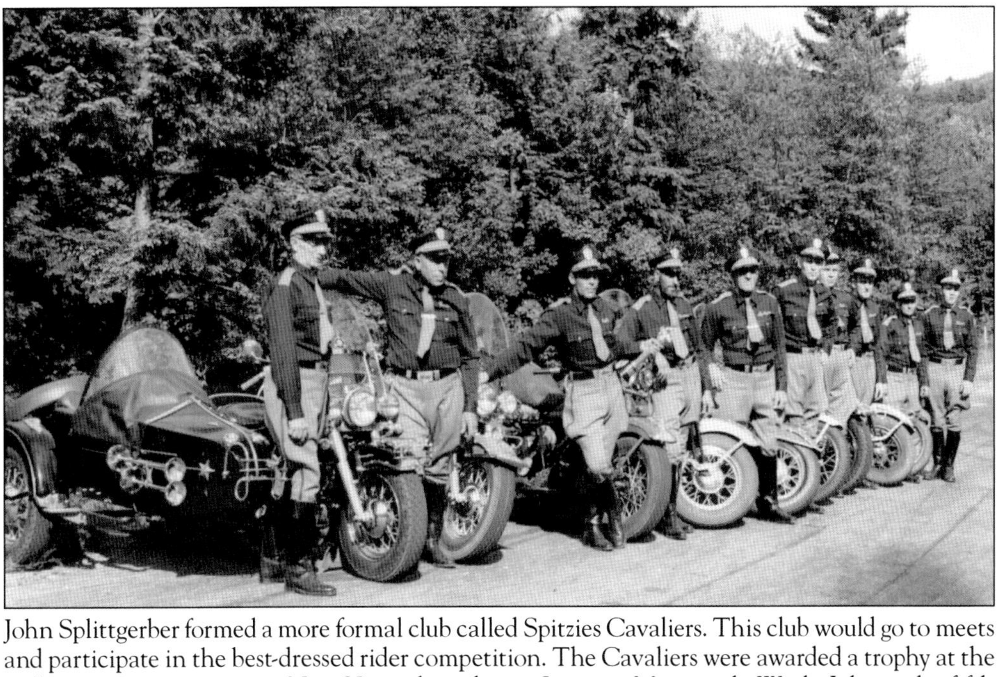

John Splittgerber formed a more formal club called Spitzies Cavaliers. This club would go to meets and participate in the best-dressed rider competition. The Cavaliers were awarded a trophy at the Belknap recreation area in New Hampshire during Laconia Motorcycle Week. John is the fifth from the left; Erv is the third from the right. (Erv Splittgerber collection.)

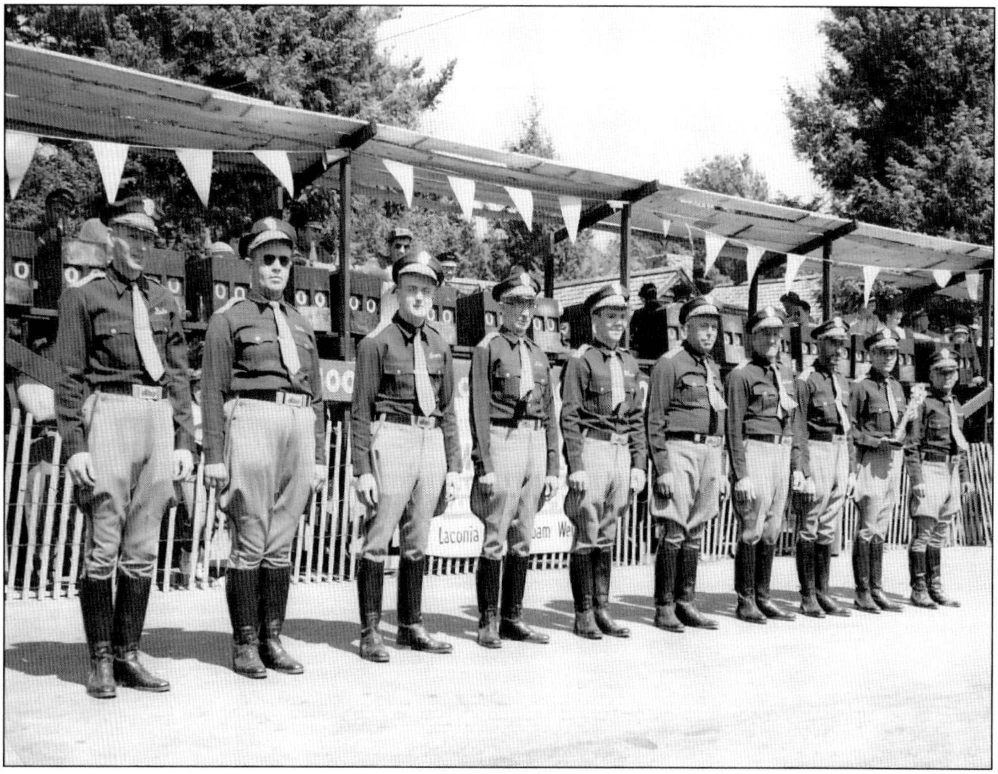

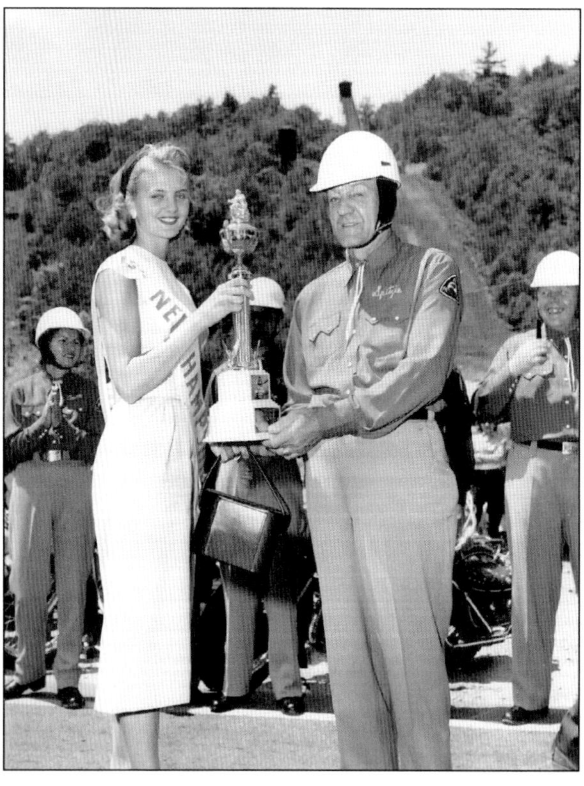

The Cavaliers line up for judging in the best-dressed rider category, held in the pit area of the racetrack at the Belknap recreation area. Clubs took this competition seriously, bringing their trophies with them to show off to the other clubs. Erv Splittgerber is the third from the left; John Splittgerber is the fourth from the right. (Erv Splittgerber collection.)

John Splittgerber receives a trophy for the best-dressed club from Miss New Hampshire in front of the 70-meter ski jump at the Belknap recreation area in the mid-1950s. The landing area for the ski jump was used for the hill climb competition until 1962 and then again beginning in 1993. (Erv Splittgerber collection.)

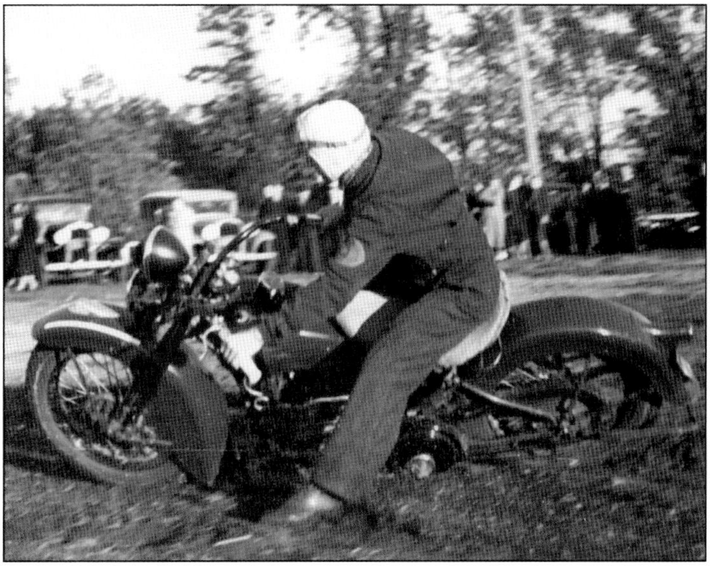

Larry Dagostino slides his Harley-Davidson during an Australian pursuit race in the late 1940s. Larry was one of the founding members of the Electric City Riders Club, holding the treasurer position for many years. Protective riding gear had not yet been developed, as the cloth helmet shows in this photograph. (Larry Dagostino Jr. collection.)

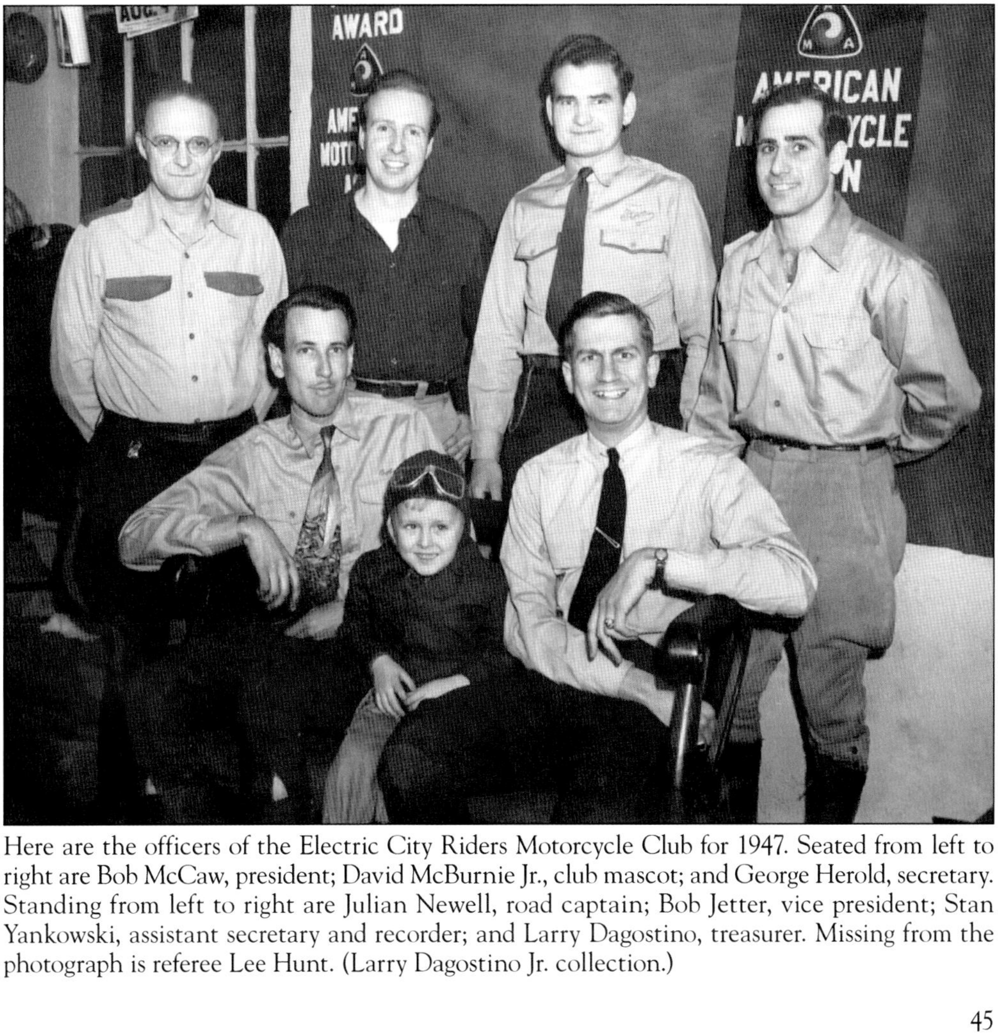

Here are the officers of the Electric City Riders Motorcycle Club for 1947. Seated from left to right are Bob McCaw, president; David McBurnie Jr., club mascot; and George Herold, secretary. Standing from left to right are Julian Newell, road captain; Bob Jetter, vice president; Stan Yankowski, assistant secretary and recorder; and Larry Dagostino, treasurer. Missing from the photograph is referee Lee Hunt. (Larry Dagostino Jr. collection.)

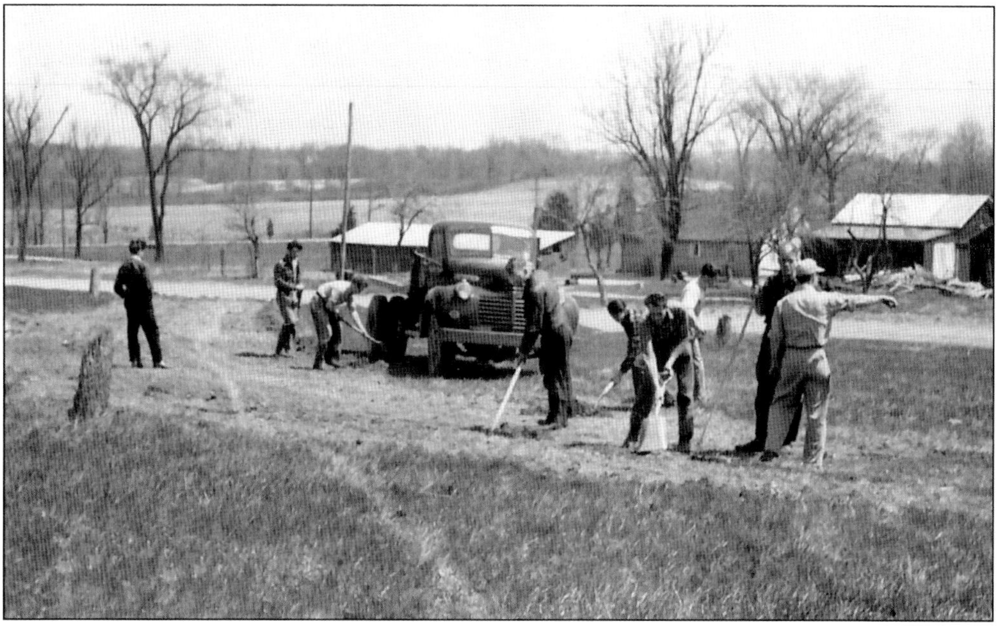

In 1946, the Electric City Riders started to build the Long Meadow Speedway in Rexford. The main investors were landowners Ken Williams, Howard Bigelow, and Charlie Smith. Smith is second from the right. (Larry Dagostino Jr. collection.)

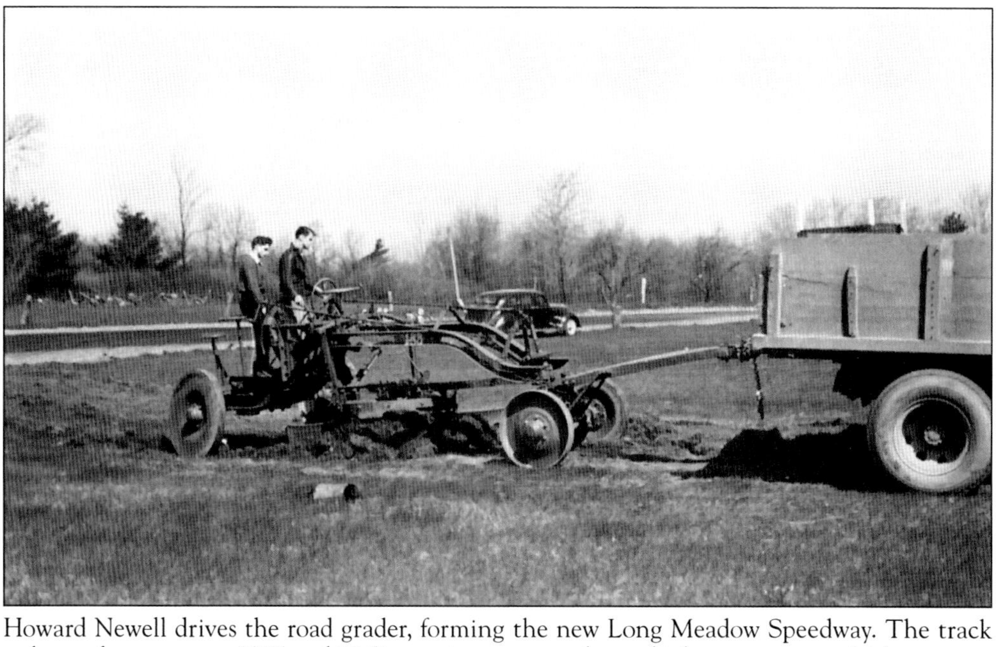

Howard Newell drives the road grader, forming the new Long Meadow Speedway. The track only ran for two years, 1946 and 1947, running motorcycles and jalopy race cars, which were cut down Model T's and A's. The track was a quarter-mile-long dirt oval just off of Garnsey Road in Rexford. Oil was used to quell the dust. It is said "if you dug there today you would still strike oil." This location is now a housing development. (Larry Dagostino Jr. collection.)

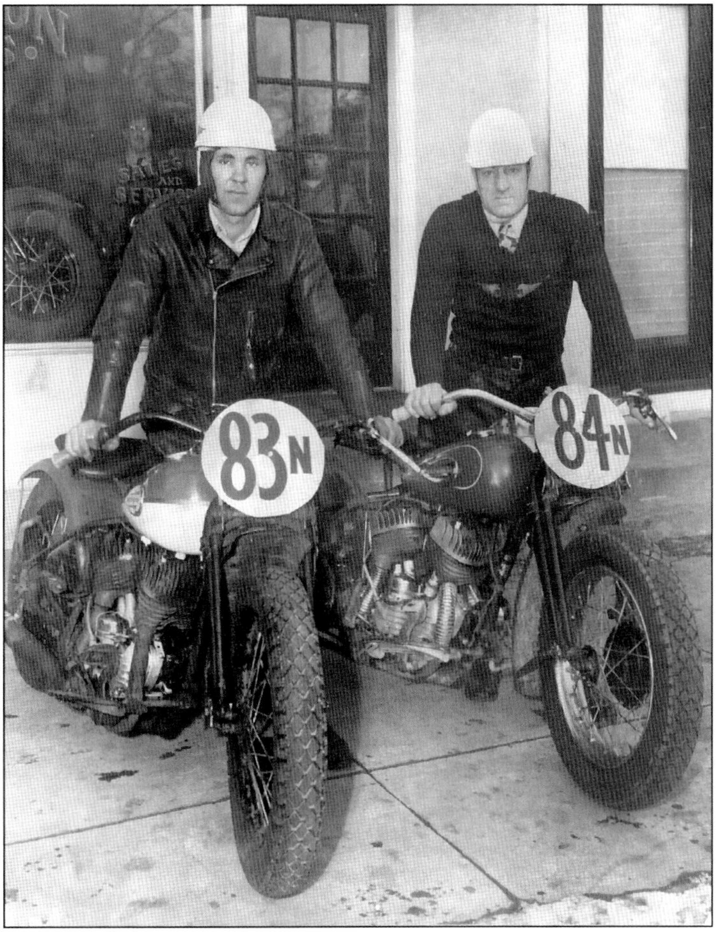

In 1948, Enoch Jones and John Splittgerber pose in front of the Spitzies store in Scotia. They are getting ready to leave for Daytona, Florida, to compete in the second annual Motorcycle Speed Week. The races were held on the old beach course, which used part of Route 1A and Daytona Beach to form the track. (Erv Splittgerber collection.)

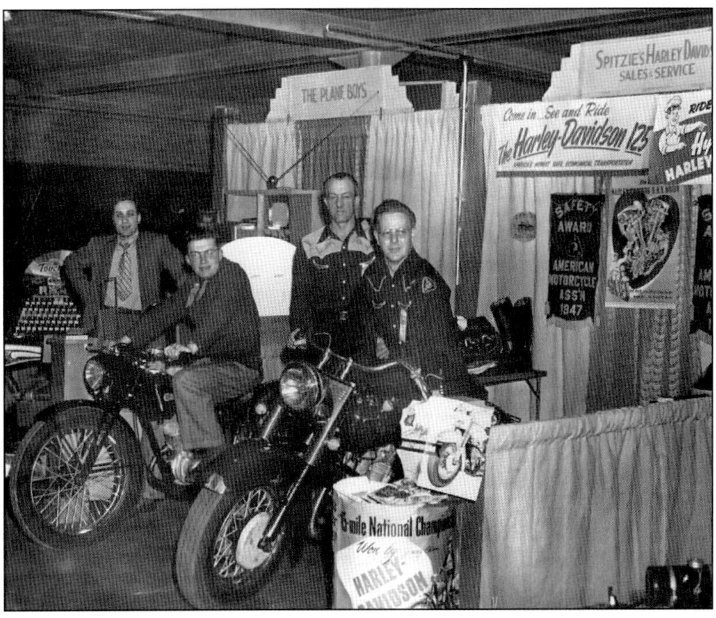

Lou Plane, on the left, and John Splittgerber, second from the right, participate in the Schenectady Sportsman Show at the Armory in 1948. John has the new Harley-Davidson Hydra-Glide on display in the Spitzies booth, along with a 125cc Harley Hummer. The Plane Boys store on State Street was a popular spot for kids as it always had a good supply of the newest bicycles. (Dean Splittgerber collection.)

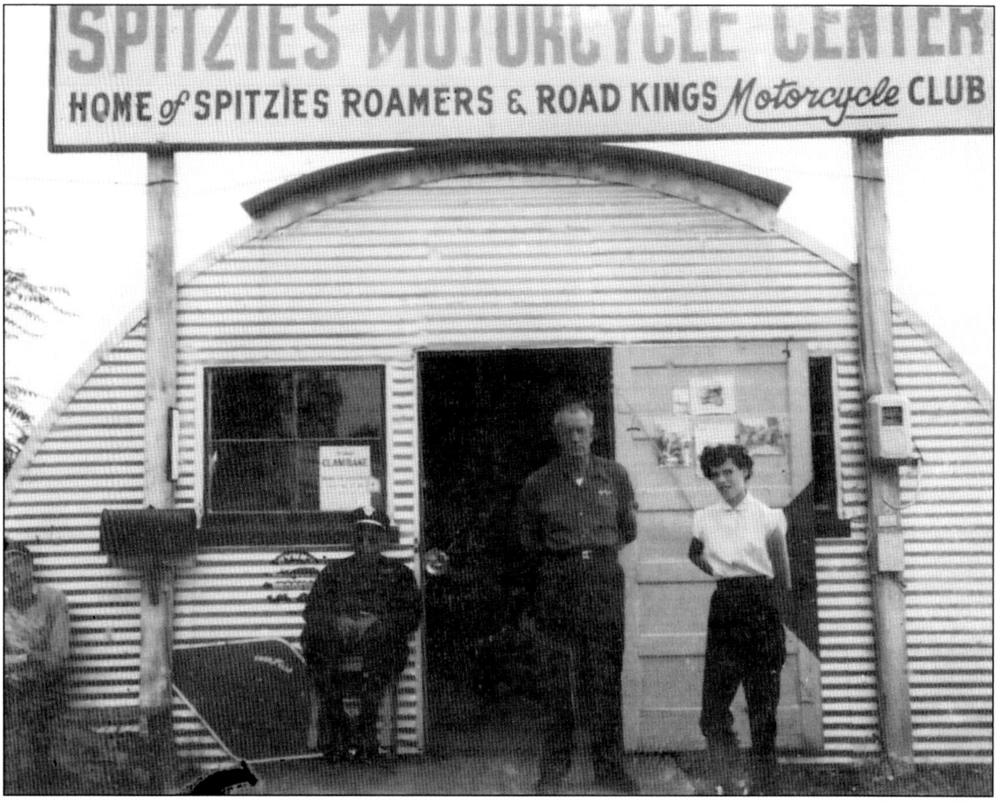

John and Joyce Splittgerber, standing, moved the Spitzies motorcycle dealership to a Quonset hut on Central Avenue in Colonie in 1952. The location currently hosts a U-Haul trailer business. (Dean Splittgerber collection.)

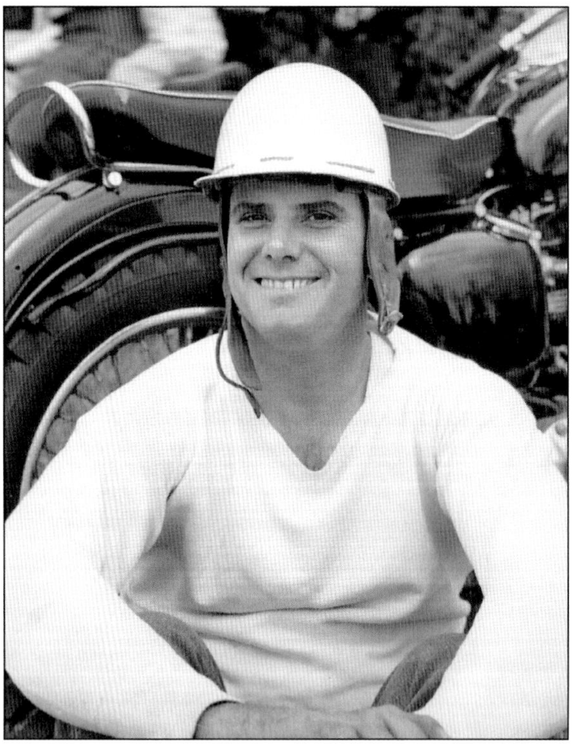

Howard Newell was an early member of the Electric City Riders Club. He participated in polo, field meets, scrambles, and ice racing. He went on to form Howard's Cycle Shop in Ballston Lake. Howard's started out selling Triumph and Ossa brand bikes, then became a Honda motorcycle dealer in the 1960s. He sponsored many riders through the years, helping to keep the sport alive. (Photograph by C.B. Sellers Jr.)

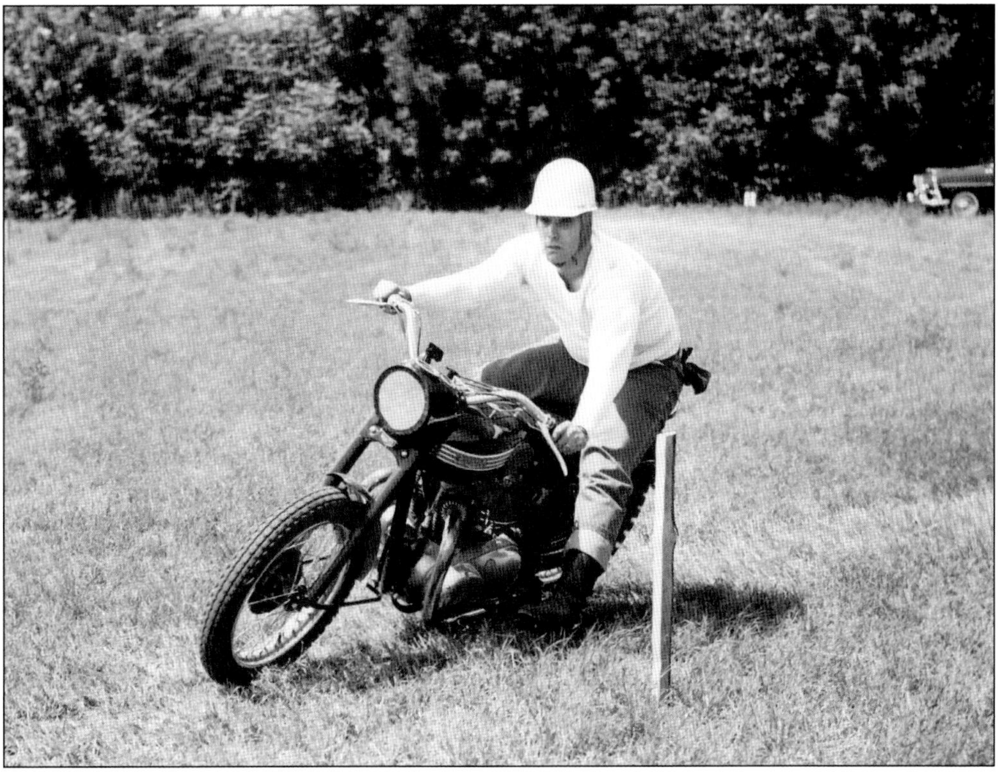

Howard Newell, on a Triumph, weaves his way through the slalom course in a field meet held in the Glenville Hills. This field meet was covered in a full-page spread in the *Schenectady Gazette* in July 1956. (Photograph by C.B. Sellers Jr.)

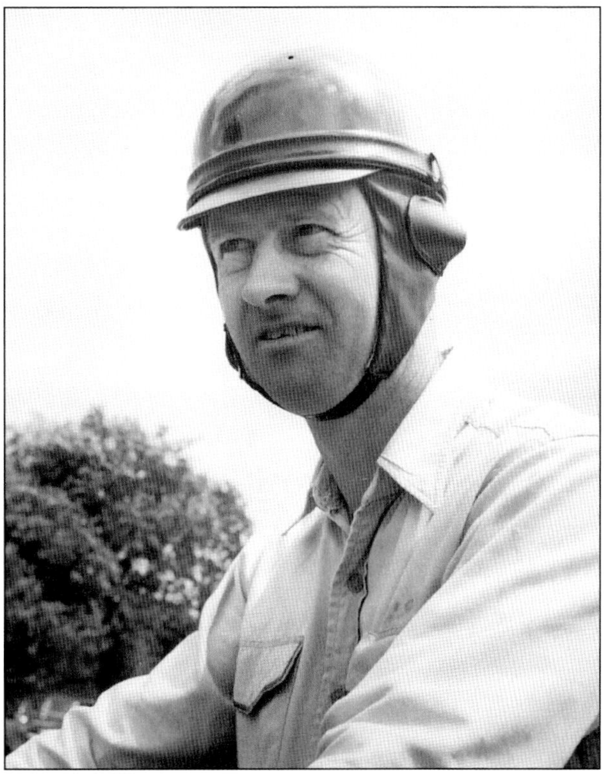

Joe Debie ran a body and welding shop on Maple Avenue in Scotia. He also sold Triumph motorcycles, and his building advertised for the Electric City Riders. Joe became the official starter when the club built its first scrambles track in 1962. His wife, Mary, and their daughters ran the concession stand. (Photograph by C.B. Sellers Jr.)

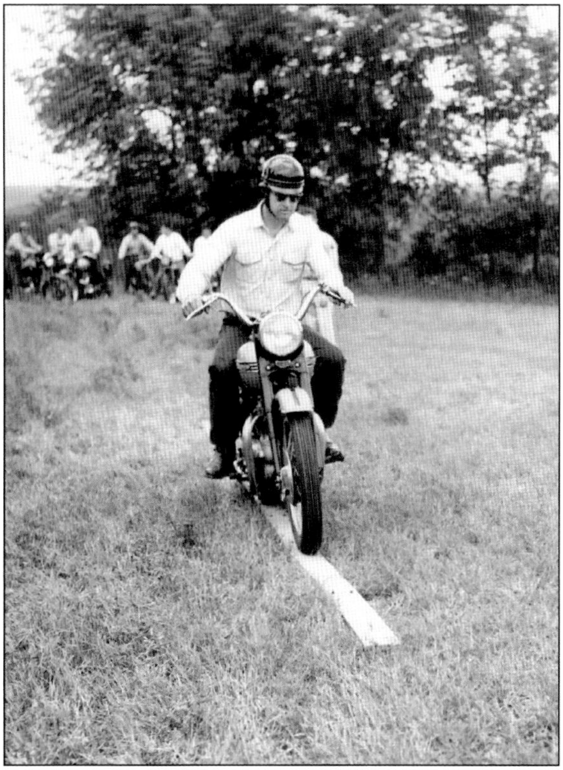

Joe Debie competes in the plank riding competition on his Triumph motorcycle. The idea is to ride the slowest across the plank without falling off or putting your feet down. At the time, Joe was the oldest rider at 46 years old. (Photograph by C.B. Sellers Jr.)

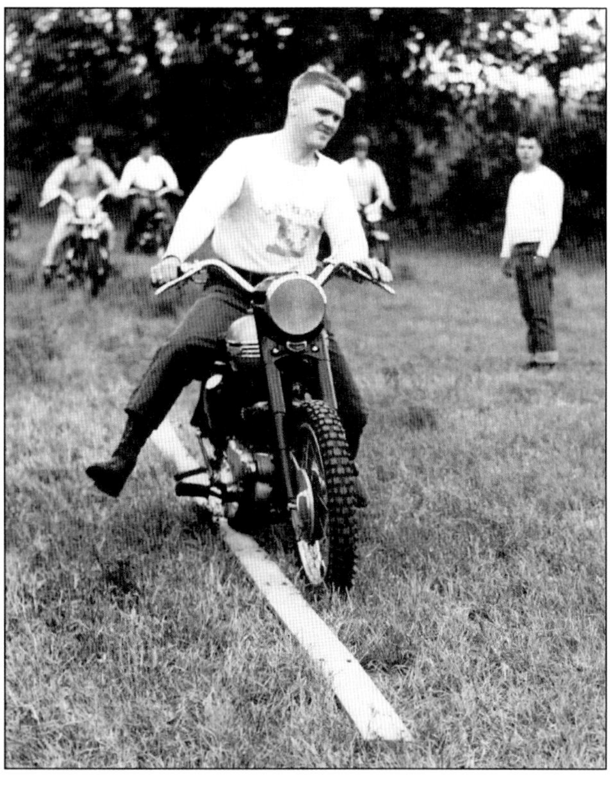

Joe's son, Dick, shows how not to ride the plank as other club members look on. Dick went on to be the high point scorer for the day and became a champion scramble racer in the 1960s. (Photograph by C.B. Sellers Jr.)

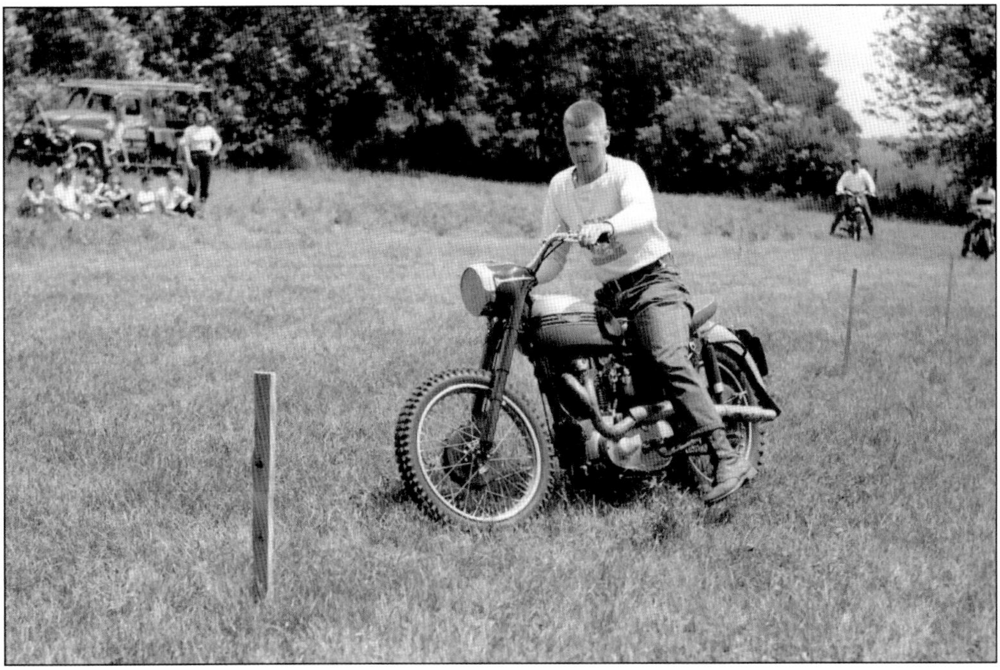

The slalom course takes good concentration, as seen with Dick Debie as he navigates the course on his Triumph motorcycle. These events were all in fun and had a family atmosphere. (Photograph by C.B. Sellers Jr.)

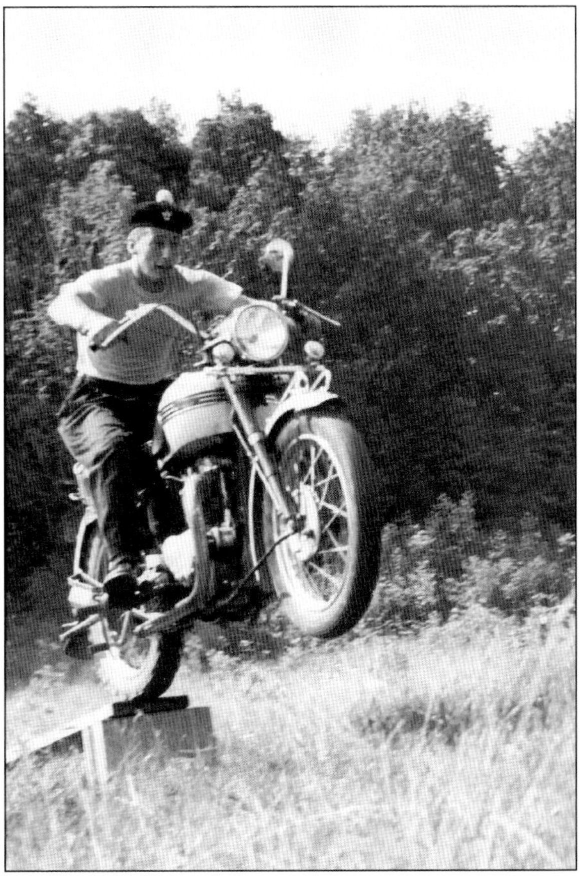

Chuck Hebert jumps his Triumph in the long jump competition. This field meet was for Electric City Rider members only. Hebert went on to be an expert rider in scramble competitions. (Photograph by C.B. Sellers Jr.)

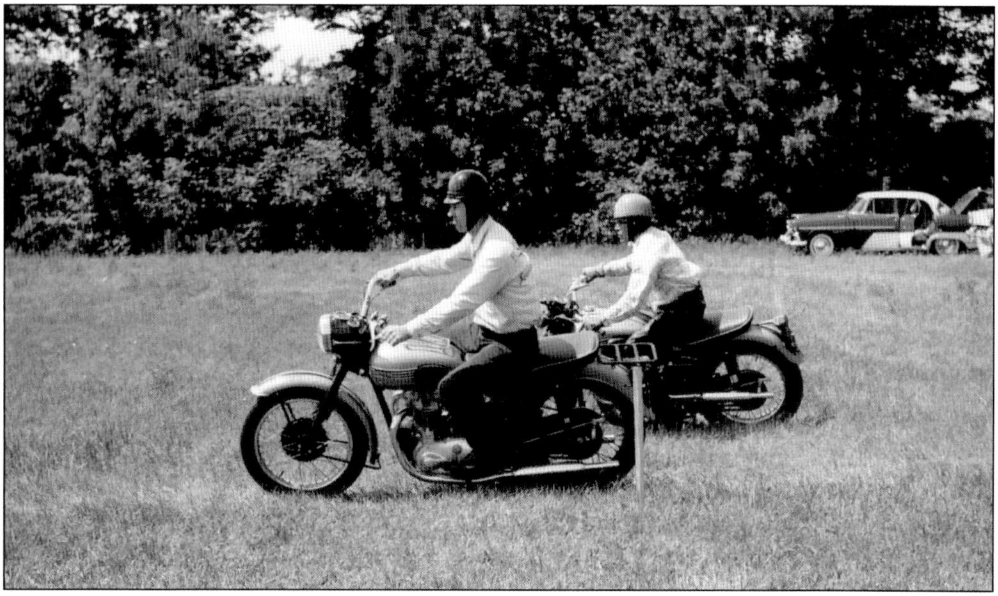

Joe Debie passes an unidentified rider while participating in a TT scramble event. TT or tourist trophy scrambles were derived from the British form of racing that was held on a road course, which in the early part of the 20th century was predominantly dirt. In America, TT events were held in a field where contestants raced around sticks or barrels that marked the course. TT gave way to scrambles, which were held on a prepared dirt track with at least one jump. (Photograph by C.B. Sellers Jr.)

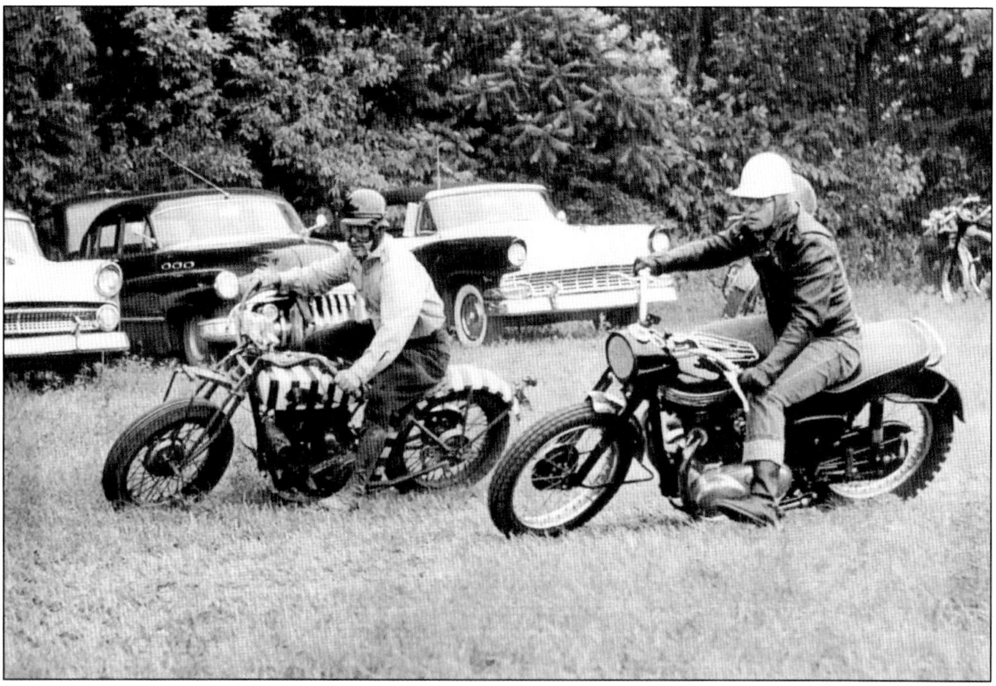

Larry Dagostino goes wide on his Indian while Howard Newell passes on the inside on a Triumph during a TT scrambles event. Larry's Indian had been previously used in motorcycle polo, as indicated by the striped paint job. (Photograph by C.B. Sellers Jr.)

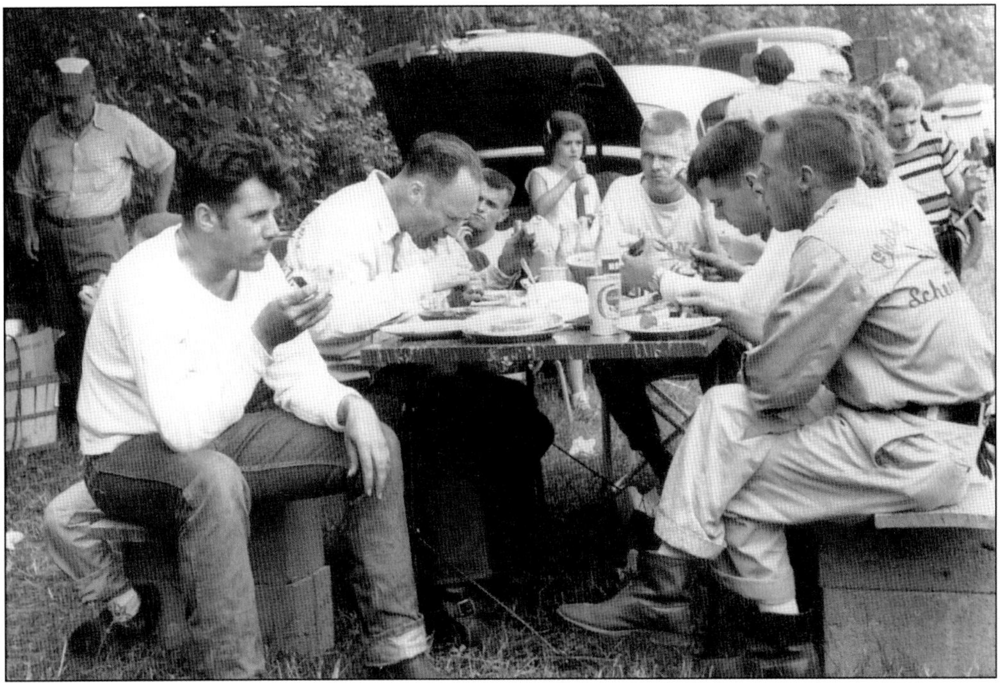

Electric City Riders Club members stop for lunch. From left to right are Bob Newell, Joe Debie, Wayne Hovey, Marilynn Dagostino, Dick Debie, Howard Newell, and Chuck Hebert. In the background on the left is Frank Dagostino, grandfather of Marilynn. (Photograph by C.B. Sellers Jr.)

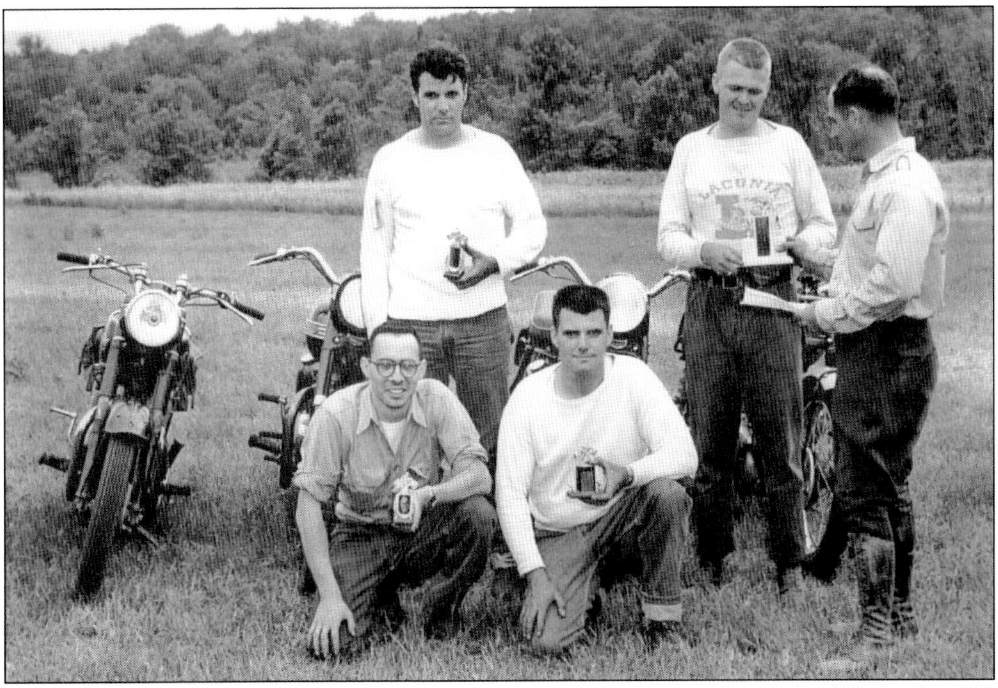

Larry Dagostino hands out the trophies for the winners of the day's field meet. Dick Debie finished first in the day's events. From left to right are Fred Samolovich, Bob Newell, Howard Newell, and Dick Debie. (Larry Dagostino Jr. collection.)

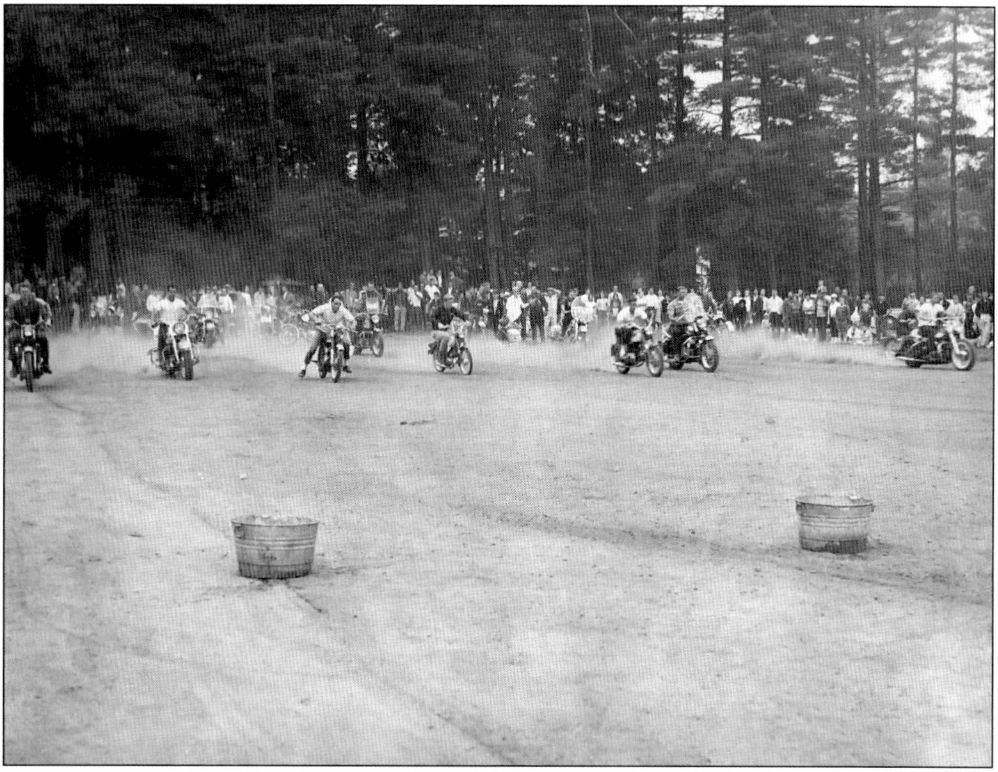

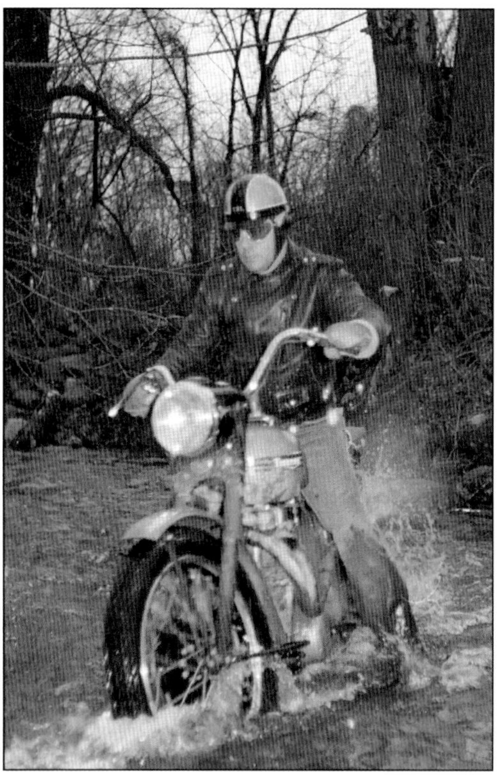

During the gypsy tour held at Caroga Lake, the riders would compete in the bob for the apple event. Each rider would have to race to the bucket and grab an apple with his mouth and then race to the finish line. These events, put on by the AMA, were always well attended. (Erv Splittgerber collection.)

Another form of competition was the motorcycle enduro. Riders have to ride their bikes through a course laid out in the woods. Riders with the fastest time were the winners. Here, Howard Newell crosses a frigid stream on his Triumph. (Bob Newell collection.)

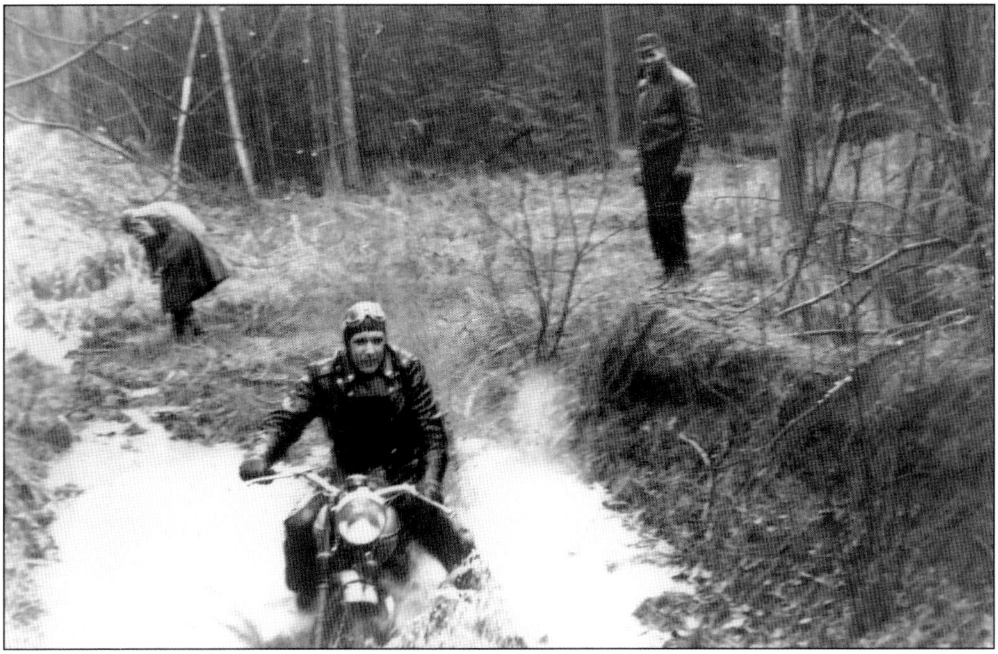

Bob Newell tries his luck at riding his Triumph through a swamp in a cold and wet enduro event. These events helped improve the waterproof ability and reliability of the machines that entered. This lead to a club member, John Taylor, developing a motorcycle years later that could better handle this kind of event. The bike was called the Yankee and was built in Schenectady. (Bob Newell collection.)

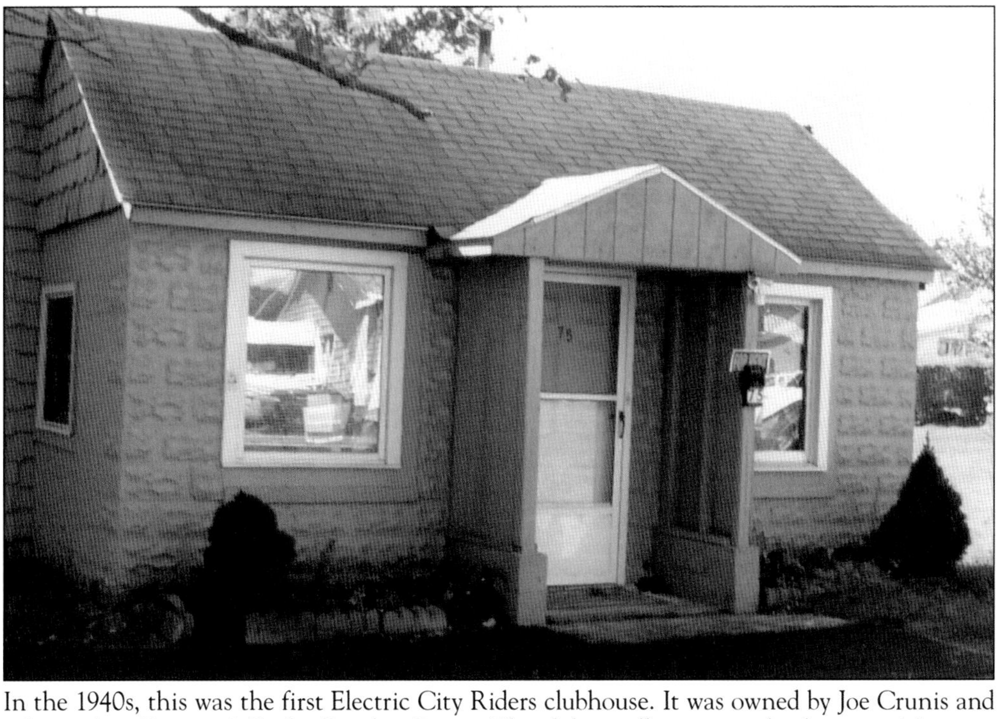

In the 1940s, this was the first Electric City Riders clubhouse. It was owned by Joe Crunis and is located on Freeman's Bridge Road in Scotia. The club rapidly outgrew this location. Meetings were later held at different locations in Schenectady. (Photograph by the author.)

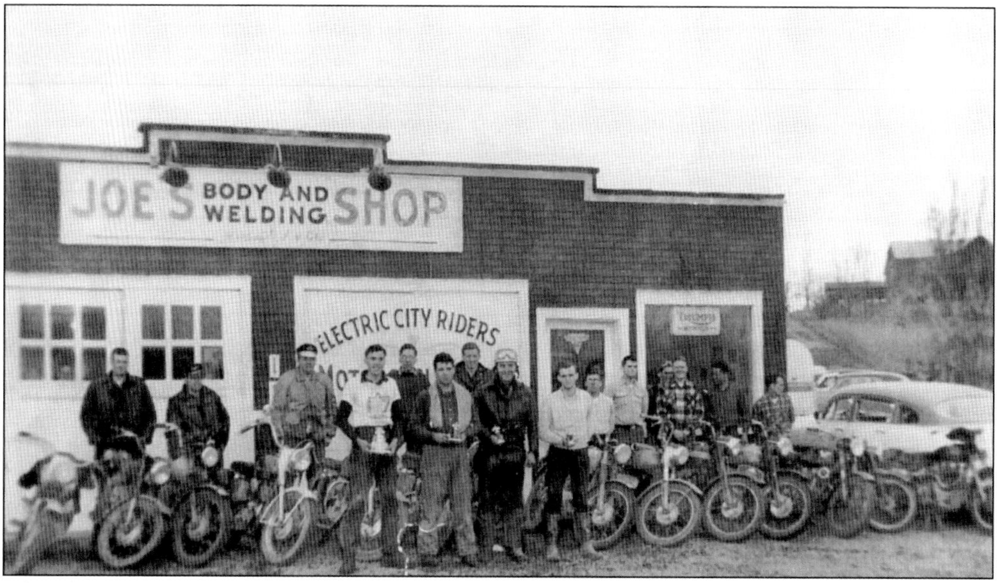

The Electric City Riders pose with their trophies in front of Joe Debie's body shop on Maple Avenue in Scotia. Joe promoted the club on his storefront and sold Triumph motorcycles until 1963. Howard Newell took over the Triumph dealership and moved it to his shop in Ballston Lake. (Tim Newell collection.)

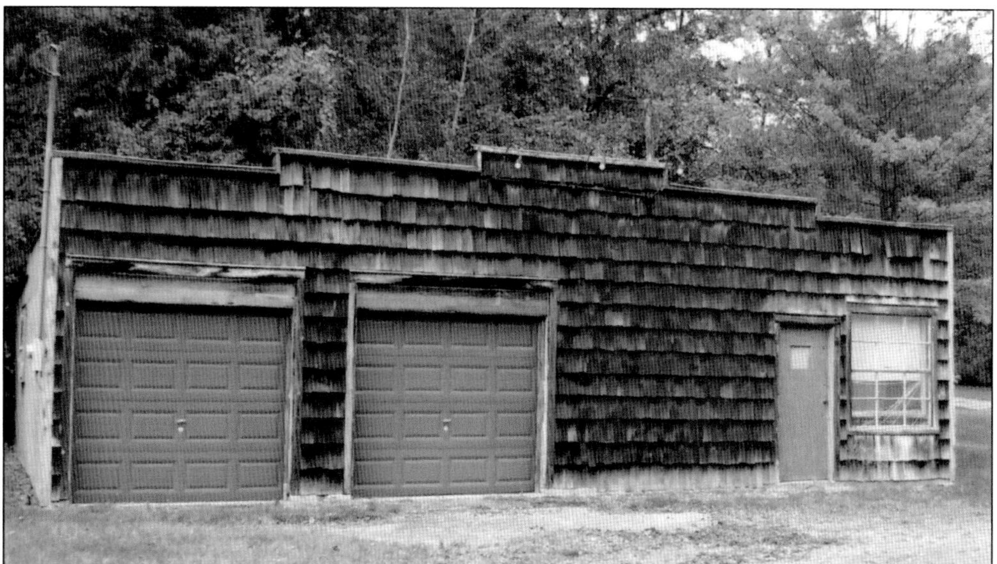

This is Joe Debie's shop as it stands today; it is used as a storage building for a rug dealer. (Photograph by the author.)

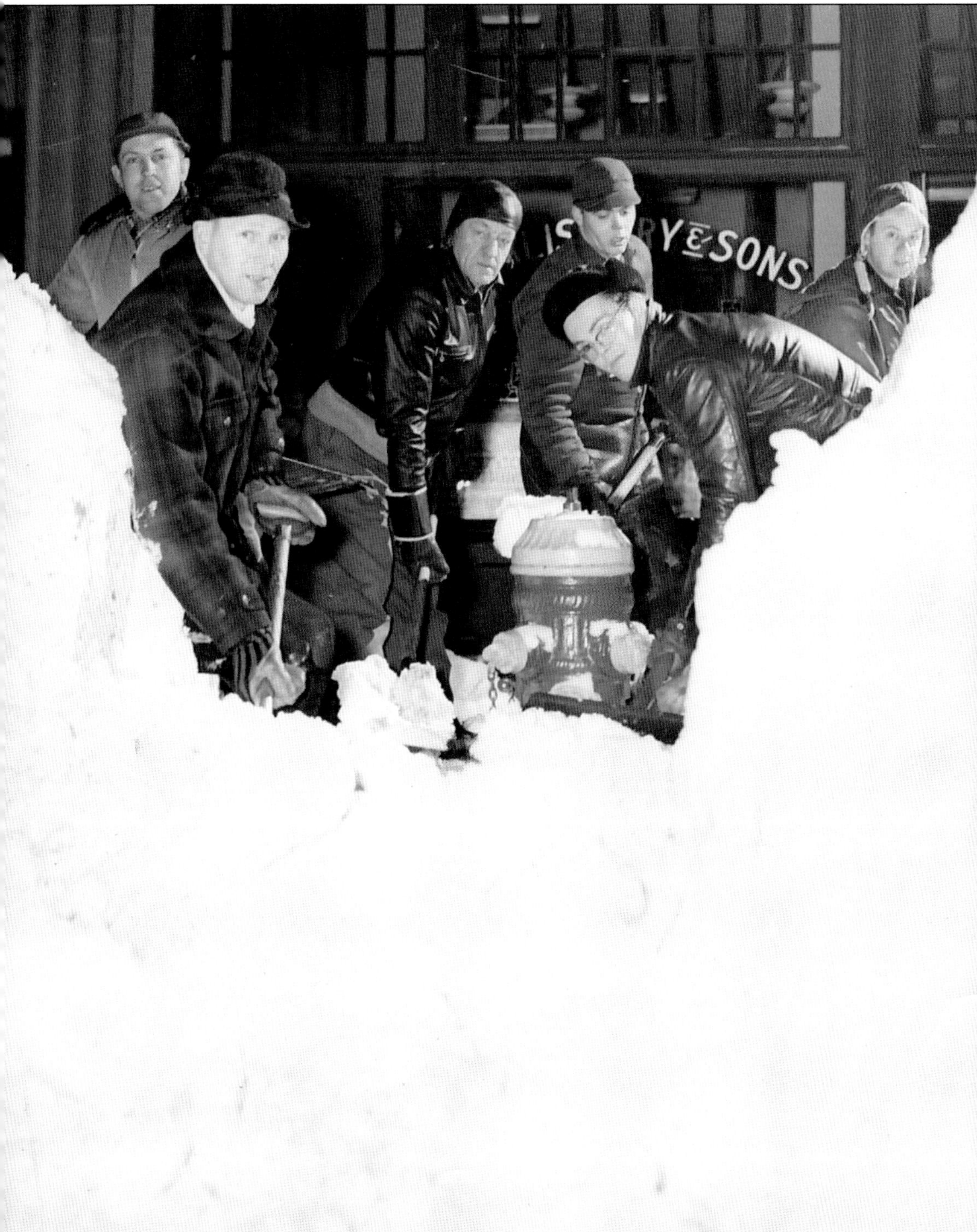

Members of the Spitzies Roamers Motorcycle Club remove snow from the fire hydrants on State Street after a snowstorm in 1958. This community service showed motorcyclists in a positive light. (Dean Splittgerber collection.)

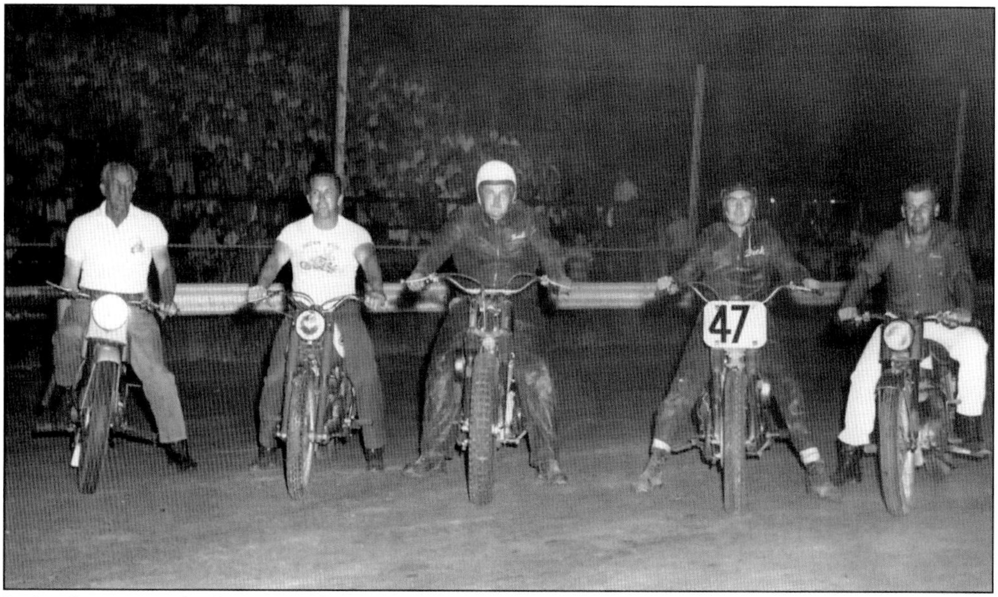

Riders line up on the front stretch of Victoria Speedway to perform a stunt show during intermission. Victoria Speedway was a half-mile dirt track located on Route 20 in Dunnsville. The track ran Sportsman stockcars from 1960 to 1966. This photograph is from the mid-1960s. From left to right are John Splittgerber, Dick Karlius, Bob "Bucky" Wertman, Dick Hickok, and Howard Wertman. (Photograph by Russ Bergh.)

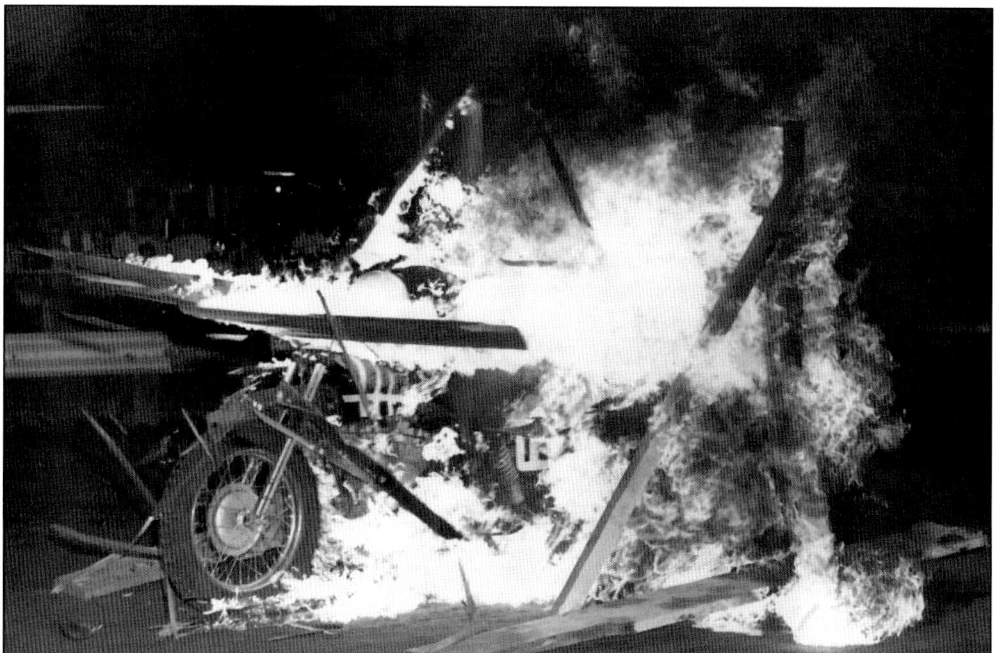

Bucky Wertman crashes his Harley-Davidson Sportster through a wall of fire for the crowd at Victoria Speedway. The boards on the wall had to be precut to insure that they would give way without knocking the rider off the bike. One of the biggest concerns was having a flaming board land in the rider's lap. (Dean Splittgerber collection.)

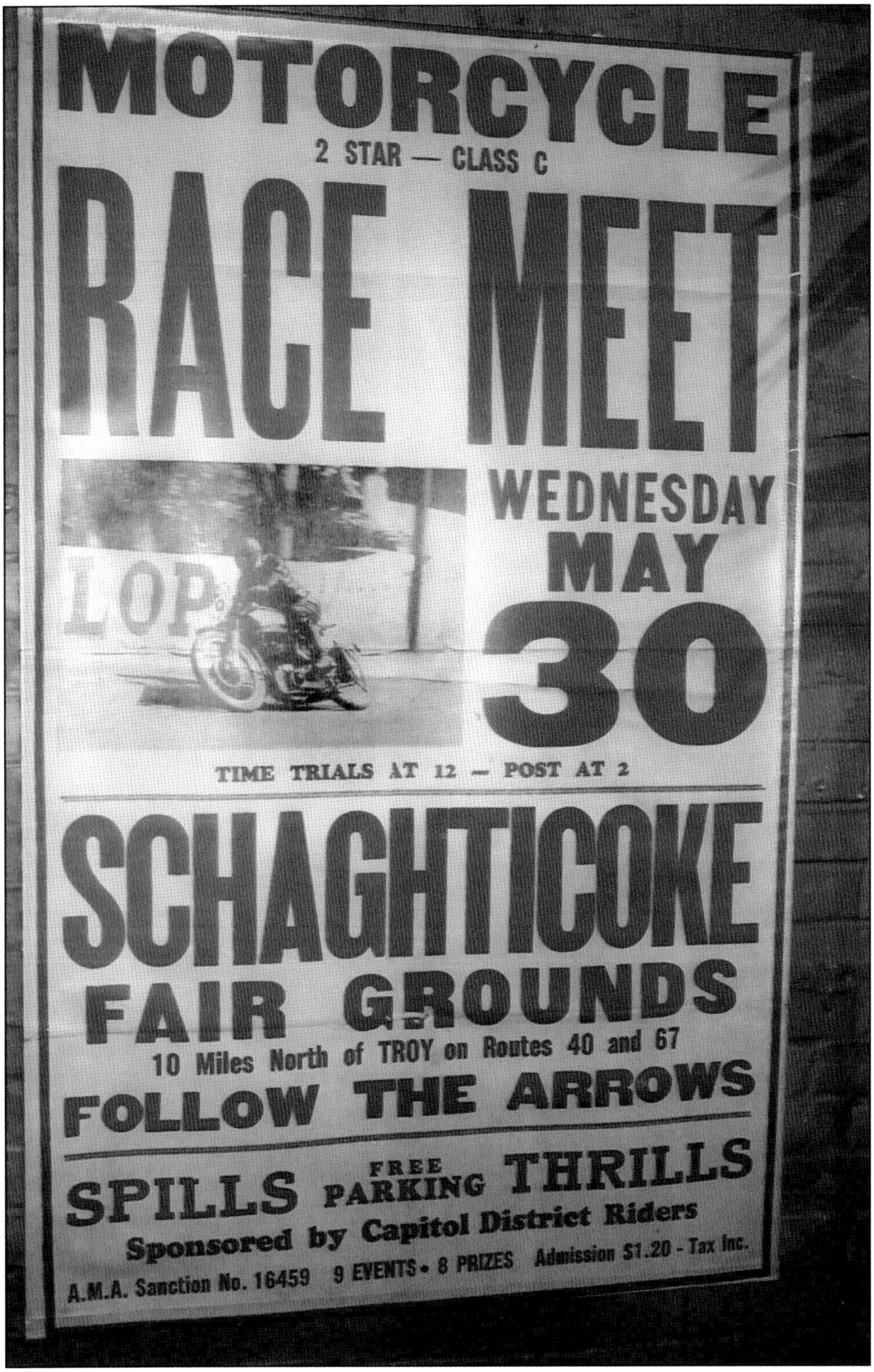

Brownie Betar's club, the Capital District Riders, was based out of Albany. It held Class C motorcycle races at the Schaghticoke Fairgrounds. Class C events were for stock-production motorcycles with the head- and taillights removed. The idea was to provide close, competitive racing on nearly identical machines. The race took place on the horse track, which was dusty and dangerous. The outside wooden fence was hard to see and a few riders crashed through it. (Photograph by the author.)

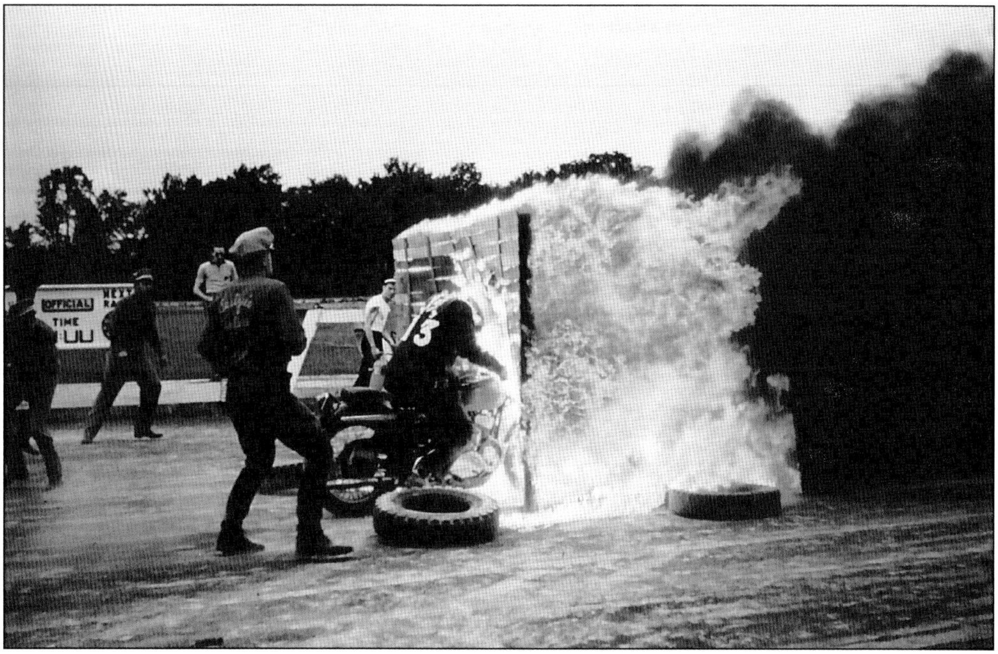

John Splittgerber jumps back as Bucky Wertman blast his K Model Sportster through a wall and tunnel of fire at the Schaghticoke Fairgrounds during an intermission. This event advertised nine events with spills and thrills; the admission cost $1.20. (Erv Splittgerber collection.)

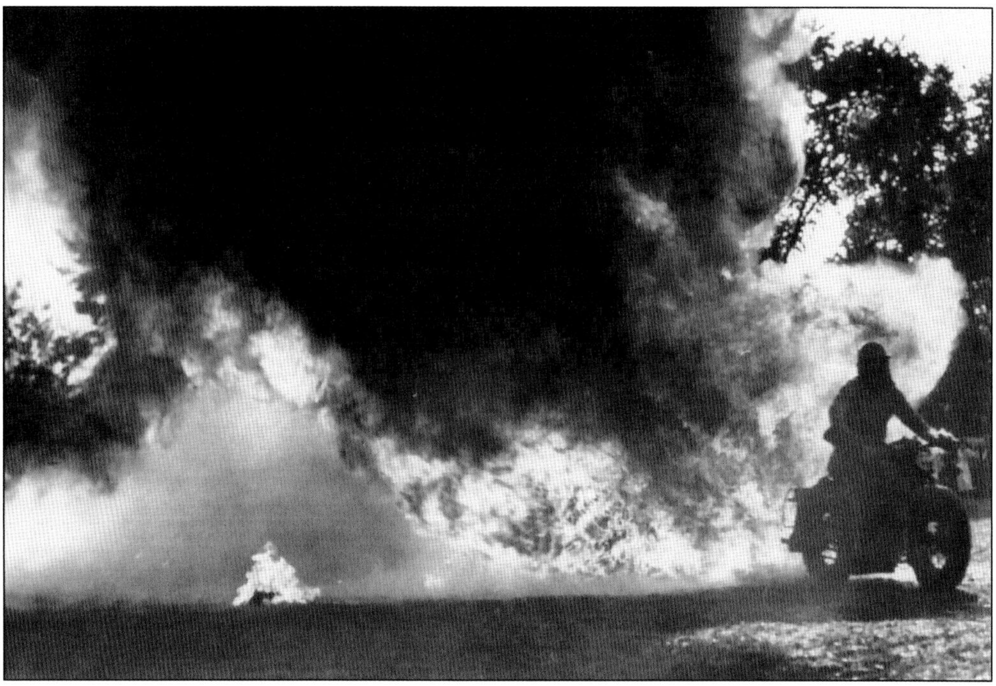

At a motorcycle meeting for the Harley-Davidson dealers in Central Bridge, John Splittgerber performed the tunnel of fire exhibition. During the performance, the fire got out of control; as John went through the fire, the oxygen was depleted, causing the engine to stall. He just barely made it out the other side. (Erv Splittgerber collection.)

New York state troopers look over their new Harley-Davidson police bikes in front of Spitzies motorcycle shop on Central Avenue. John Splittgerber, in the center, sold and maintained the motorcycle fleet for many years. (Dean Splittgerber collection.)

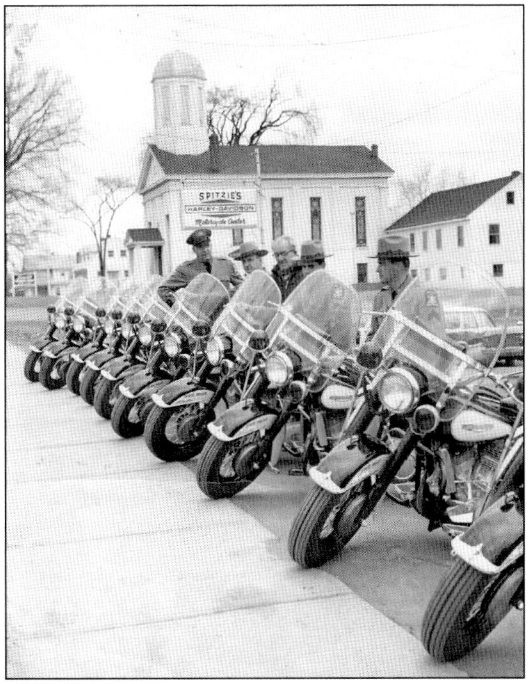

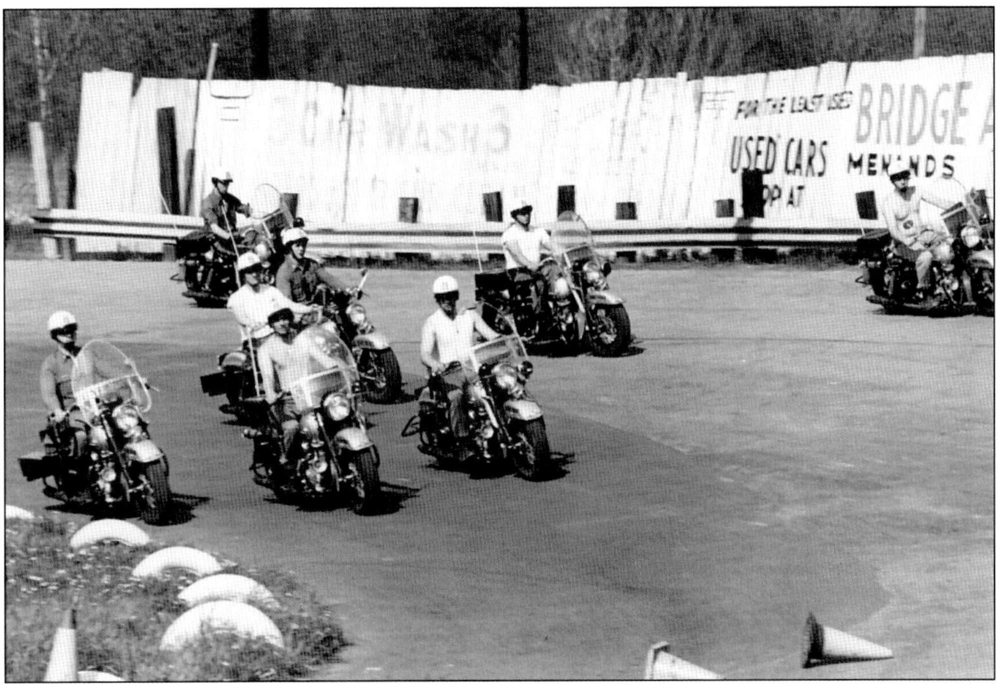

New York state troopers try out their new Harley-Davidson police bikes at the Empire Speedway in Menands. It must have been a hot day, as some of the riders are out of uniform. Empire Speedway, also known as Menands Speedway, operated from 1949 until 1961. When a drive-in theater was built next to the racetrack, the owners complained that the races were too loud. The racetrack officials moved their events from Friday nights to Wednesday nights to accommodate the drive-in. Attendance declined, and the track closed shortly after. It was replaced by a shopping plaza. (Photograph by Joe Alper.)

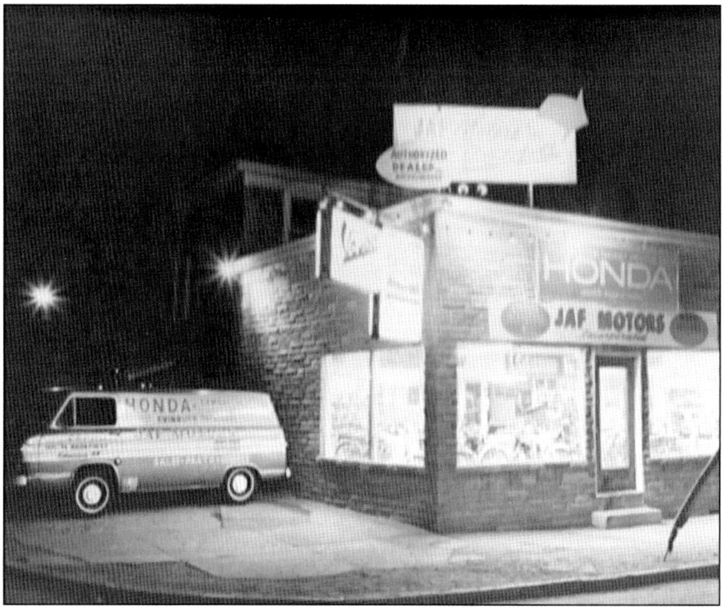

Joseph A. Farina started JAF Motors in 1959. It was located just off of Broadway on Kusie Avenue. He started by selling boats and Evinrude outboard motors. In the early 1960s, he took on Lambretta and Vespa scooters. In 1965, he became a Honda motorcycle dealer. At the time, this was a good location, as the General Electric workers would walk past on the way to and from work. (Charlie Farina collection.)

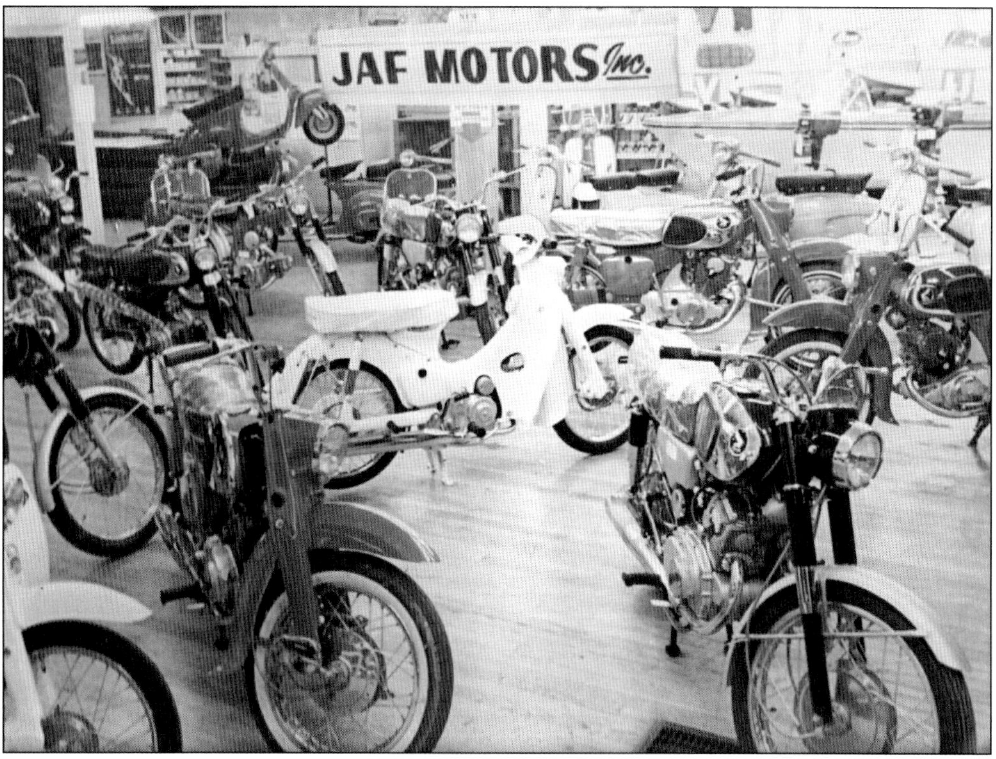

The showroom inside JAF Honda in 1965 shows a Glastron boat and a selection of scooters and Honda motorcycles. JAF stayed in this location until moving to Route 50 in Glenville in 1992. Joe's son Charlie runs the business and still sells Honda products, as well as Yamahas. (Charlie Farina collection.)

Five

Scrambles

Motorcycle scrambles, also know as tourist trophy (TT) events, were originally held on a grassy field. The riders would race around a marked-off course. By the 1960s, scramble racing really took hold. The races were held on a prepared dirt track that included both right and left turns and usually contained at least one jump. Many tracks sprang up in the Capital Area: Berne Knox, run by the Spitzies Roamers; Tribes Hill, run by Ken Hanson; Argyle, run by the Northway Riders; Chatam, run by the Columbia County Riders; and Keck Center, run by the Rolling Mohawk Motorcycle Club.

With the influx of smaller-displacement motorcycles, like Bultaco and Ossa from Spain and Zundapp from Germany, this form of racing became very popular.

The next big influx of motorcycles from Japan, produced by the big three (Kawasaki, Honda, and Yamaha), made scramble racing available to anyone who wished to try it. The bikes came ready to race; all the riders had to do was add gas and a number plate and they were ready to go.

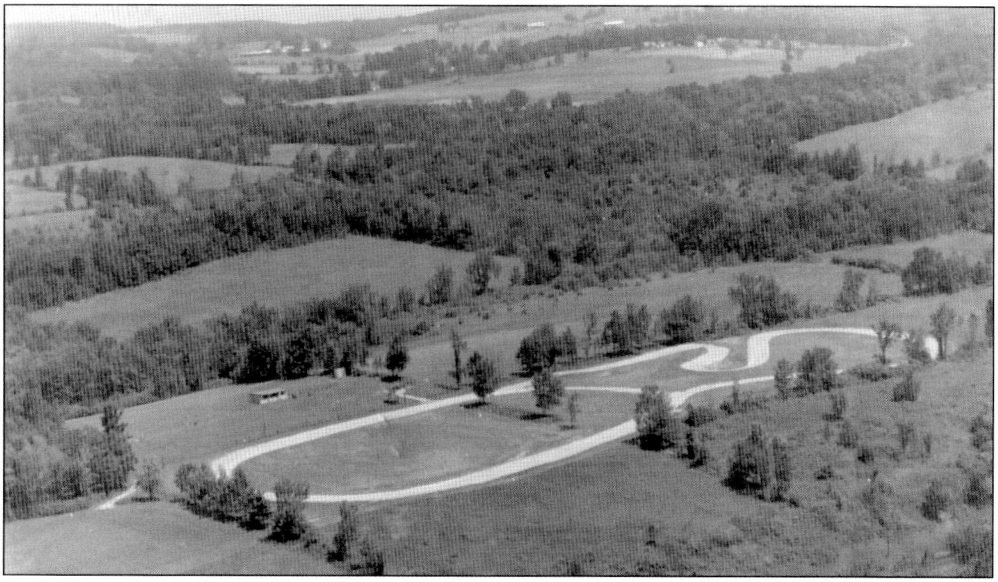

The Electric City Riders decided to build a track in 1962 on rented land in Duanesburg. The landowner, William Lee, and club treasurer, Larry Dagostino, had a gentlemen's agreement that as long as people wanted to race they could race here. When both men passed away, so did the agreement. The track existed until 2008, when the new landowners decided to sell. The earlier track was located in the field near the concession stand in this photograph. (Larry Dagostino Jr. collection.)

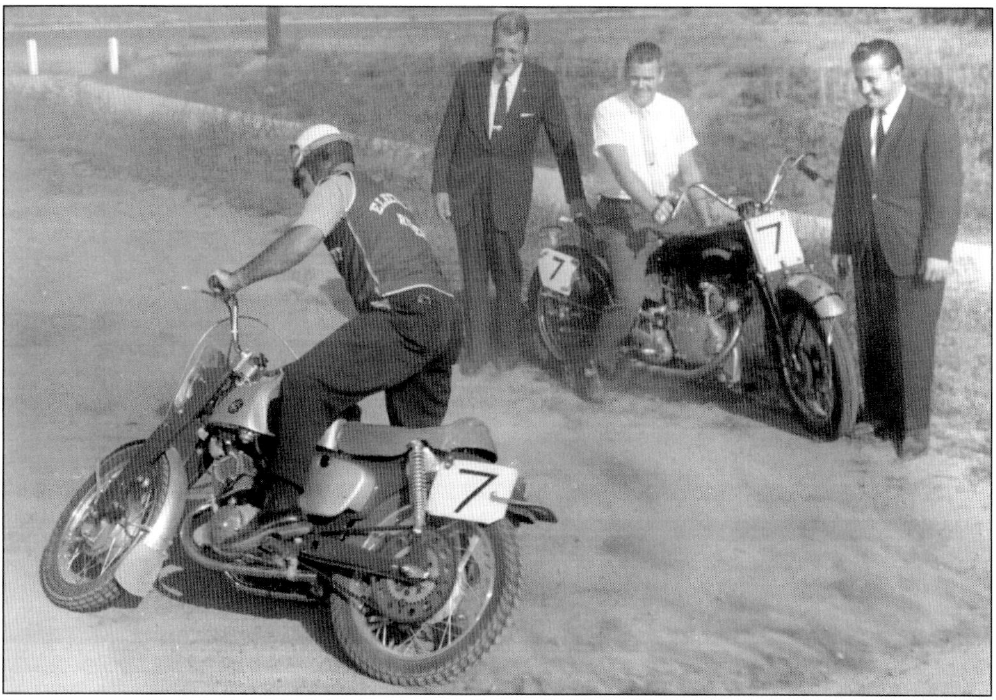

Two Kiwanis Club members in suits watch as Larry Dagostino does a donut on his Honda. This photograph was used in the *Schenectady Gazette* to promote an upcoming race. Looking on from left to right are an unidentified man; Dick Debie, sitting on the 500cc Vincent motorcycle, and Ken Dagostino. (Larry Dagostino Jr. collection.)

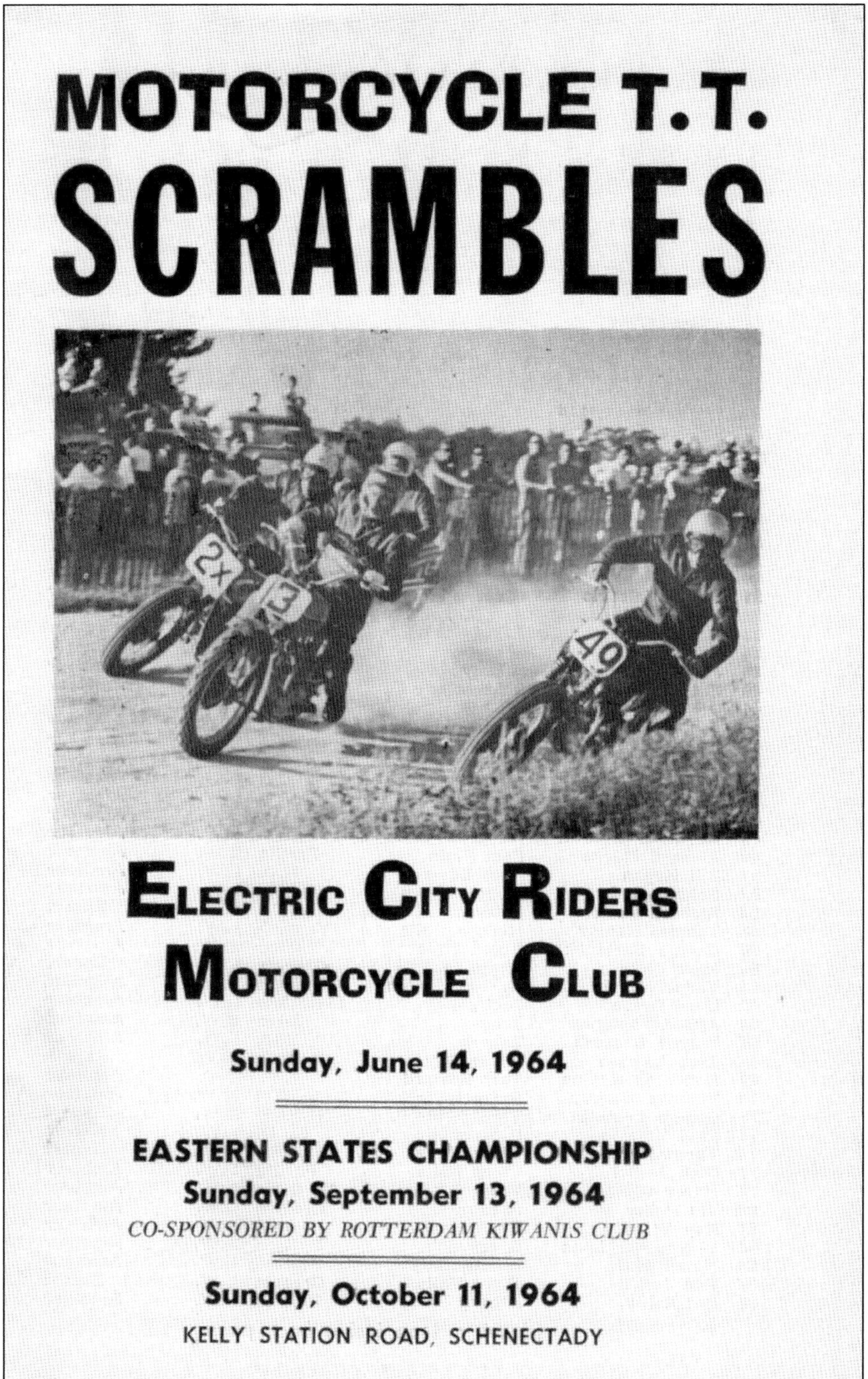

In 1964, the Electric City Riders track was elected by the Eastern New York State Sports Committee to hold the Eastern State Championships, which drew the top riders in the Northeast. The Rotterdam Kiwanis Club cosponsored these events, helping with advertising and ticket sales. (Author's collection.)

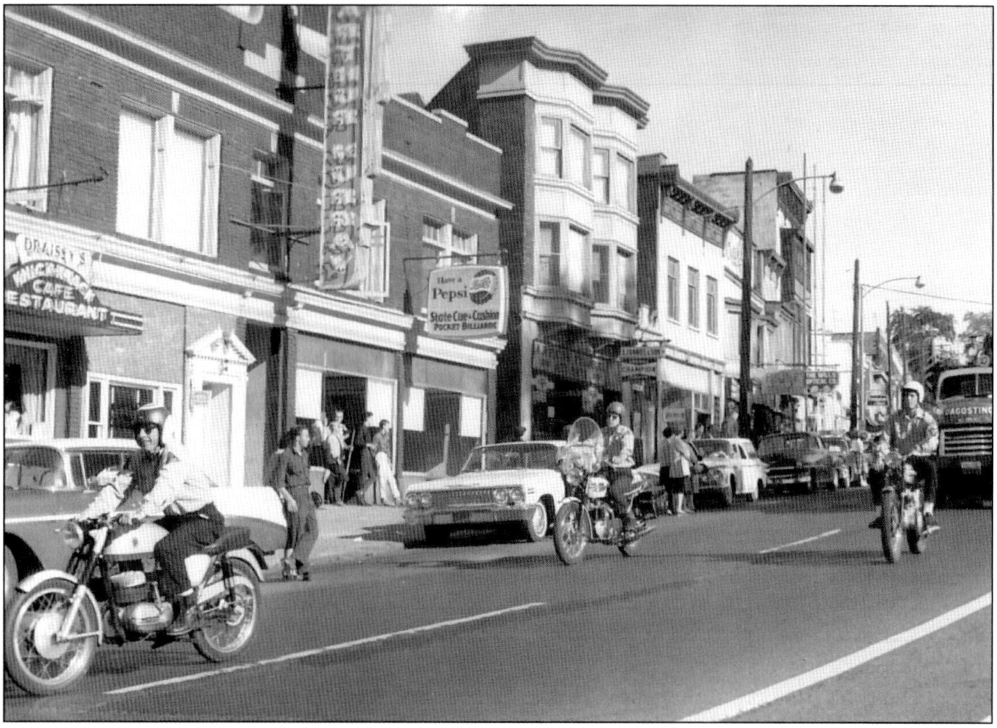

On September 14, 1963, the Electric City Riders were in a parade in Schenectady. Chuck Hebert, on a Bultaco, leads Howard Newell and John Parks on their Triumphs down State Street. (Randi Hebert collection.)

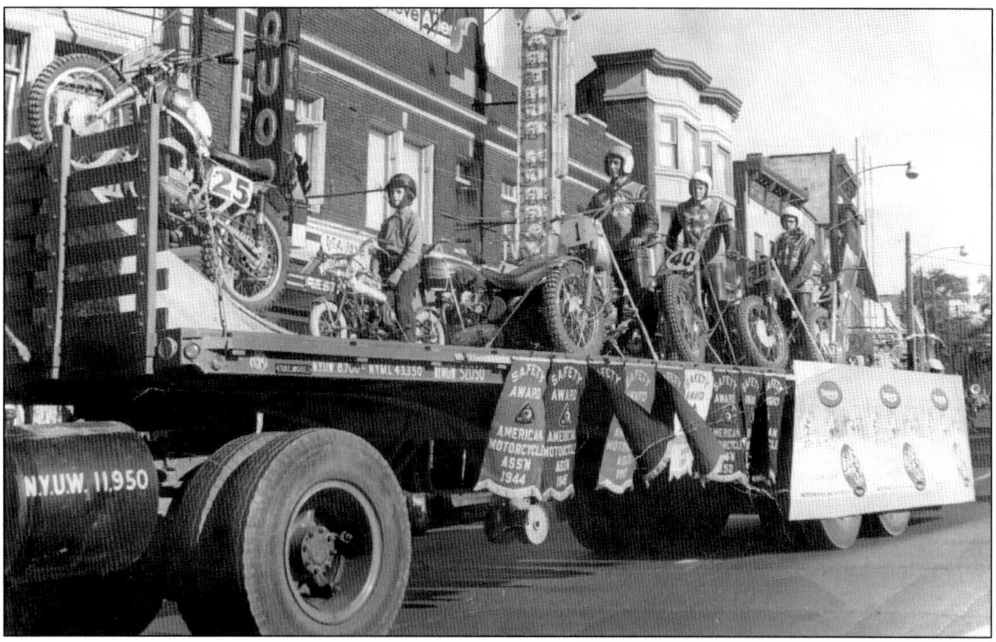

American Motorcycle Association Safety Award banners proudly hang from the Electric City Riders' float as it passes by the Arthur Murray Dance Studio. From left to right, Tim Newell, George Bartzak, John Green, and Dave Green enjoy the ride. (Howard Newell collection.)

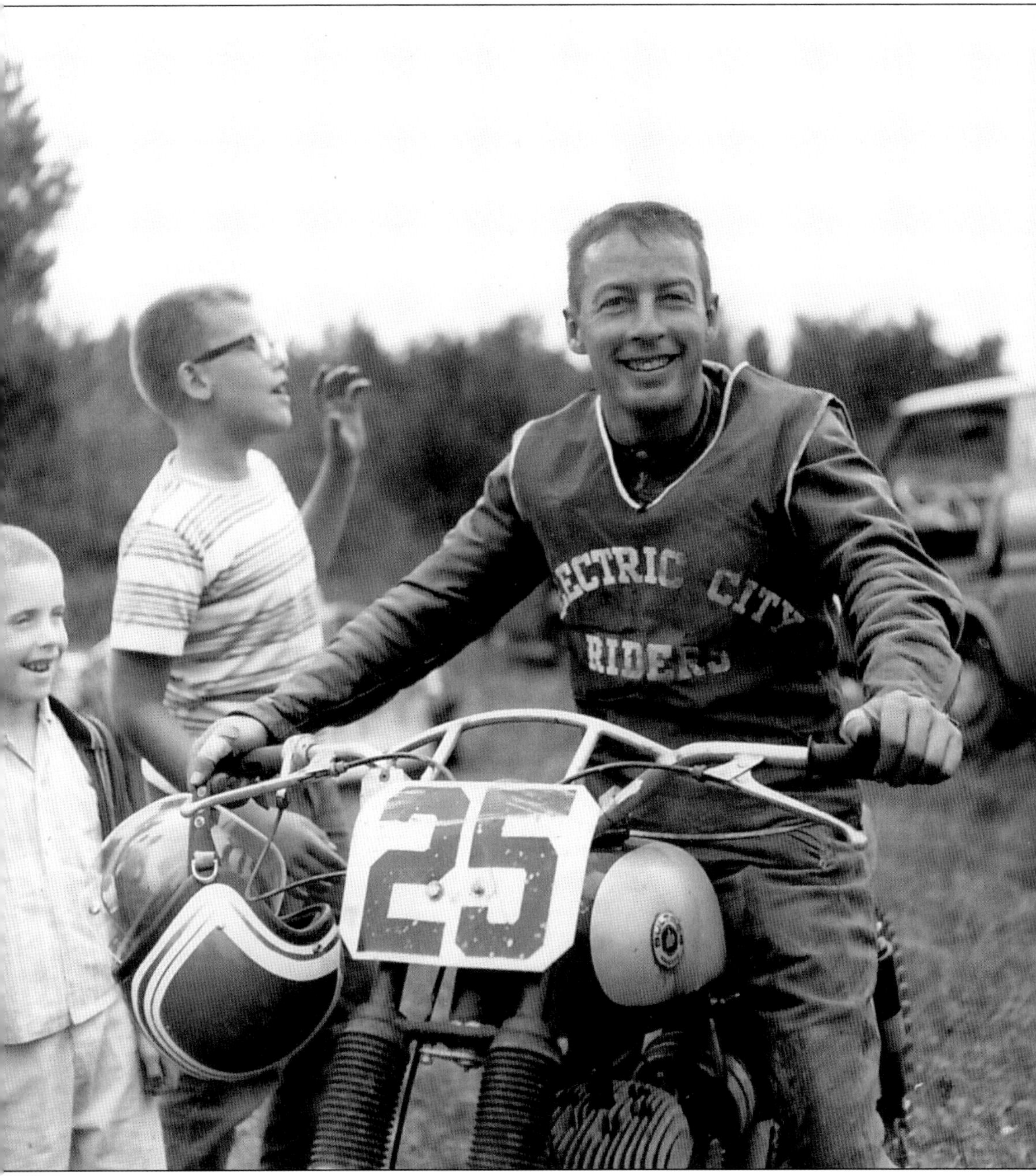

Trent Taylor (left) and Dean Splittgerber congratulate Chuck Hebert after a win on his Bultaco. Chuck was sponsored by Spitzies, who was a new distributor for the brand. (Randi Hebert collection.)

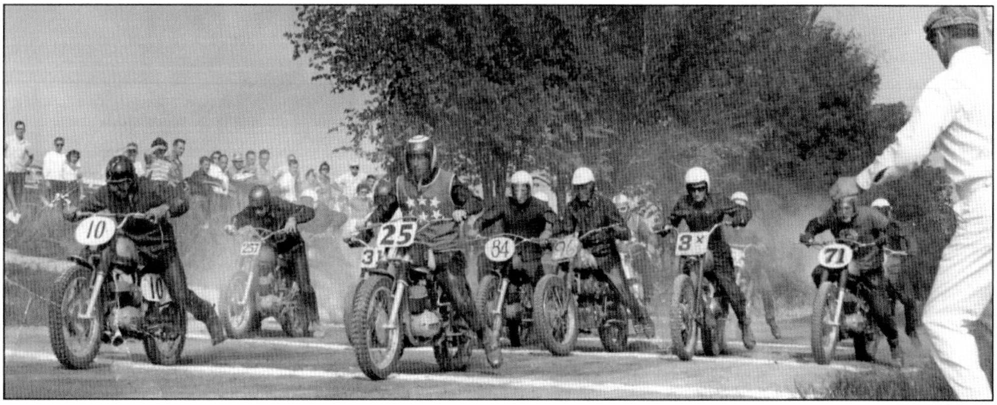

Joe Debie waves the flag to start the very competitive 185cc Bantam Class. Chuck Hebert gets a good start on number 25 to lead the pack into turn one. Don Dillman, 10; Jim Valovic, 31; Nolan Hill, 84; Johnny "Fast" Wiedman, 96; three unidentified racers; and George Crosetta, 71, are close behind. (Randi Hebert collection.)

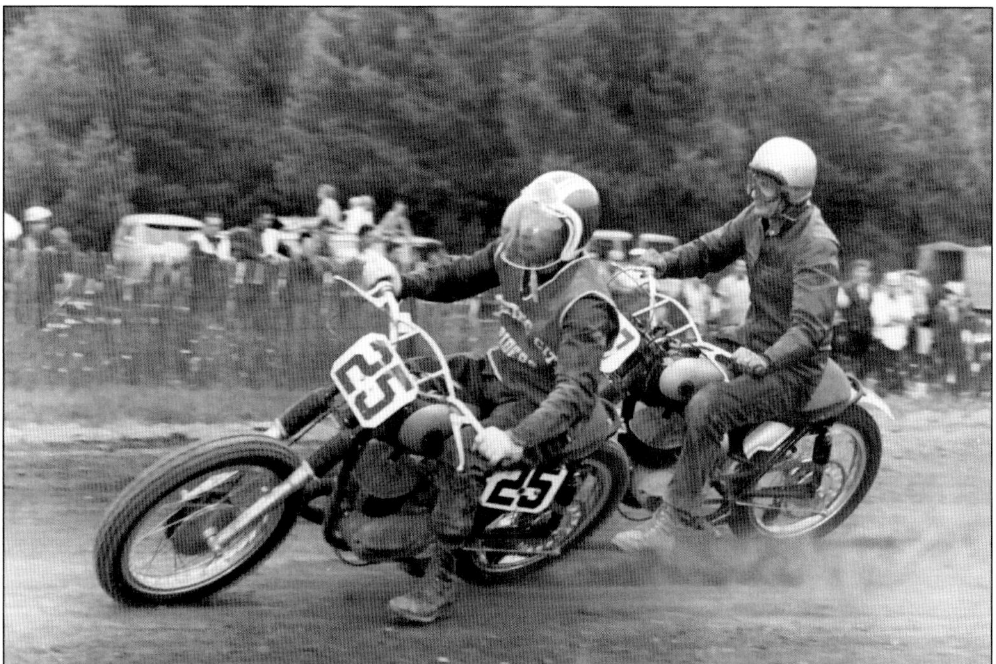

Chuck Hebert leads Ray Palen at the Knox track. Ray was killed in 1964 at Orange County Speedway when he missed a gear and hit the wall in turn three. He died from broken ribs and a collapsed lung. (Randi Hebert collection.)

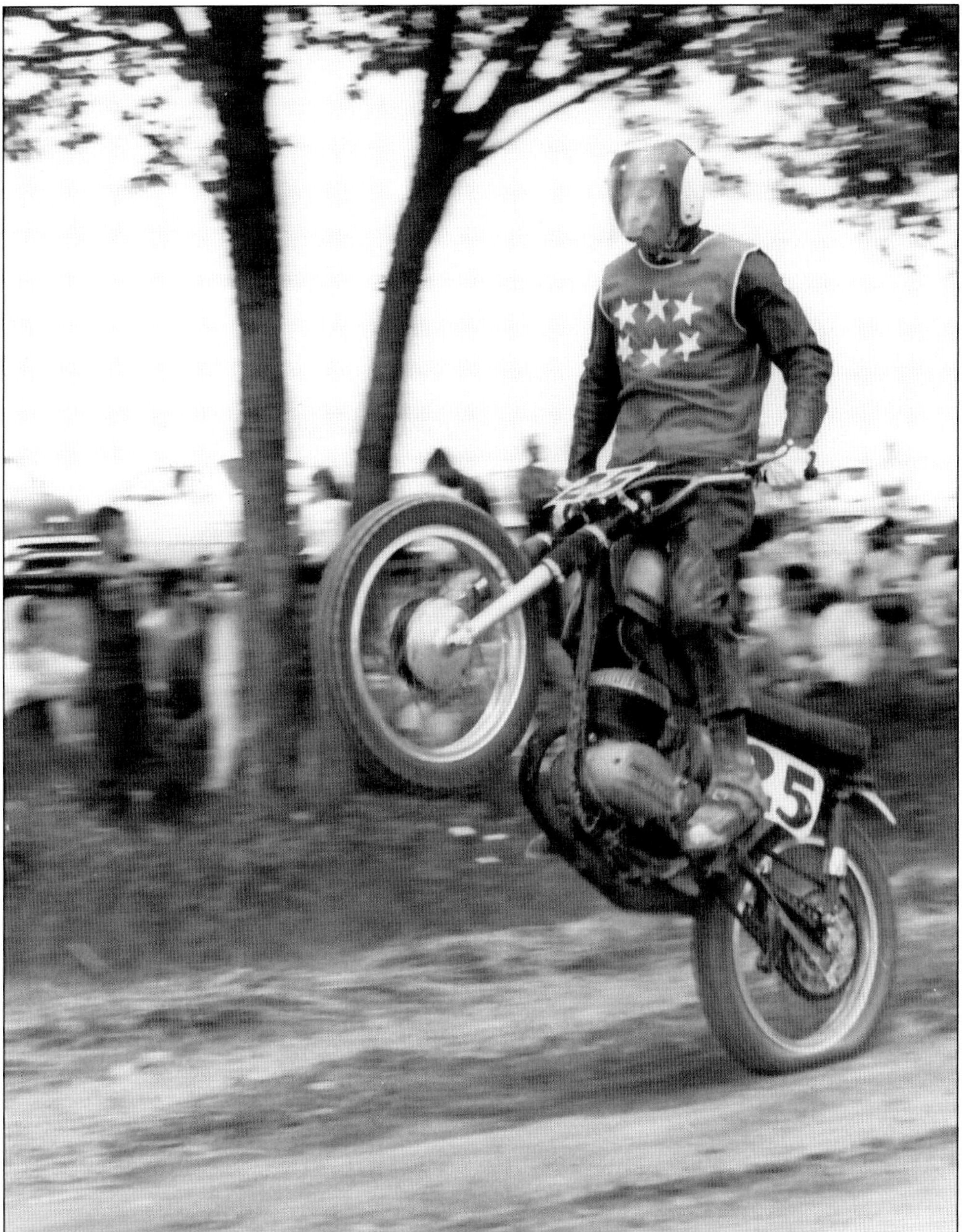

Chuck Hebert wheelies his Bultaco over the jump in the front stretch at the Electric City track in 1963. Riders' bibs were used to designate what club they were affiliated with. Each club had its own design. Electric City Riders had bibs with stars; some also had the club name. That tradition faded in the 1970s due to an influx of riders that were not in a club. (Randi Hebert collection.)

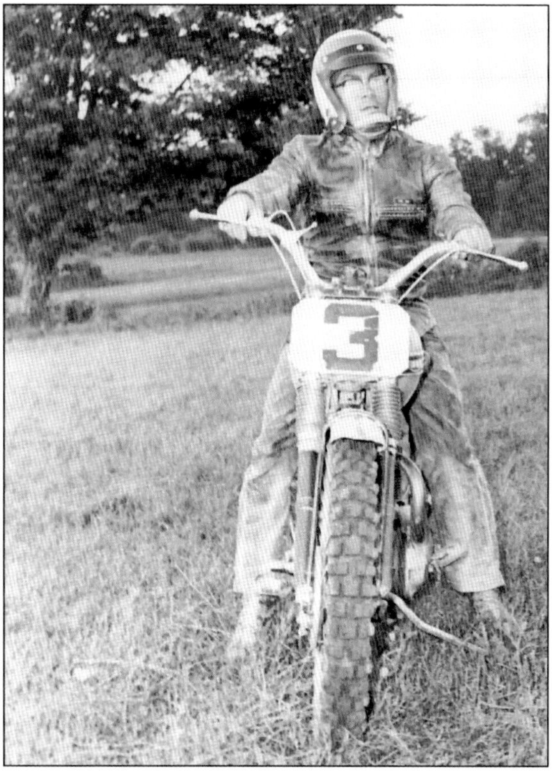

Harold "Pee Wee" North prepares to do battle in 1962 on his 500cc Triumph. North had many good races with Bob Lanfear, Wayne Hovey, and Marty Kvinlaug. (Photograph by Larry Dagostino.)

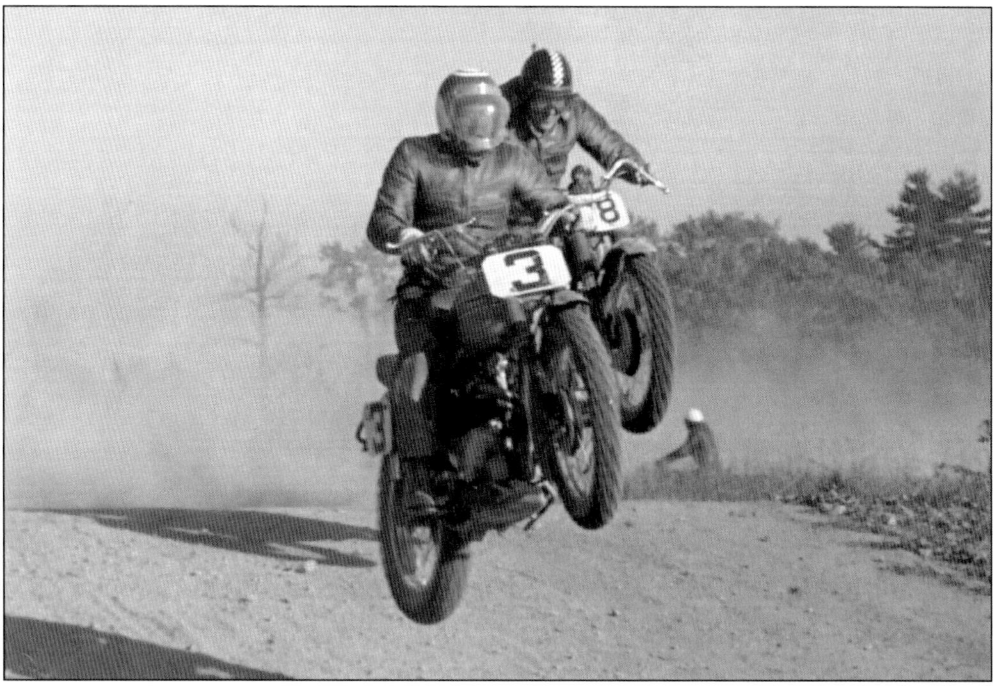

Pee Wee leads Marty Kvinlaug over the jump during the 500cc expert event at the Electric City Riders track. North was the stepson of Louie Lichva, who helped form the Antique Motorcycle Club of America. (Marty Kvinlaug collection.)

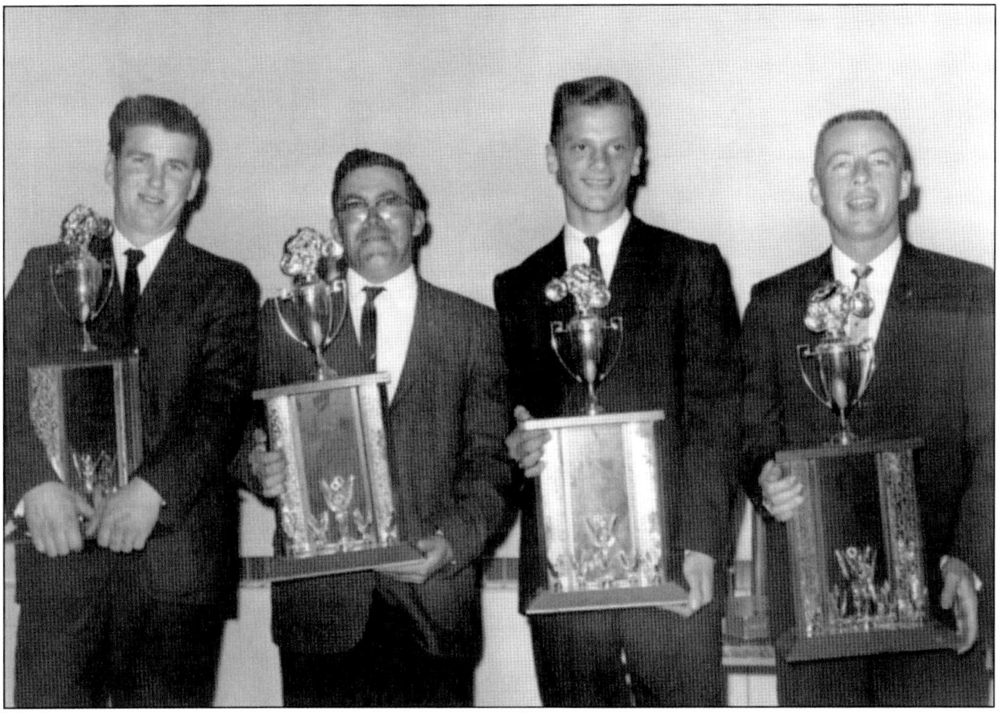

The Eastern New York State Sports Committee awards were handed out at the Electric City Riders awards banquet in 1962 for the 1961 season. The champions were, from left to right, Ron Gleason, Harold North, John Valovic, and Chuck Hebert. (Randi Hebert collection.)

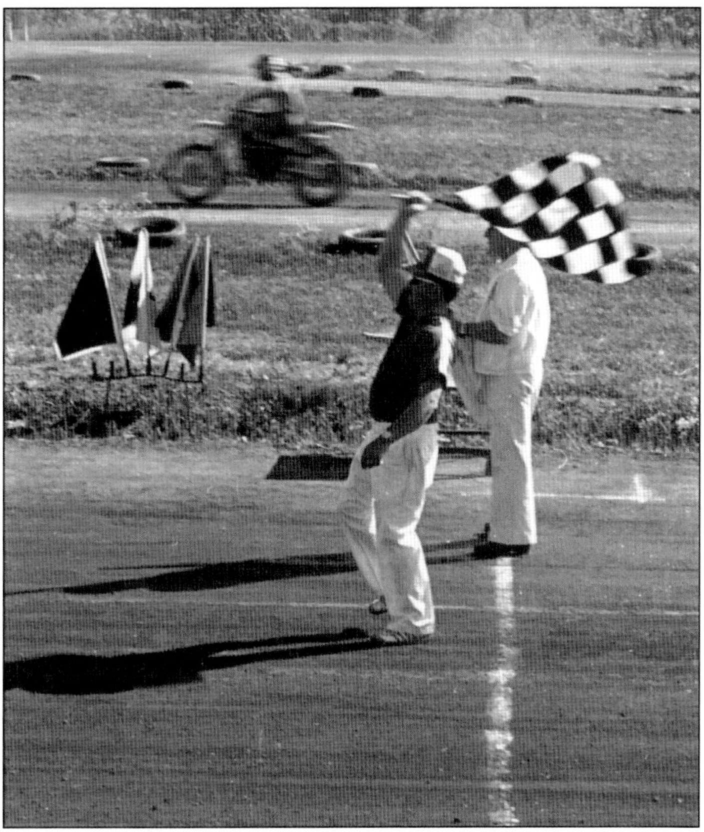

In later years, Pee Wee went on to be the official starter for the Electric City Riders Club, flagging both dirt and ice races for many years. He was always chewing on his trademark cigar. (Joe Corbett collection.)

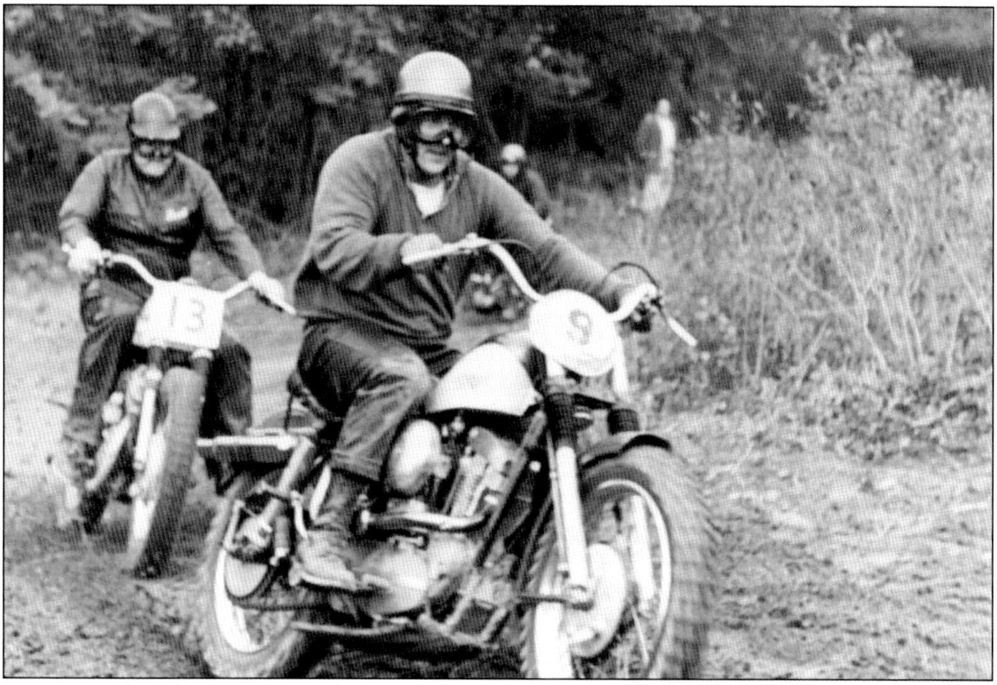

Marty Kvinlaug leads Bob "Bucky" Wertman in the Open Expert Class. Both men are riding Harley-Davidson Sportsters. Marty is on an XLCH and Bucky is on a K Model. This was on the old TT track prior to 1962, before the new track was built. (Marty Kvinlaug collection.)

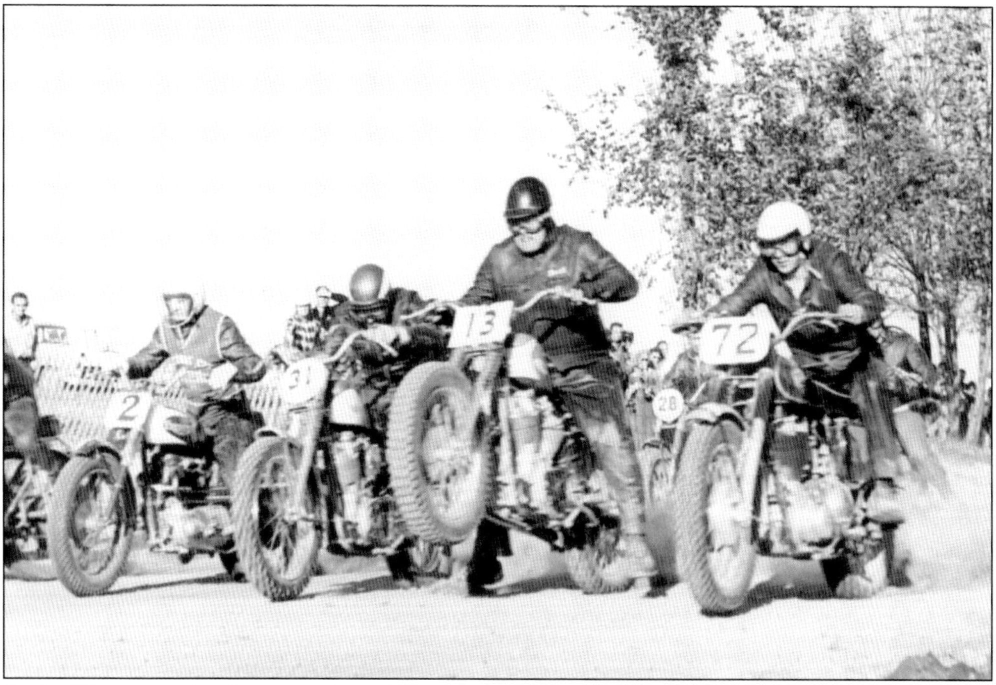

Bucky Wertman wheelies away from the start on his Harley-Davidson in the Open Expert Class. Dick Debie, 2, is on a Triumph; Marty Kvinlaug, 31, is on a Harley. Bucky became the starter for the club in the early 1960s, replacing Dick Hickok. (Marty Kvinlaug collection.)

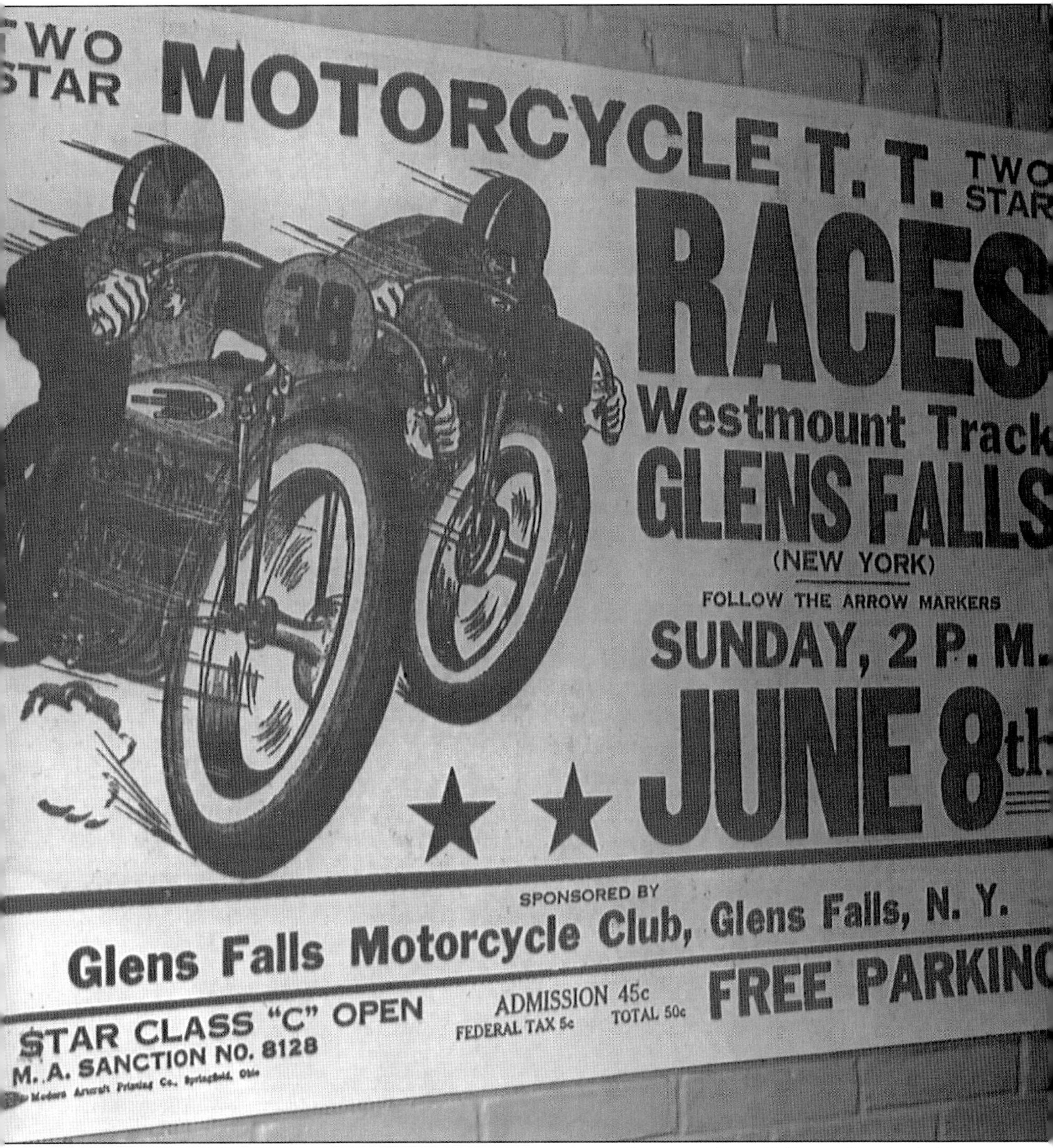

Motorcycle TT races were held at the Westmount racetrack in the late 1940s and early 1950s. The Glens Falls Motorcycle Club sponsored the races, which were AMA sanctioned and featured Class C open events. The track was relocated in the 1960s to Argyle and was run by the Northway Riders Club. (Author's collection.)

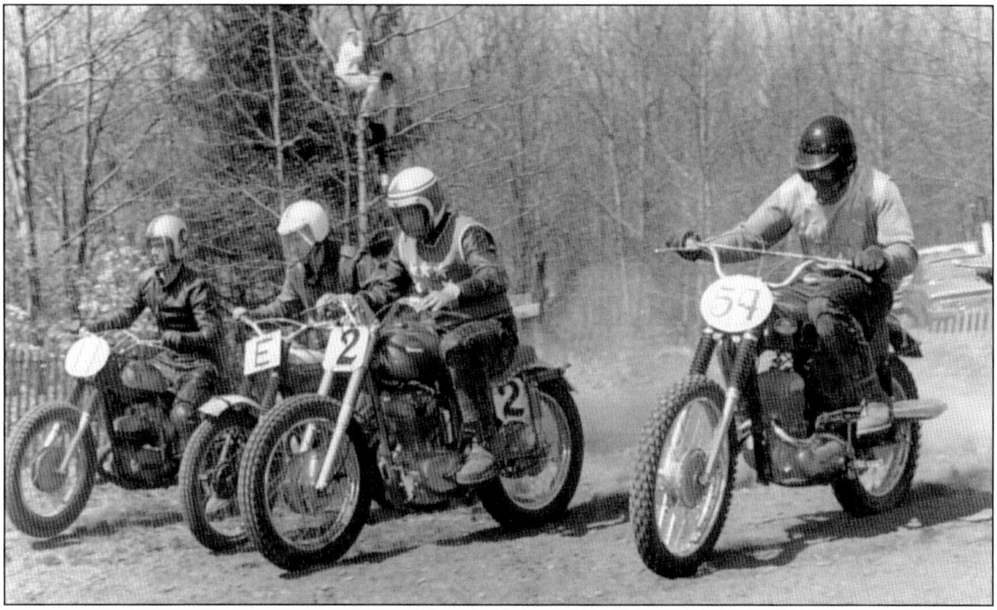

The 250cc Expert Class takes off at the Knox track. From left to right are John Taylor, Sky Brown, Dick Debie, and Joe Bolger. In 1962, John Taylor became the eastern United States distributor for the Bultaco Motorcycle Company. He later became the chief executive officer of the Cemoto East Importing Company and dropped Bultaco for the Ossa brand of motorcycles. He later formed the Yankee Motorcycle Company to manufacture motorcycles under the Yankee name. (Marty Kvinlaug collection.)

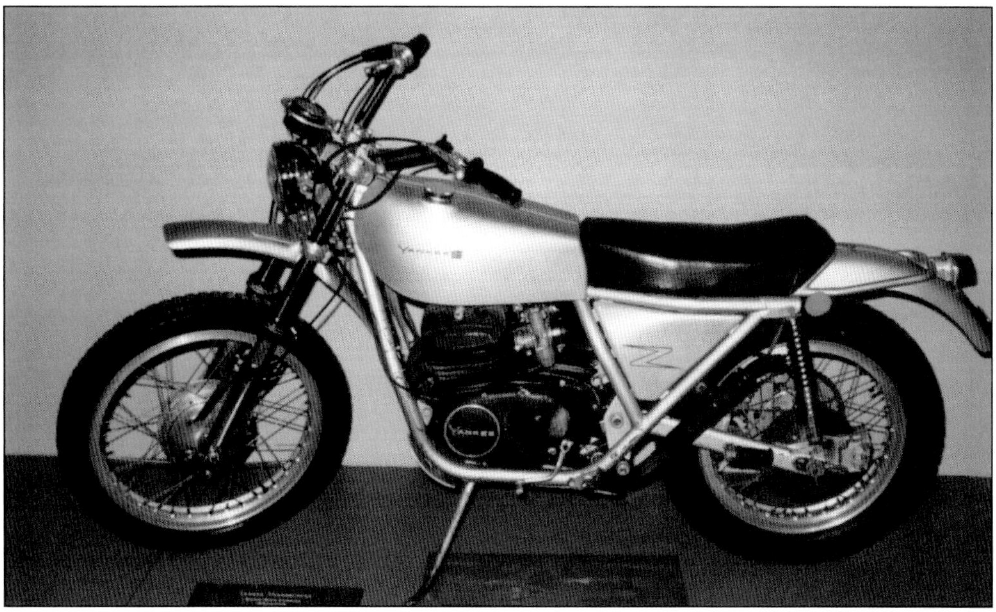
Yankee motorcycles were built at 2910 Campbell Avenue in Schenectady in 1968. This Yankee 500cc Z enduro model made its debut in 1972. It carried the first new American motorcycle trade name in 30 years. The machine was late getting to the market and was plagued by lack of development. The death of John Taylor's son, Trent, in the crash of a motorcycle he was testing may have also led to the demise of the brand. A total of 750 machines were manufactured, ending in 1973. (Photograph by the author.)

Marty Kvinlaug, from Albany, was known as the "Terror of the Northeast." He rode many brands of bikes, both big and small. Harley-Davidsons, BSA, Greeves, Bultaco: it did not matter, he won on them all. (Marty Kvinlaug collection.)

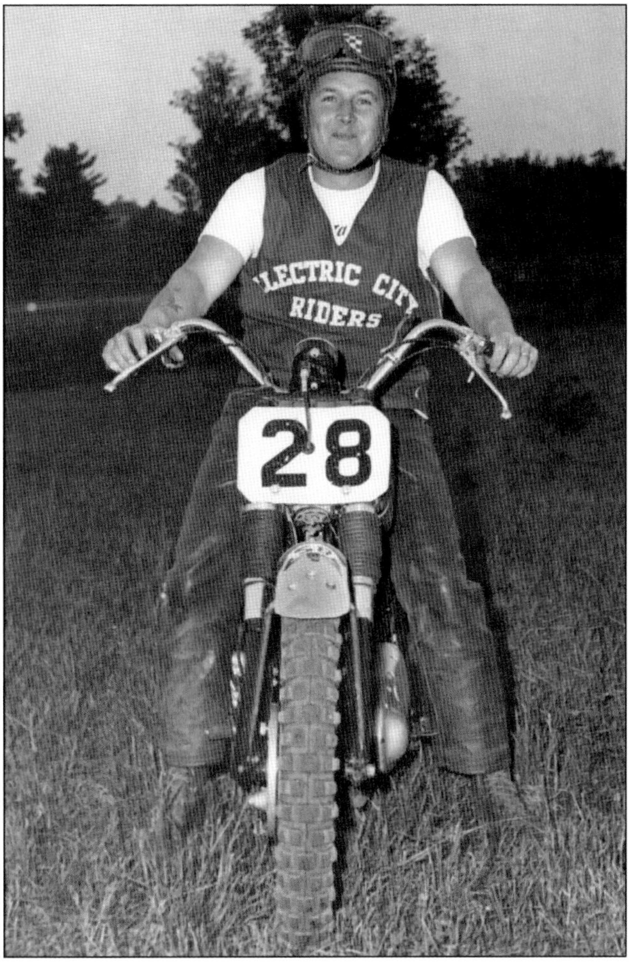

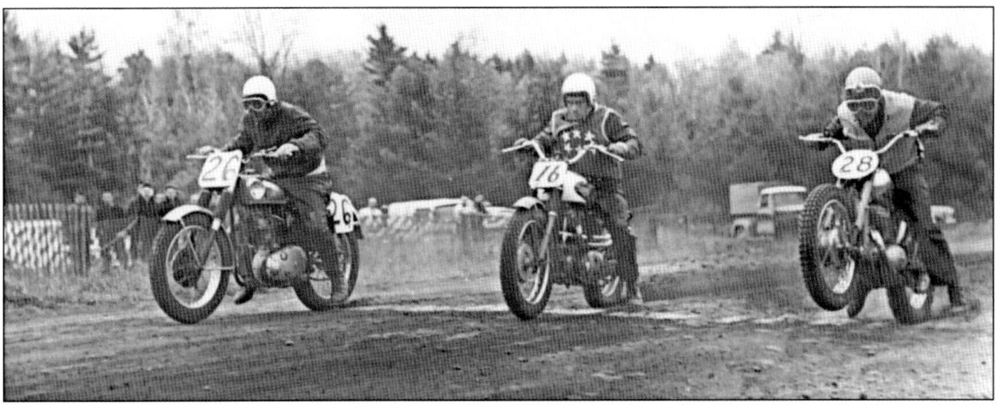

The headline in the December 1962 *Cycle Sport* magazine read "Kvinlaug Beats the Big Bikes." The winner of the High Point Trophy at Knox TT Track for 1962 had to be determined in a runoff on October 21, 1962, as three riders were tied on the season's points. These were Mike Dahlin on a Triumph 650, Bob Lanfear on a BSA 500, and Marty Kvinlaug on a 250 Greeves. It turned out to be a big afternoon for Marty. Off the line is Bob Lanfear, 26; Mike Dahlin, 16; and Marty Kvinlaug, 28. (Marty Kvinlaug collection.)

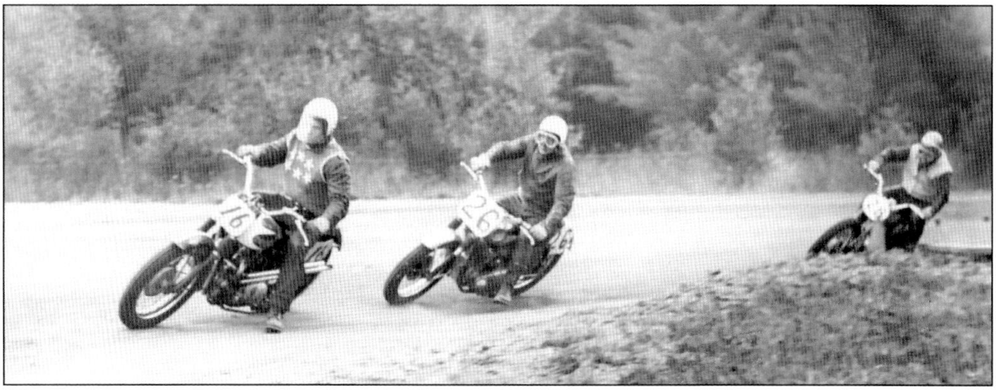

At the first turn of the eight-lap race, Kvinlaug has been outpowered by the bigger bikes and trails Dahlin and Lanfear. (Marty Kvinlaug collection.)

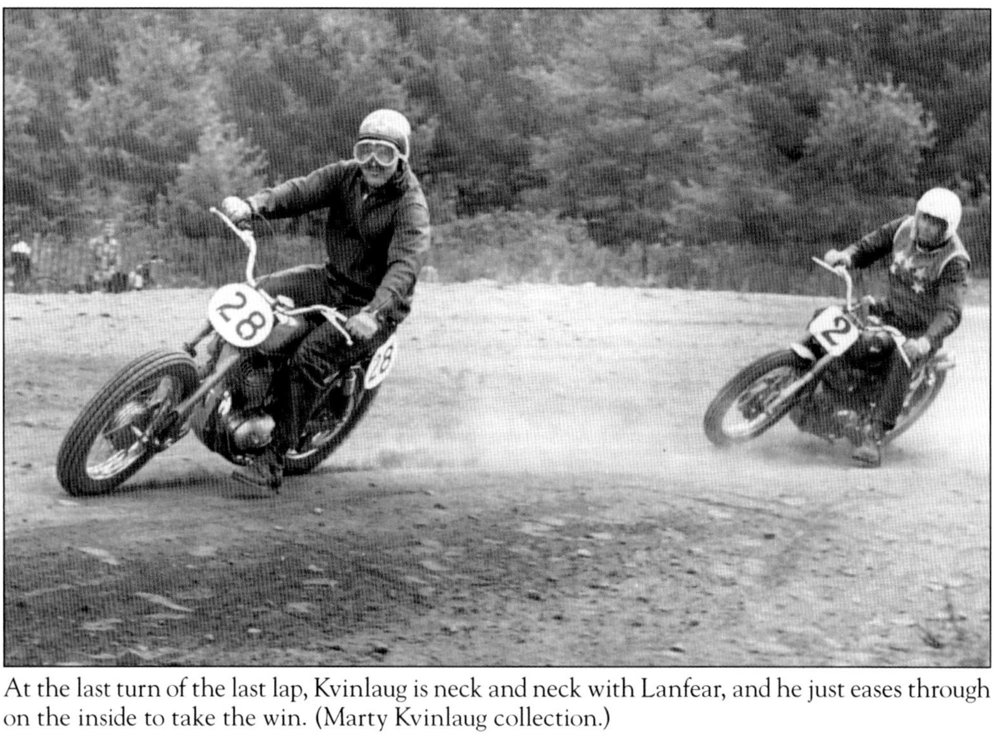

At the last turn of the last lap, Kvinlaug is neck and neck with Lanfear, and he just eases through on the inside to take the win. (Marty Kvinlaug collection.)

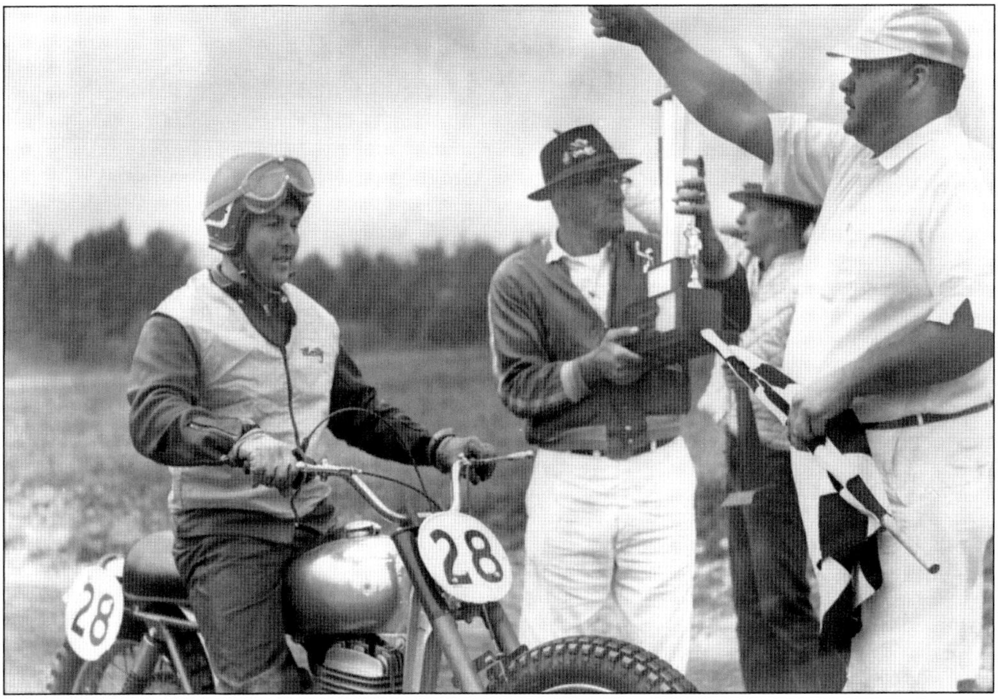

Marty receives the checkered flag from Bob Wertman as John Splittgerber gets ready to present the High Point Trophy. (Marty Kvinlaug collection.)

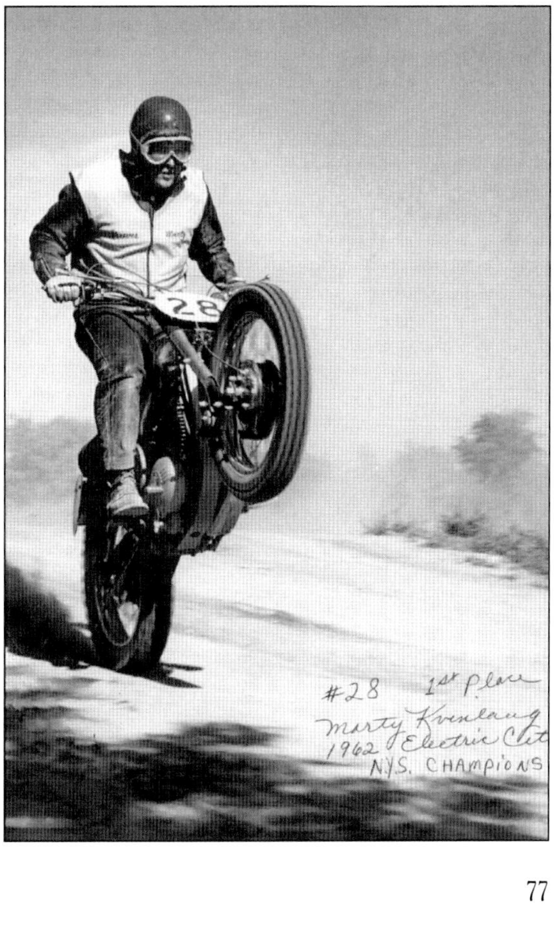

In 1962, Marty also won the New York State Championship, held at the Electric City Riders track, aboard a square-barrel 250 Greeves. (Marty Kvinlaug collection.)

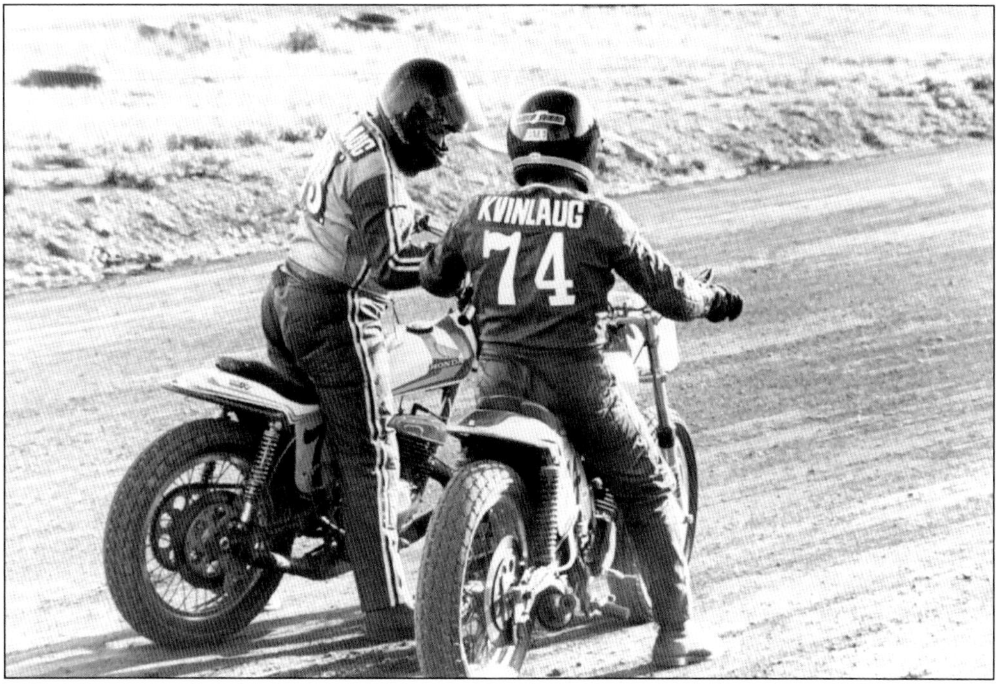

Jeff and Eric Kvinlaug kept the tradition going in the 1970s and 1980s. Now, both of their sons, Evan and Eric, are the third generation to compete. (Joe Corbett collection.)

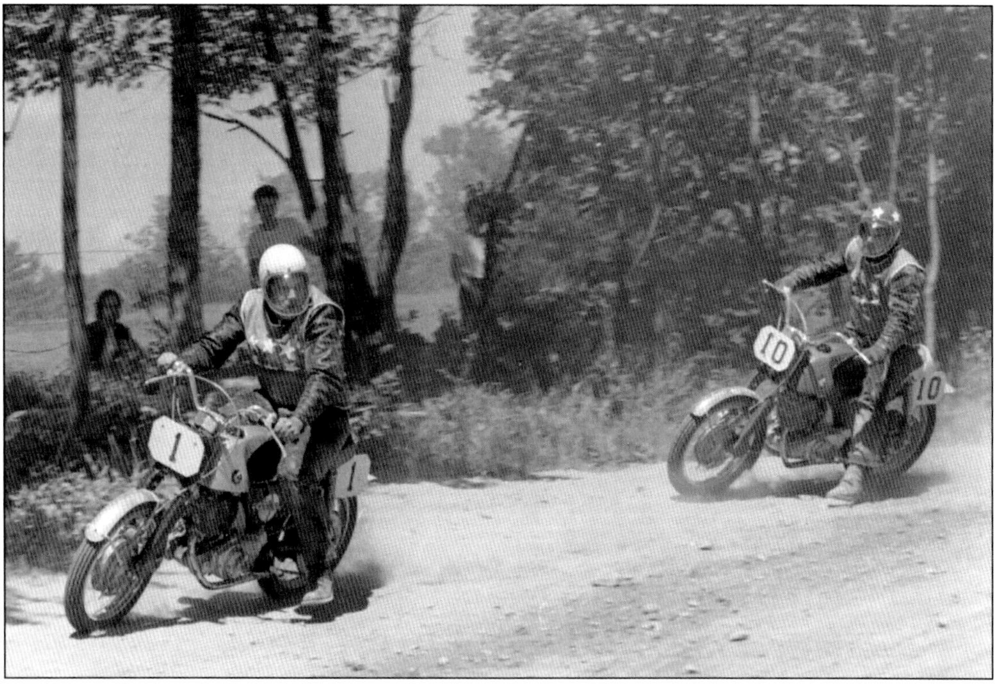

Bob Newell carries the number one plate that he won during the 1966 season. He leads his brother, Howard; they were both riding Honda Benly 125cc machines, also known as CB-92s. Notice they are both wearing the starred club vests to identify them as Electric City Riders. (Bob Newell collection.)

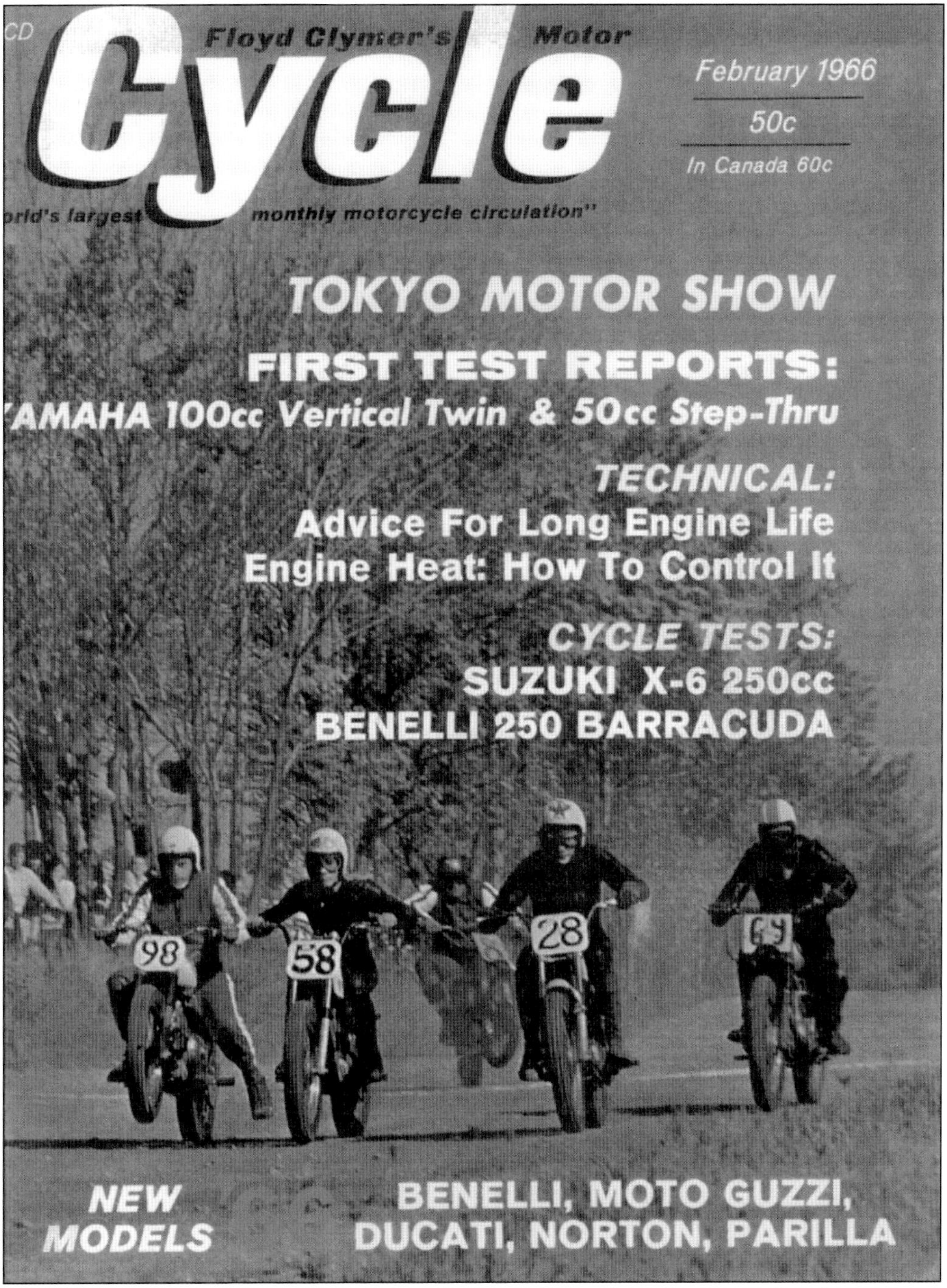

In February 1966, the Electric City Riders track was featured on the cover of *Cycle* magazine, promoting the popularity of scramble racing. Jess Thomas, 28, takes the lead off the starting line, with Tom Courtney, 98; Jody Nicholas, 58; and Clem Nash, 69, in hot pursuit. Both Courtney and Nicholas were working for Cemoto East and John Taylor at the time. (Tim Newell collection.)

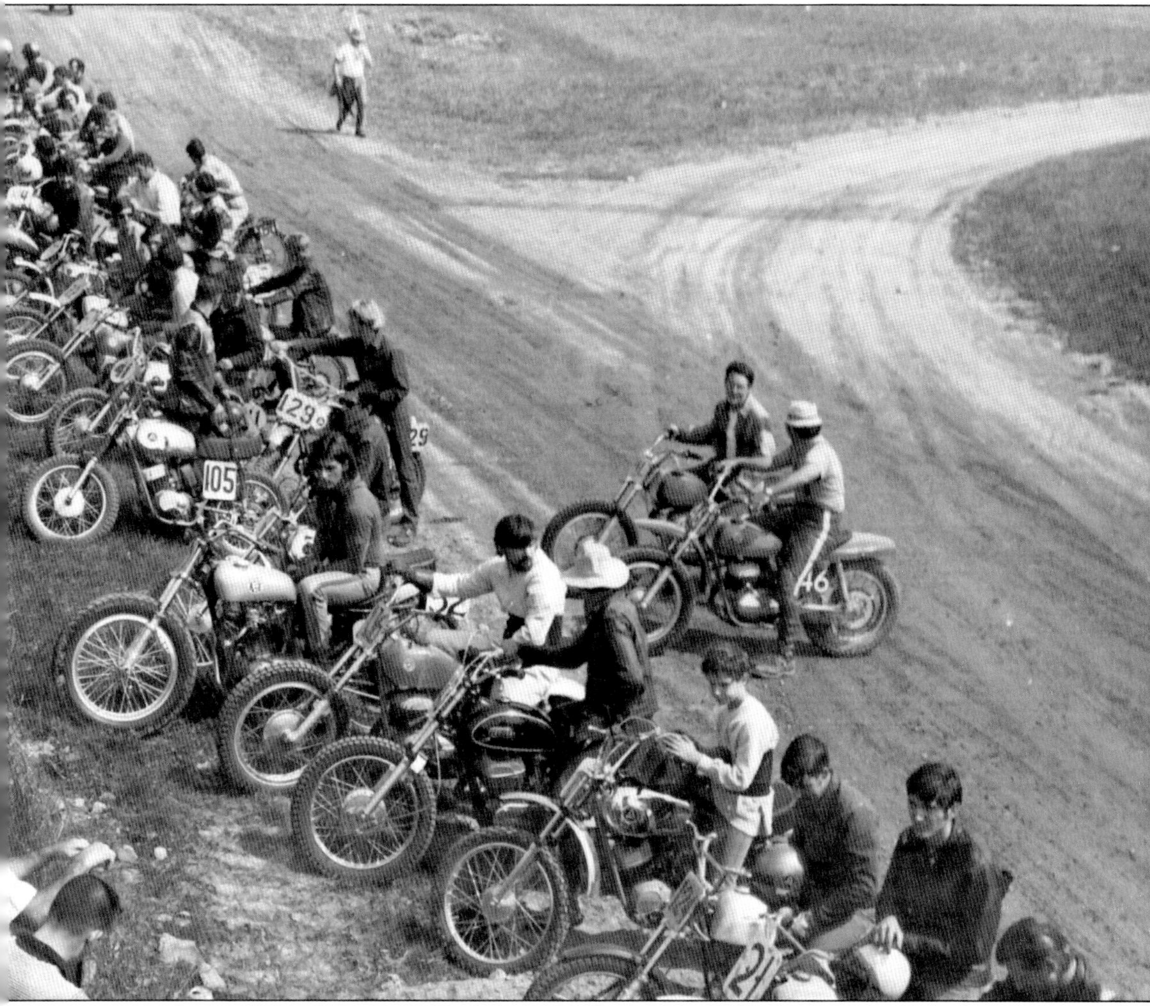

Racers line up for rider introduction prior to the day's scramble event. This was a tradition until the rider count got too large. It took too long to announce all the riders, so it was dropped from the program. This photograph is from the early 1970s. Notice the brands of bikes ready to compete, including Bultaco, Hodaka, Kawasaki, Triumph, Honda, Yamaha, and Bridgestone. (Larry Dagostino Jr. collection.)

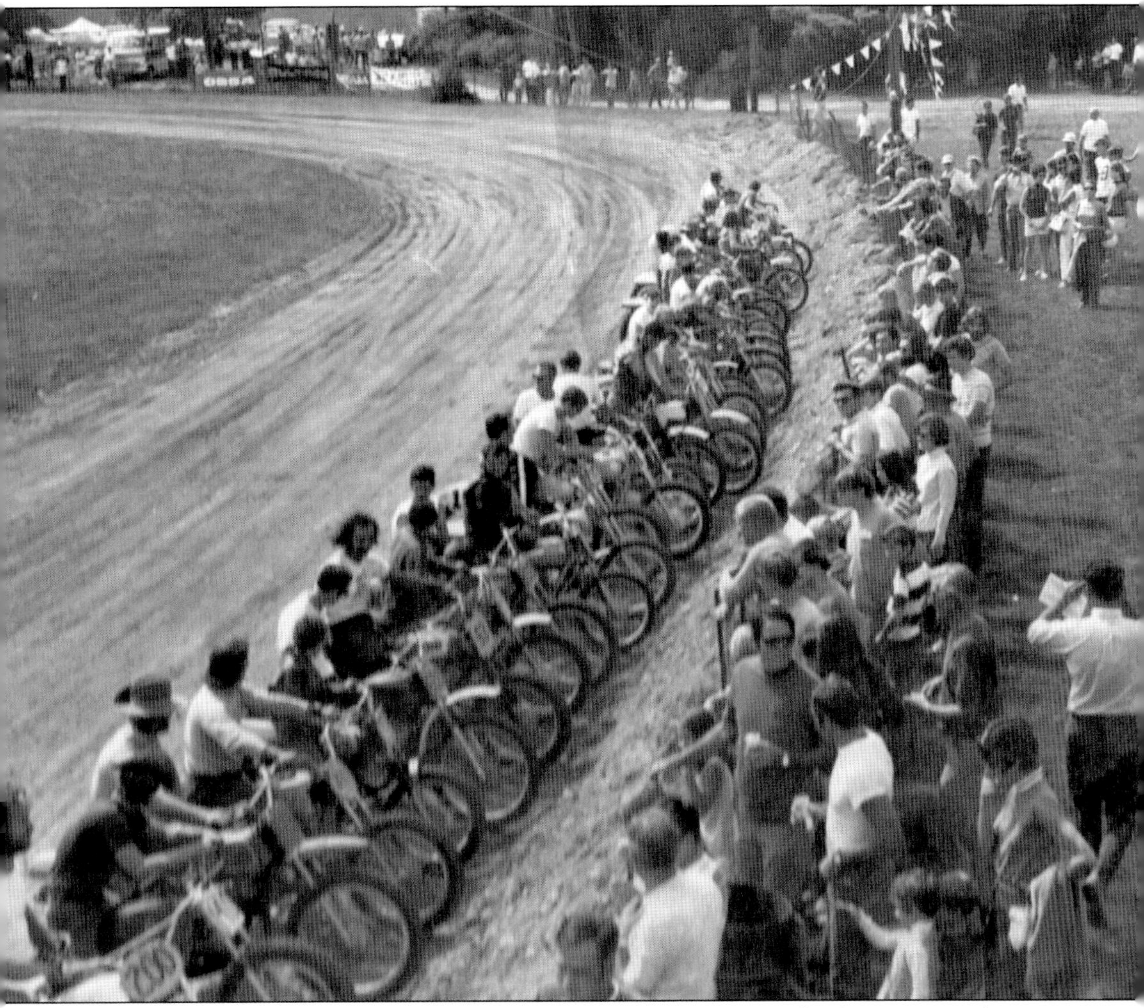

The early to mid-1970s saw the peak in scramble-style racing. Large crowds of spectators and racers showed up to spend the day at the track. Cookouts and tailgating were a big part of the attraction; it was the place to be on a Sunday afternoon. During intermission, there would be a motorcycle show and a competition for the best-dressed riders. (Larry Dagostino Jr. collection.)

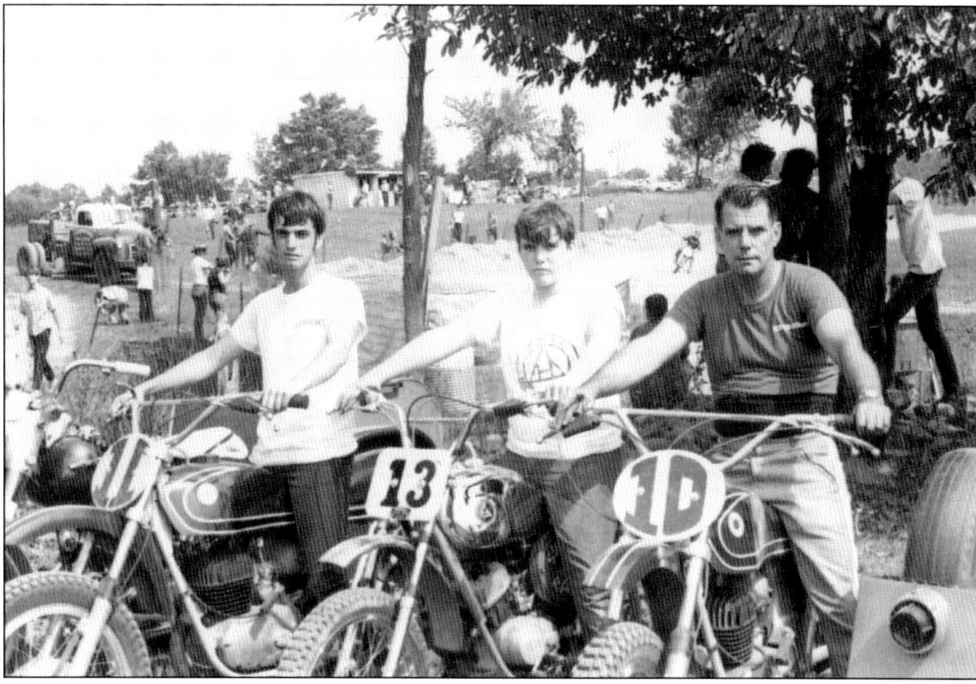

Tim, Bill, and Howard Newell pose with their machines prior to competing in the day's scramble events. Bill is on a Hodaka Super Rat 100. Tim and Howard are both on 175cc Ossa Stilettos. Howard was an Ossa dealer in 1970 in Ballston Lake. (Tim Newell collection.)

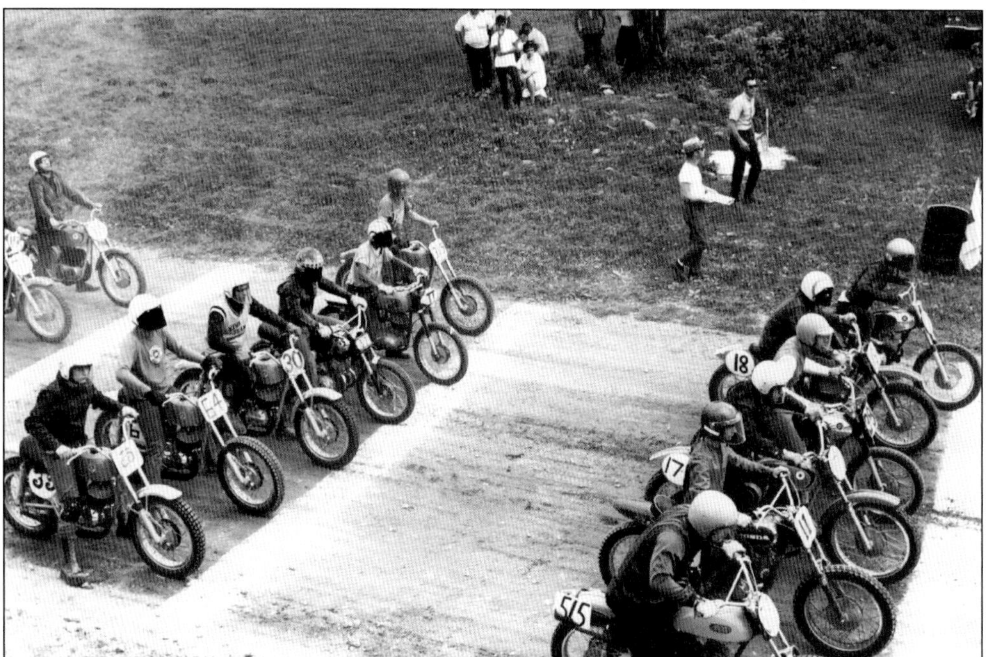

The 185cc Class is ready for the start. In the front row are Tim Newell, 11; Roger Sperling, 38; Gordon Kirby, 18; and Rick Curtis, 12. In the second row are Keith Green, 35; Dean Splittgerber, 64; and Dave Knoll, 57. The year is 1969. (Bob Newell collection.)

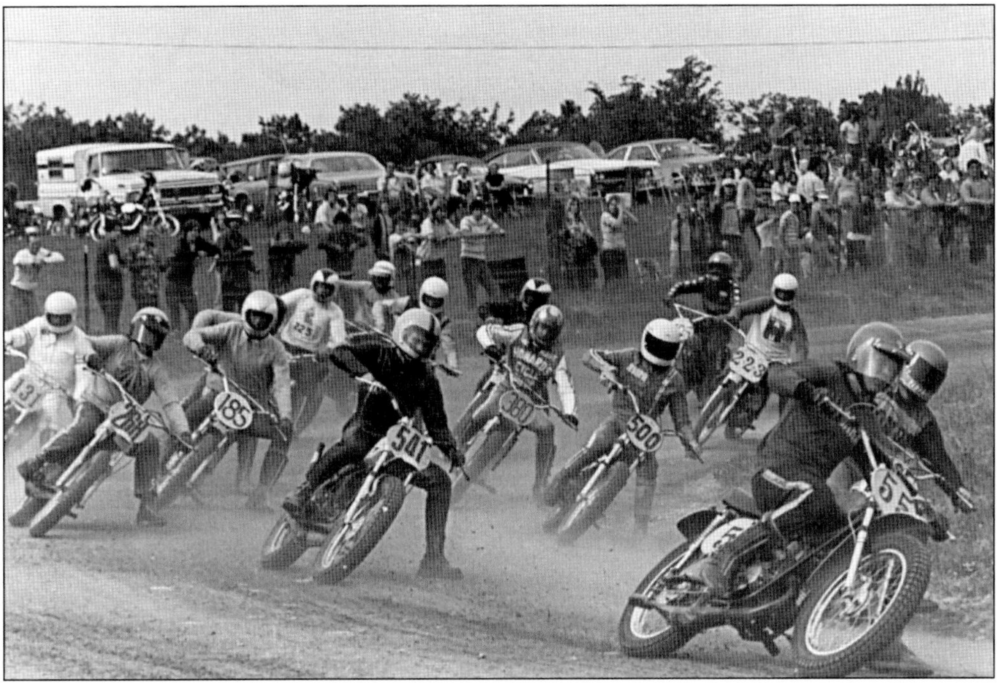

The 125cc Class dives into turn one, led by Emmett Watkins, 55. Watkins was the man to beat, no matter what class he rode in. He is chased by Richard Murphy, 500; Mark Supley, 380; Ronald Relfare, 268; and Carl Baragelata, 137. The 125 Class was a very competitive class in the early 1970s; numerous heat races were run to determine the lineup for the feature event. (Larry Dagostino Jr. collection.)

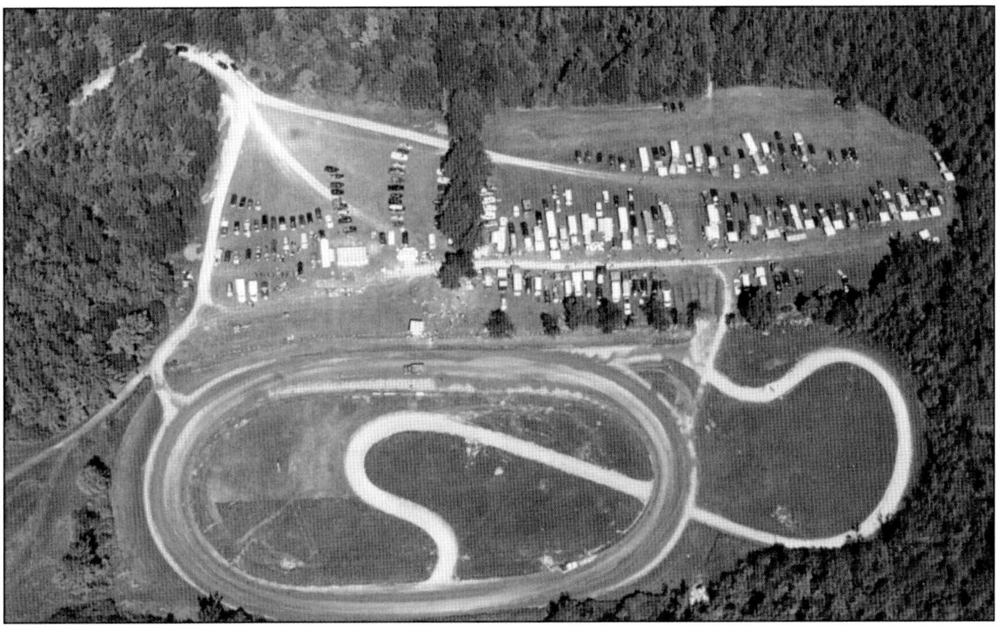

Due to the popularity of short track racing, the Electric City Riders Club reconfigured the track in 1976. The quarter-mile oval was made, and the jump and part of the scramble track was moved to the infield. Both events were held on the same day, making for a full day of racing. (Bob Newell collection.)

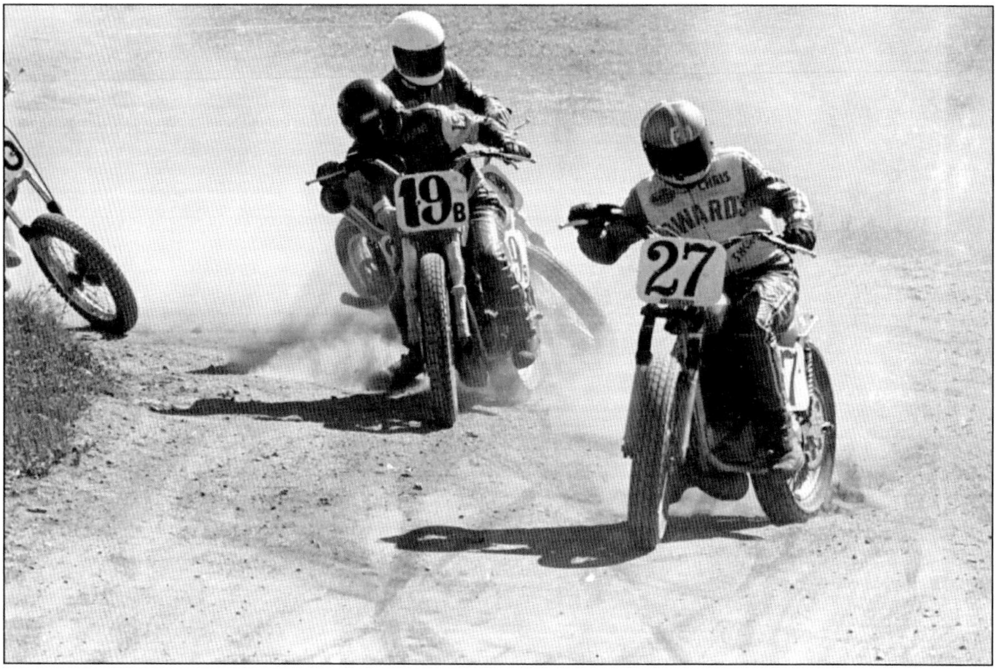

Chris Eberle leads Duane Vedder through the new infield switchback during the 250cc Expert Scramble event. Reconfiguring the track made it easier for the spectators to enjoy the action. (Photograph by Joe Corbett.)

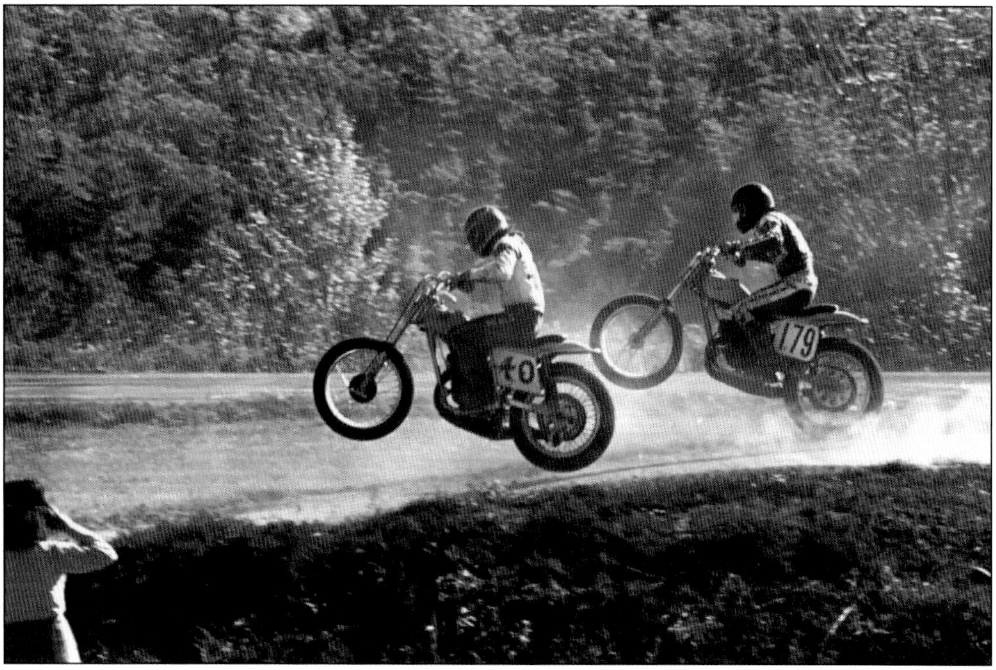

The location of the previous jump was close to the front stretch trees and fence, causing a few bad accidents. Glenn Neals leads Jim Nabinger over the new jump in the infield of the short track. (Photograph by Joe Corbett.)

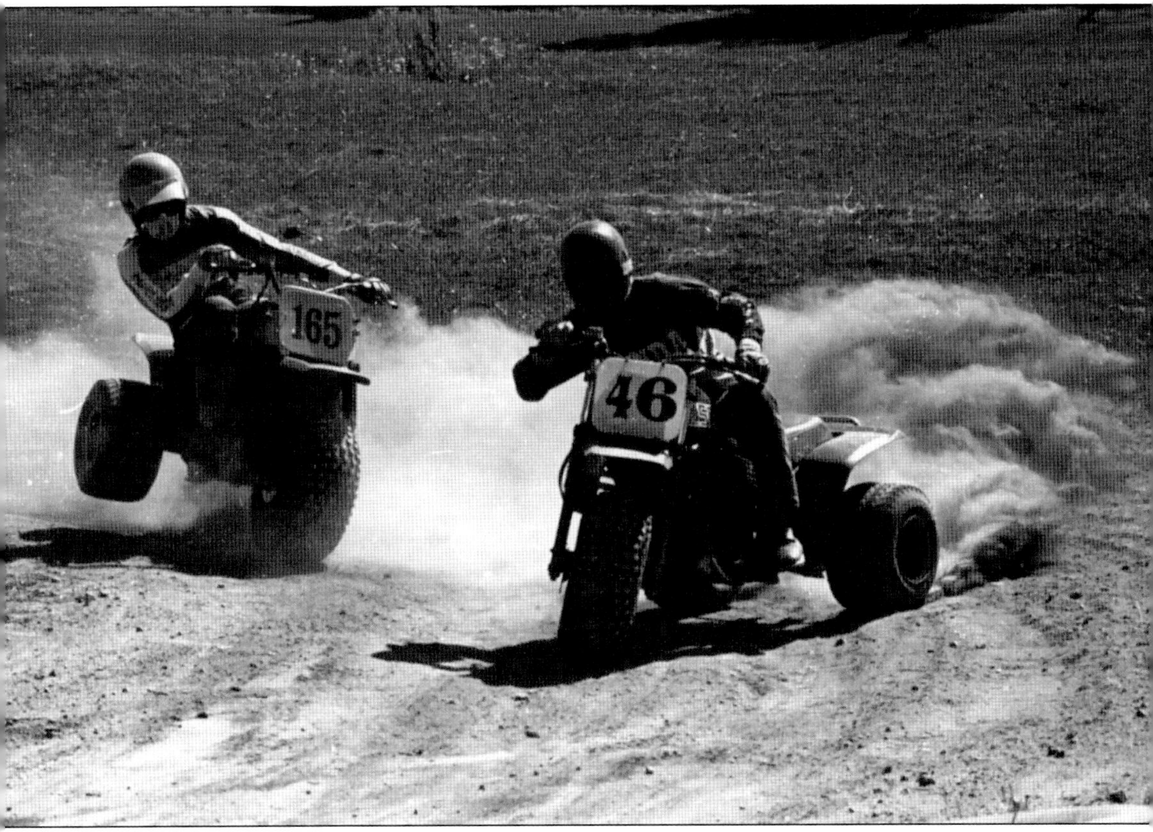

The all-terrain cycle, or ATC, became popular in the 1980s. The races were popular, as the three-wheelers provided a lot of action due to the riding style needed to be successful. (Photograph by Joe Corbett.)

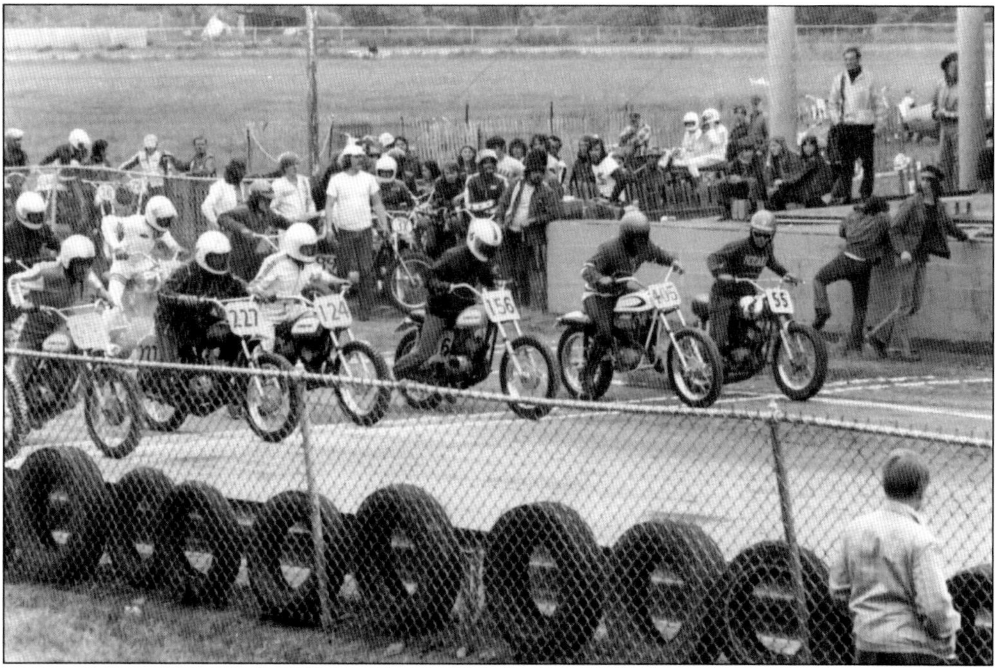

The Cobleskill Fairgrounds held numerous races on the half-mile oval during the 1970s. Here, the 100cc Class takes off from the starting line. This was at the beginning of the Japanese invasion; notice the three Kawasaki "Green Streaks" on the front row. (Larry Dagostino Jr. collection.)

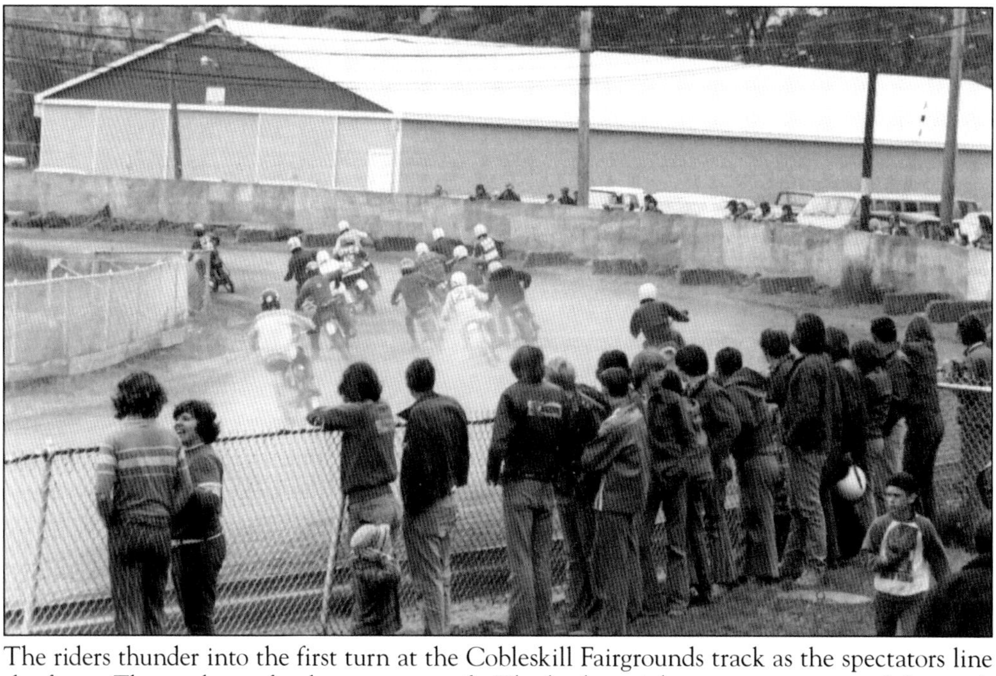

The riders thunder into the first turn at the Cobleskill Fairgrounds track as the spectators line the fence. The track was fast but not very safe. The back straightaway was wavy, and the track was usually dusty. Also, the hay bales were left on the track from race to race, causing them to grow into the ground. After a rider got killed at the track, the interest of racing there waned. The last races there were in the early 1980s. (Larry Dagostino Jr. collection.)

Six

Antique Meets

With so many early motorcycle manufacturers being located in New York and Massachusetts, there was a good supply of old motorcycles around. The Antique Motorcycle Club of America (AMCA) was founded in 1954 to help people repair and restore these old machines. Many early bikes were traded in during World War II for scrap metal to support the war effort. The bikes that did not get scrapped are sought after today.

The Empire Chapter of the AMCA held its annual meet in Duanesburg, at the Electric City Riders track. Bikes would come from all over the East Coast to show and sell parts for these old machines. In 1987, the meet was moved to the Monroe County Fairgrounds, south of Utica. Today, it is a grand national meet held at the Dutchess County Fairgrounds in Rhinebeck, supported by three additional clubs. A motorcycle timeline is formed, with bikes from 1900 to 1979 on display.

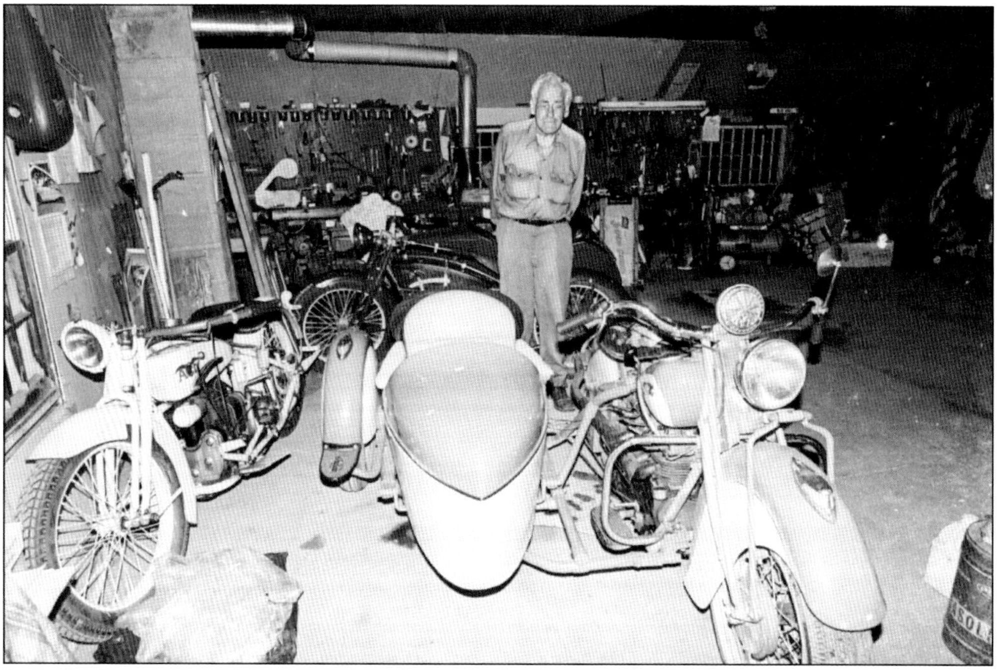

Louie Lichva was a machinist at General Electric, but his passion was antique motorcycles. Lou and his wife, Pauline, helped form the Empire Chapter of the Antique Motorcycle Club of America. Lou was also a past president of the AMCA. In this photograph are two Ace motorcycles and a four-cylinder Indian with a sidecar. These machines are on display at the Motorcyclepedia Museum in Newburgh. (Photograph by Joe Corbett.)

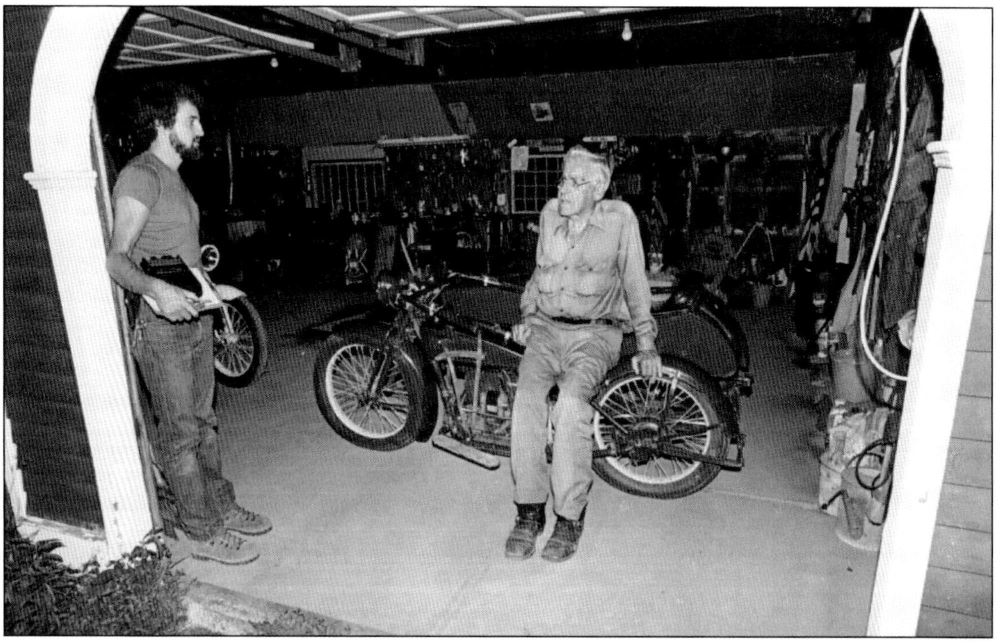

The author recorded an interview of Lou Lichva in 1980. He was more than happy to tell tales of the old days of motorcycling. Lou sits on a four-cylinder Ace motorcycle with an Ace Observer sidecar. (Photograph by Joe Corbett.)

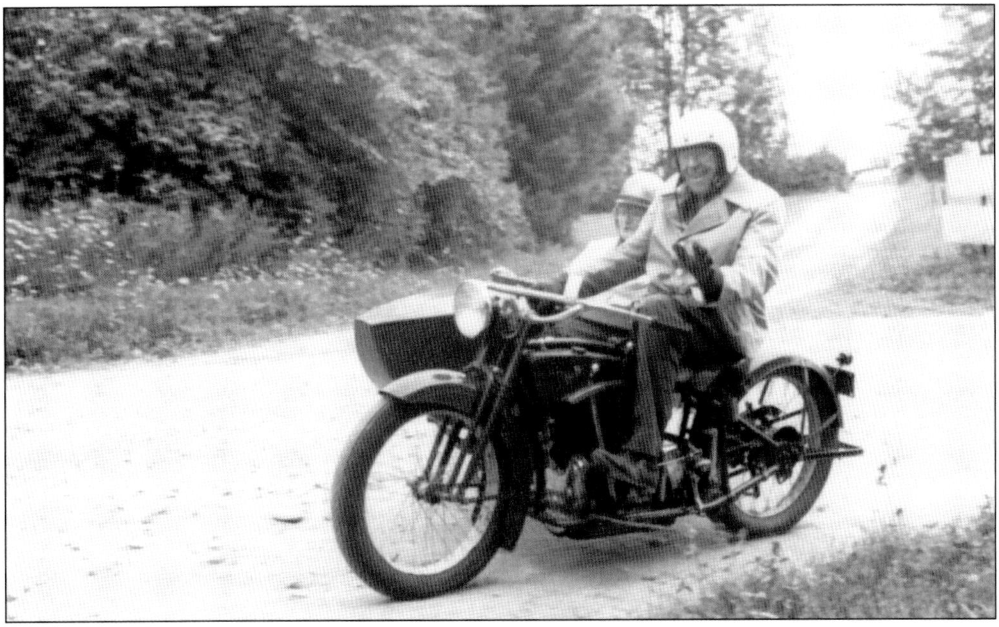

Lou Lichva heads out for a ride with his wife, Pauline, during the AMCA meet. He was happiest while giving rides and telling stories at the county fairs and antique engine shows around the area. In 1986, after Lou's passing, Pauline was the guest of honor at the AMCA meet held at the Pine Grove Farm in Duanesburg. She awarded the show winners with plaques that had Lou's likeness engraved on them. (Photograph by the author.)

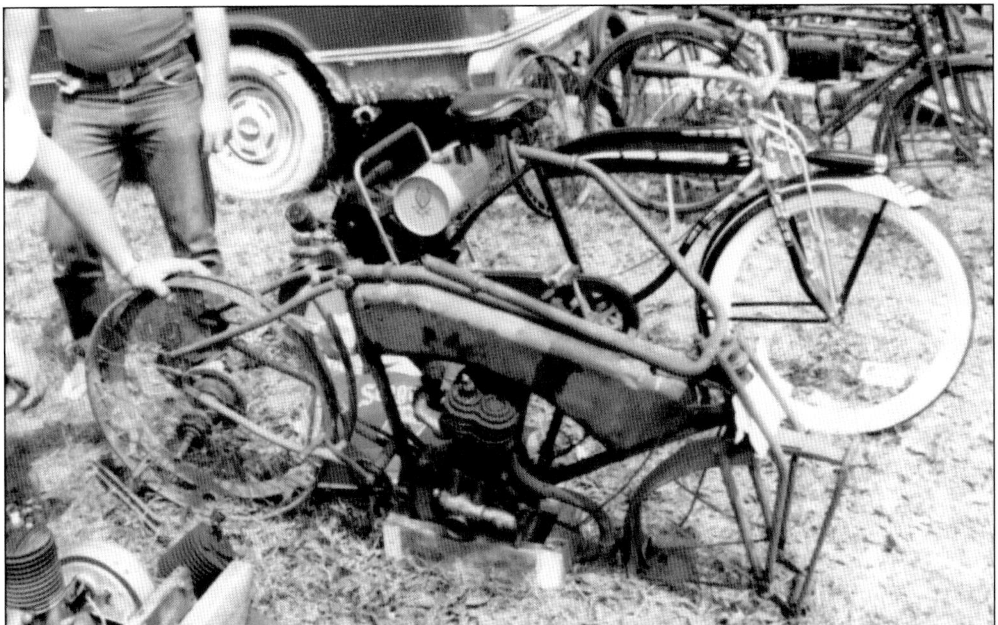

The swap meet was one of the main points of interest during the weekend. All kinds of unusual motorcycles and parts were laid out in the field for a collector or restorer to buy. In this photograph, a potential buyer looks over a 1913 Iver Johnson motorcycle built in Fitchburg, Massachusetts; in the background is a Columbia bicycle with a motor-wheel attachment installed. (Photograph by the author.)

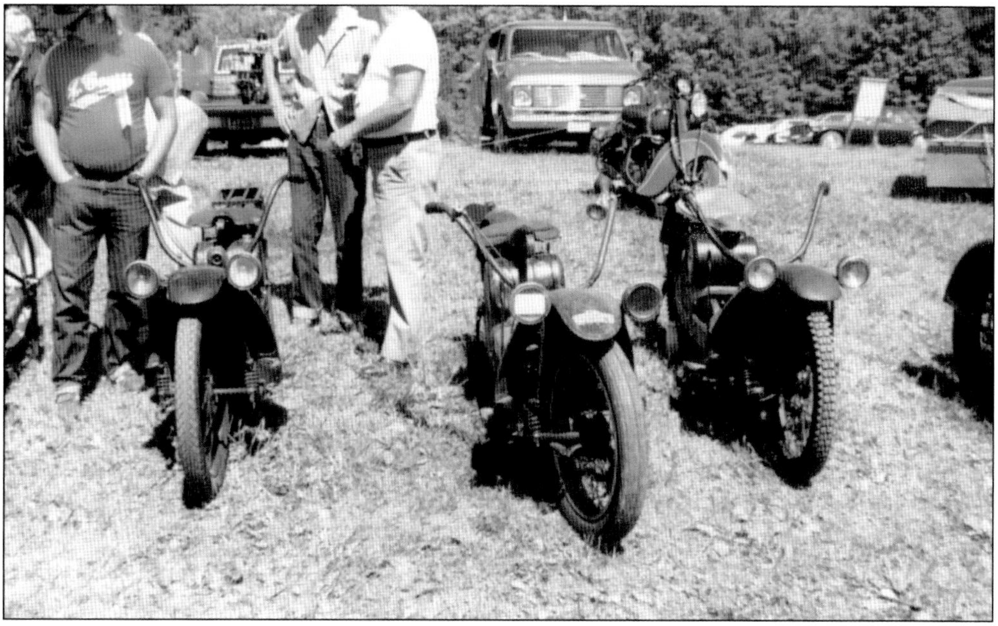

The Empire Chapter of the Antique Motorcycle Club of America held meets from 1974 to 1986 at the Electric City Riders track. The meets would include a swap meet, bike show with judging, and the opportunity to run a machine around the track. Shown here is a collection of Neracar motorcycles. (Photograph by the author.)

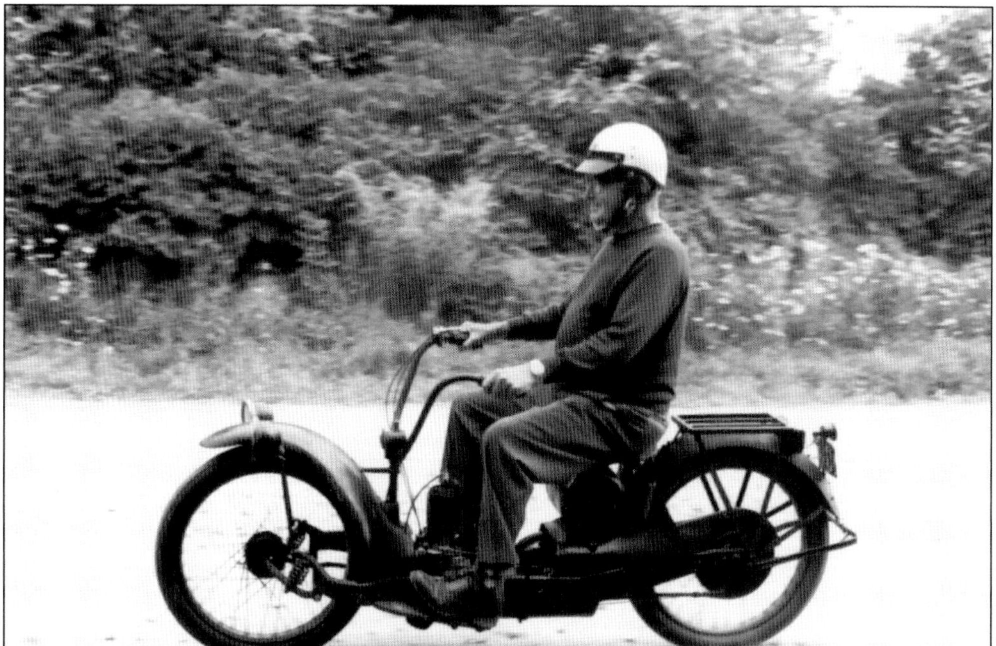

This unknown rider takes his Neracar for a ride. The Neracar was manufactured in Syracuse from 1920 to 1928. It was a distinctive motorcycle utilizing a low sheet metal frame and body, drag link steering, two-stroke engine, and a friction drive transmission. Neracars are on public display in the collections of the Buffalo and Erie County Historical Society in Buffalo. (Photograph by the author.)

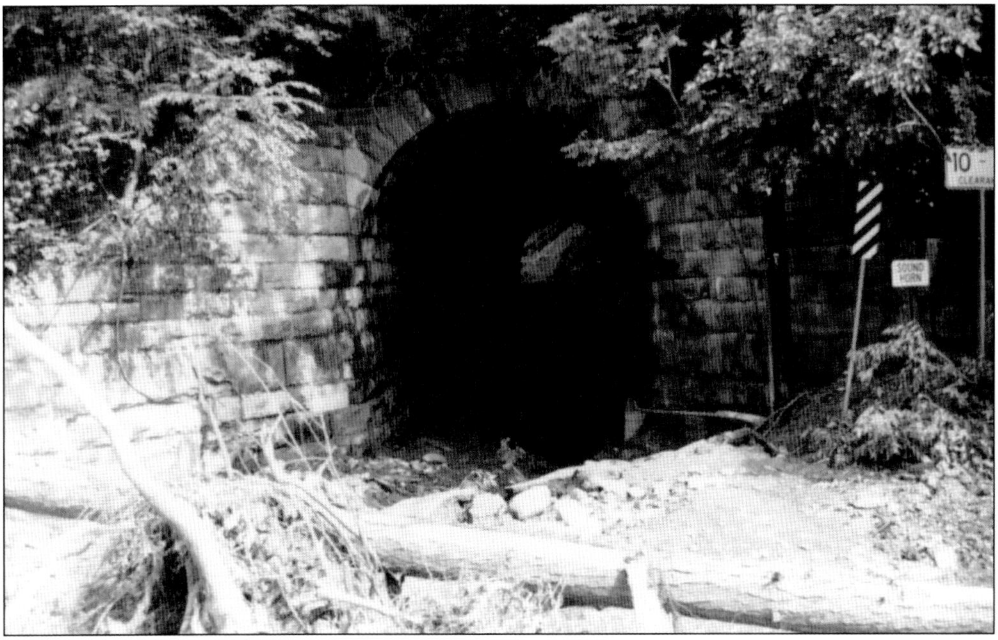

In 1986, the road leading to the club was washed out by a flood. Here is a view of the end of Kelly Station Road, looking at the tunnel. The antique meet had to be moved to Pine Grove Dairy on Route 7. Lou passed away the winter before this event. That was the last year the event was held in Schenectady. (Photograph by the author.)

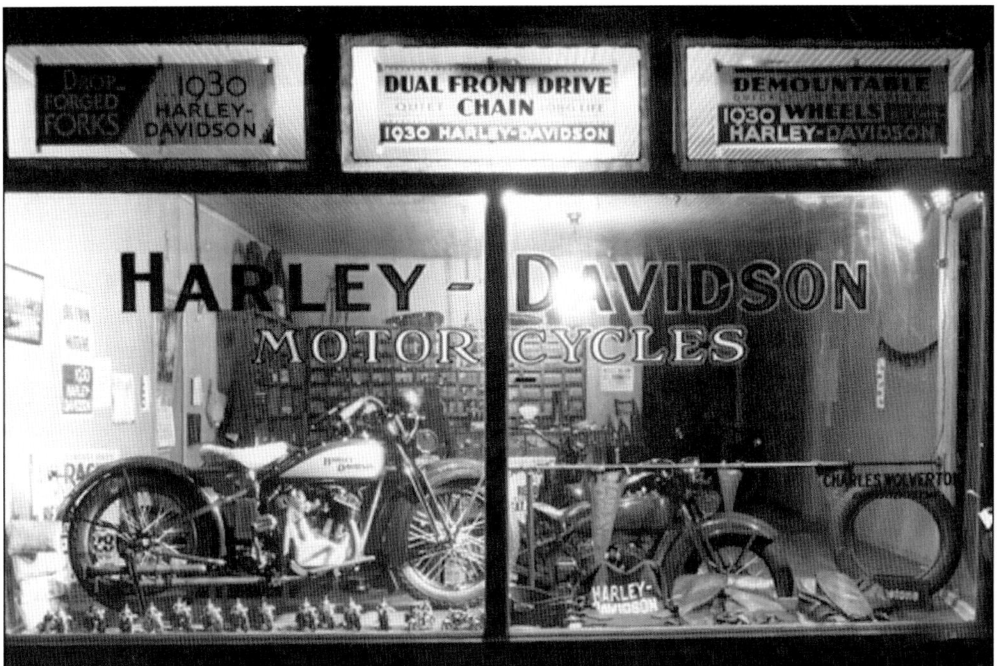

Charles "Red" Wolverton ran a Harley-Davidson dealership, first in Philadelphia and then in Reading, Pennsylvania. This photograph is from 1930; by then, Red was known to have been the first rider to go over the two-miles-per-minute mark. (Courtesy of the Harley-Davidson Company.)

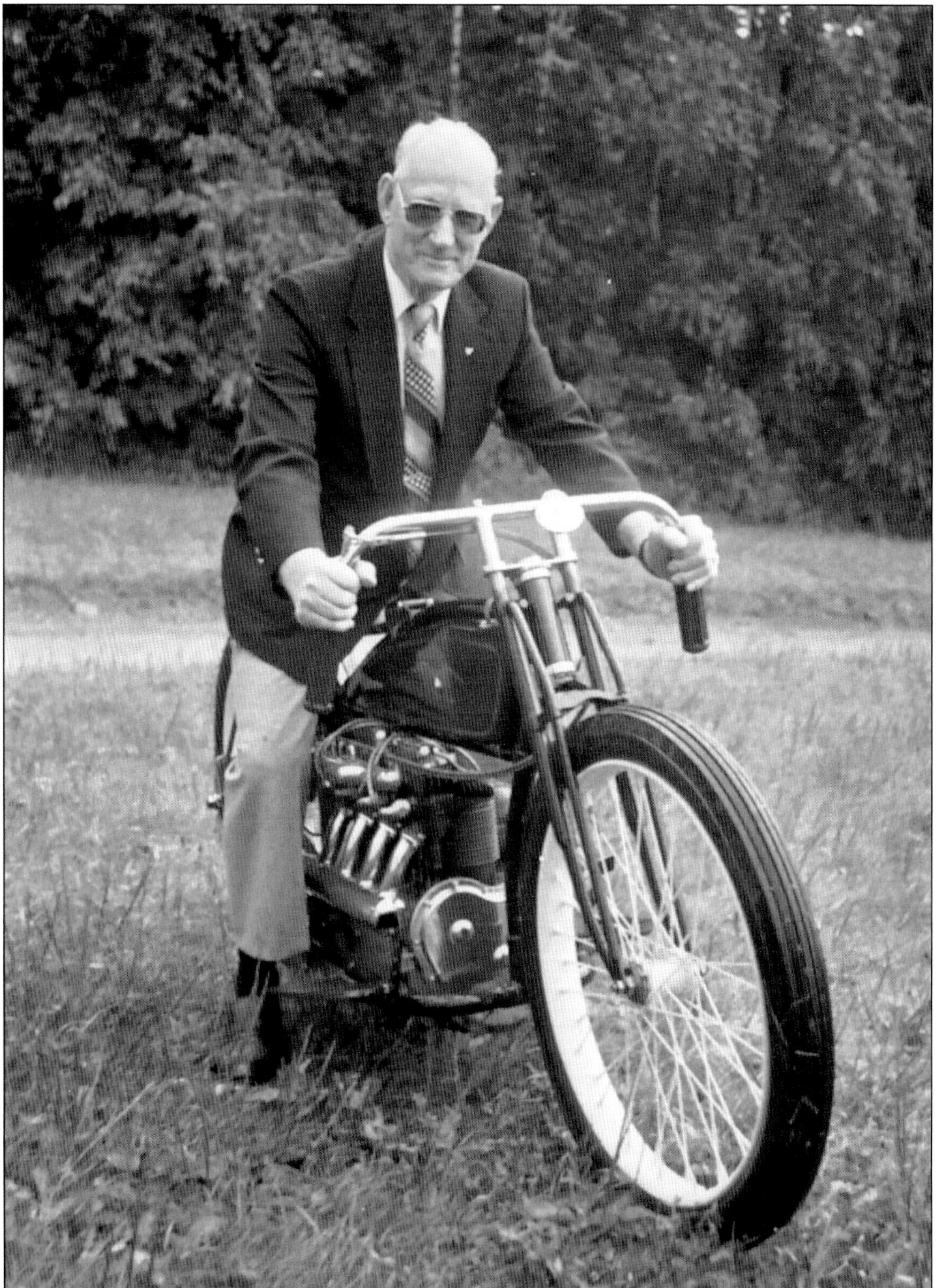

Red Wolverton was a top racer and speed-record setter in the 1920s and 1930s. He was a well-rounded rider, competing in a variety of motorcycle competitions from board track to dirt track to hill climbing. He poses with a replica of the Ace XP3 motorcycle that he set the speed record on in 1923 at 129.61 miles per hour. He was the guest of honor at the antique motorcycle meet held at the Electric City Riders track in 1984. (Photograph by Joe Corbett.)

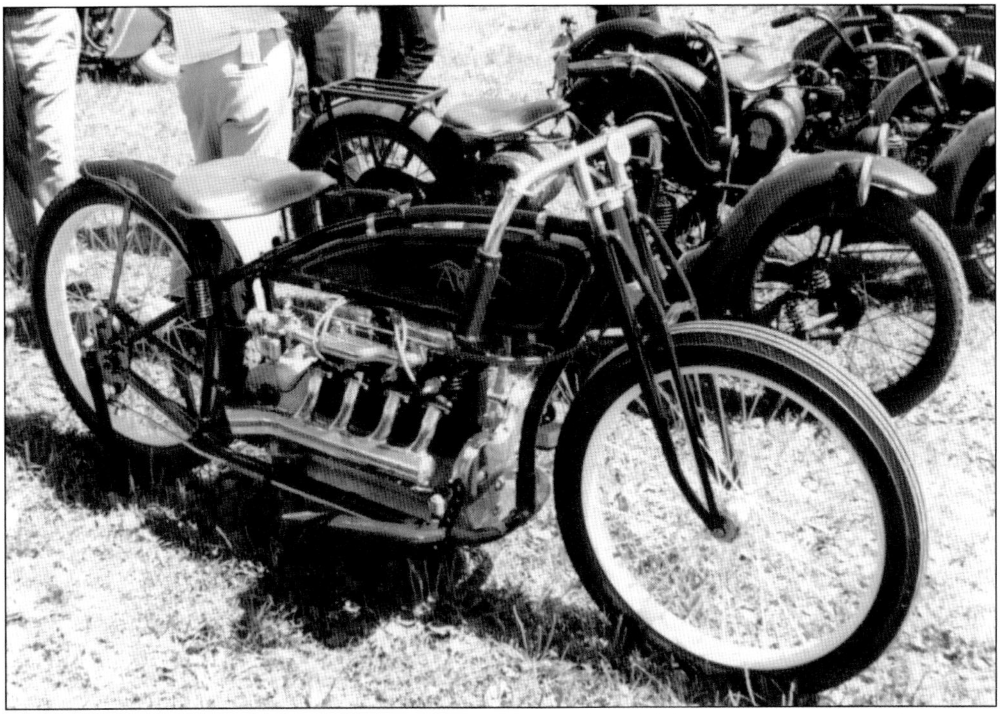

In 1923, Ace decided to build the fastest bike ever produced. No expense was spared, and the result was a bike that weighed 270 pounds and had nearly 42 horsepower. This special Ace was 100 pounds lighter than the road-going version and reportedly cost an astronomical $10,000 to build. This replica was built by Dr. John F. Patt of Pennsylvania. "Doc" Patt rode the bike during the meet to the delight of the crowd. (Photograph by Joe Corbett.)

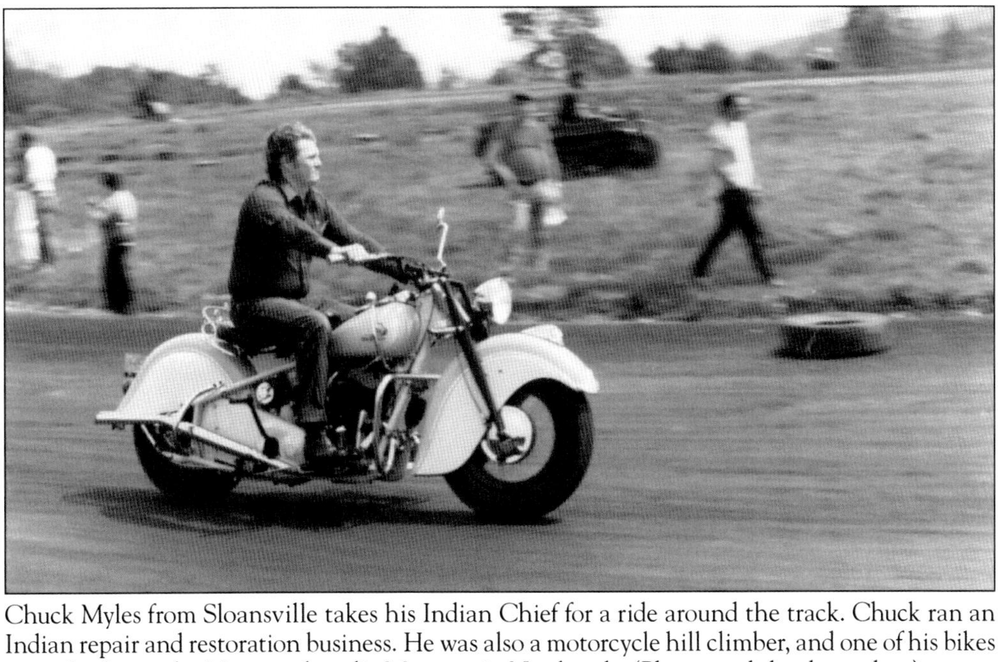

Chuck Myles from Sloansville takes his Indian Chief for a ride around the track. Chuck ran an Indian repair and restoration business. He was also a motorcycle hill climber, and one of his bikes is on display at the Motorcyclepedia Museum in Newburgh. (Photograph by the author.)

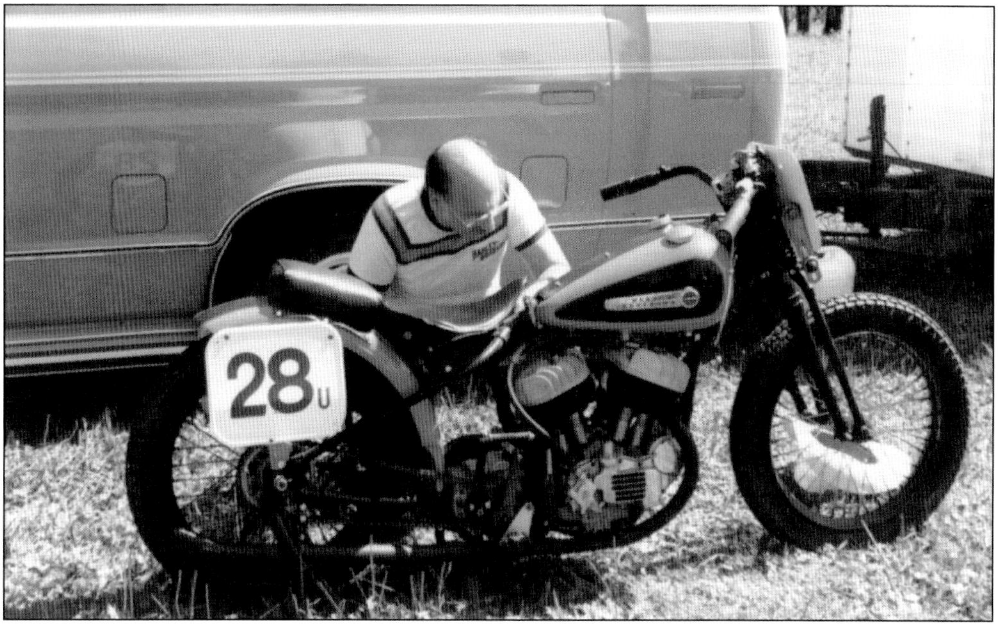

Gene Baron was a longtime Long Island Harley-Davidson dealer who raced well into his 70s. Baron was quite a collector, too; he would come to all the AMCA meets with the most unique bikes. He lived to be 83. Here, he works on an original factory race bike, a Harley WR from the early 1940s, getting ready for the day's events. (Photograph by the author.)

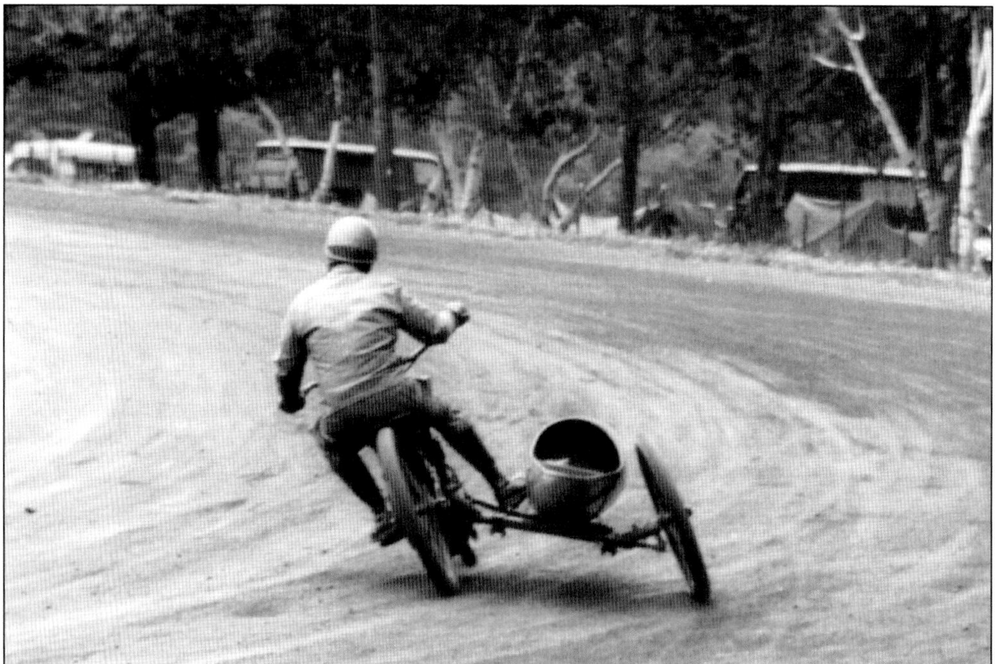
Gene Baron demonstrates how an Equalean sidecar works. Notice how the wheel leans at the same angle as the bike. This Harley-Davidson was used on board and dirt tracks around 1915 and would normally include a passenger. On this day, he used a sandbag for ballast but crashed, damaging the nose of the sidecar. (Photograph by the author.)

Seven

SHORT TRACK RACING

Oval track racing had been contested from the sport's beginning. The races were usually held on horse tracks at the county fairground. These tracks were known to be dusty and unsafe. With the development of short track racing, the bikes would race on a prepared track that had dust control and safer fencing around the perimeter.

The motorcycles were specially prepared with wider tires, higher performance motors, and no front brakes.

The races are short sprints, less than 10 laps on a track that measures less than a half-mile. This keeps the races close and exciting.

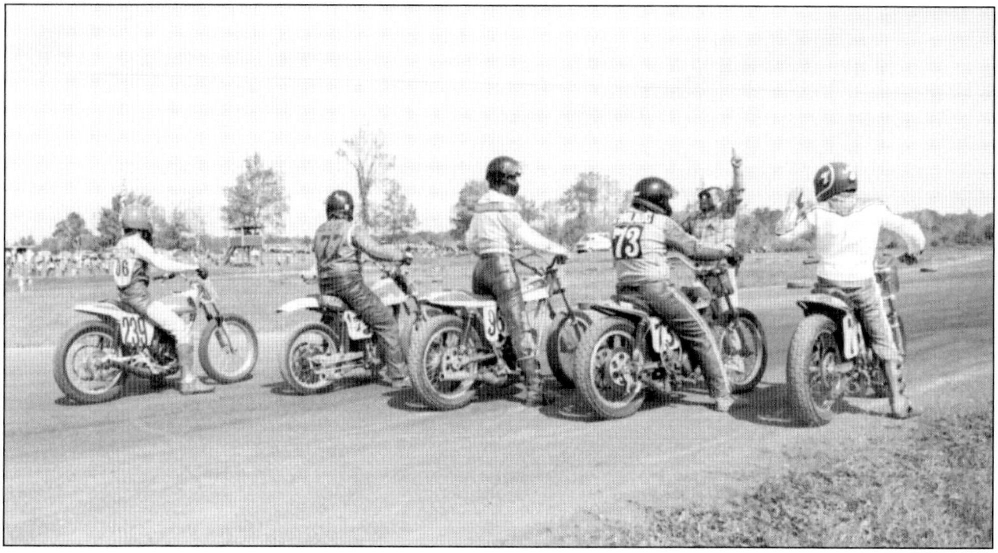

Jim Downing lines up the 250cc Expert Class before sending them to the starting line of the quarter-mile Electric City oval. From left to right are Tom Sephton, Ron Nellis, Charles Petty, Jeff Kvinlaug, and an unidentified rider. (Photograph by Joe Corbett.)

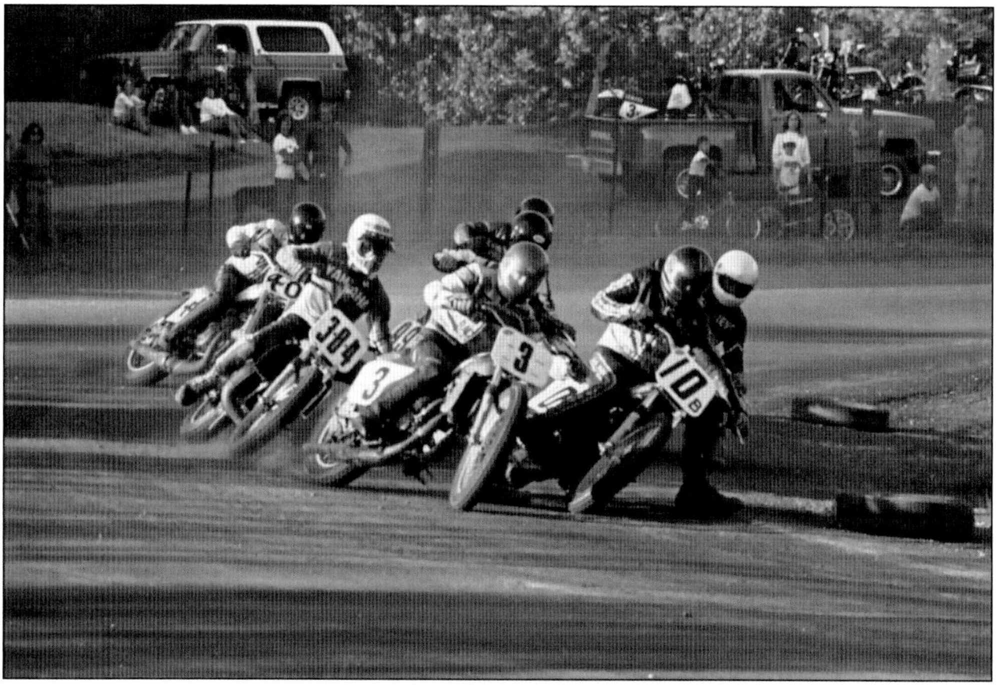

George Richtmeyer, on the 10B, leads the 250cc Expert Class into turn one. Steve Longo stays low on the inside, as number 3, Ken Myrick, and number 384, Conrad Parshalls, try to find a way by. In the 1970s, this was the premier class, which provided many exciting races. (Photograph by Joe Corbett.)

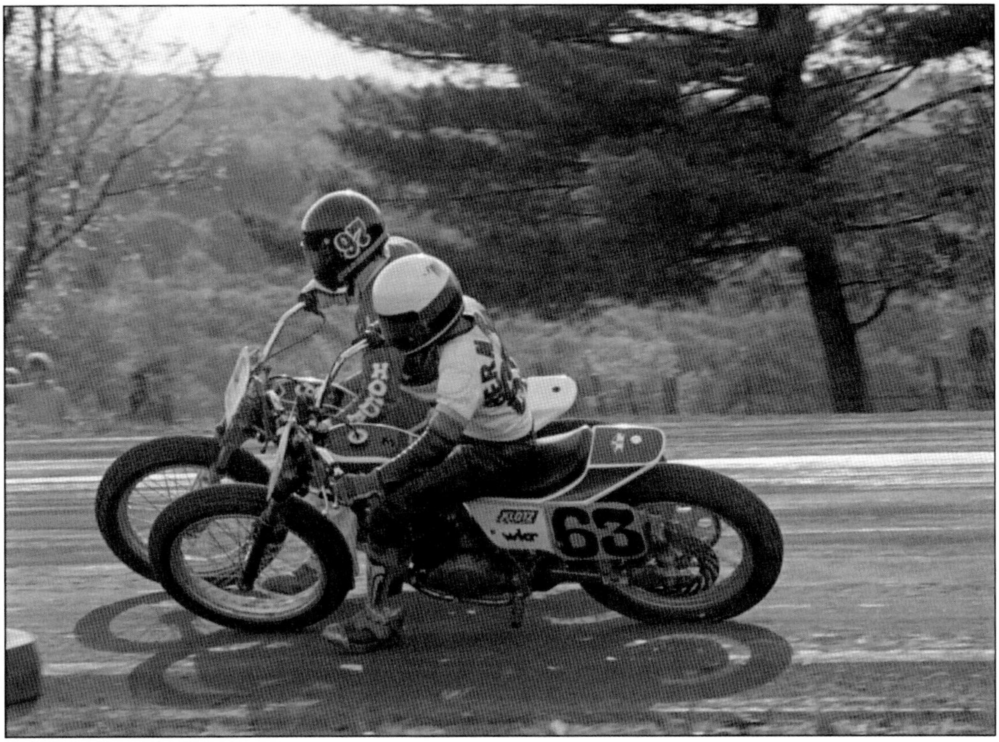

Mario Bernardini tucks inside of Kurt Spoonogle in turn two of the Electric City racetrack. Kurt's father owned the White Beach Speedway in Ballston Lake. That track ran stockcars from 1952 until 1962. (Photograph by Joe Corbett.)

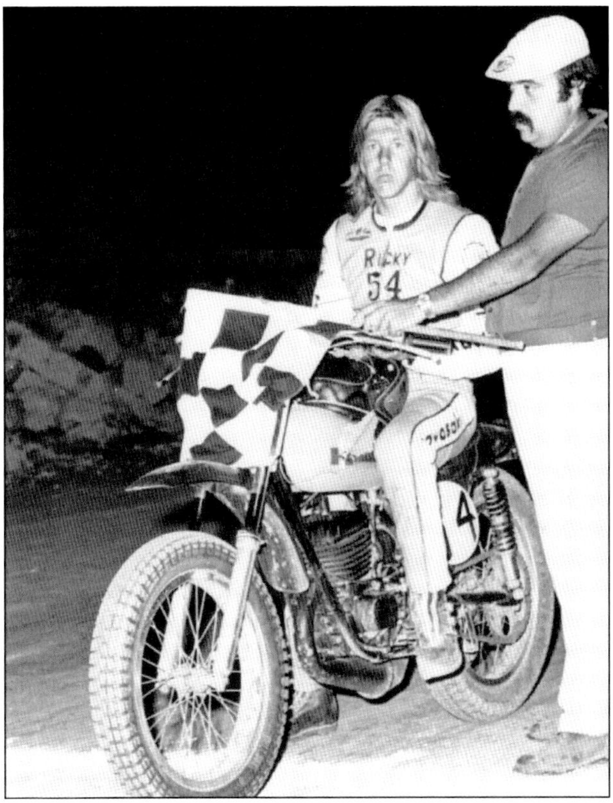

In 1972, George "Ricky" Richtmeyer breathes a sigh of relief after winning the feature at Accord Speedway. He was riding a Kawasaki 350 Bighorn. Ricky was one of the best riders to ever come out of the area, winning many 250cc and Open Expert championships. (George Richtmeyer collection.)

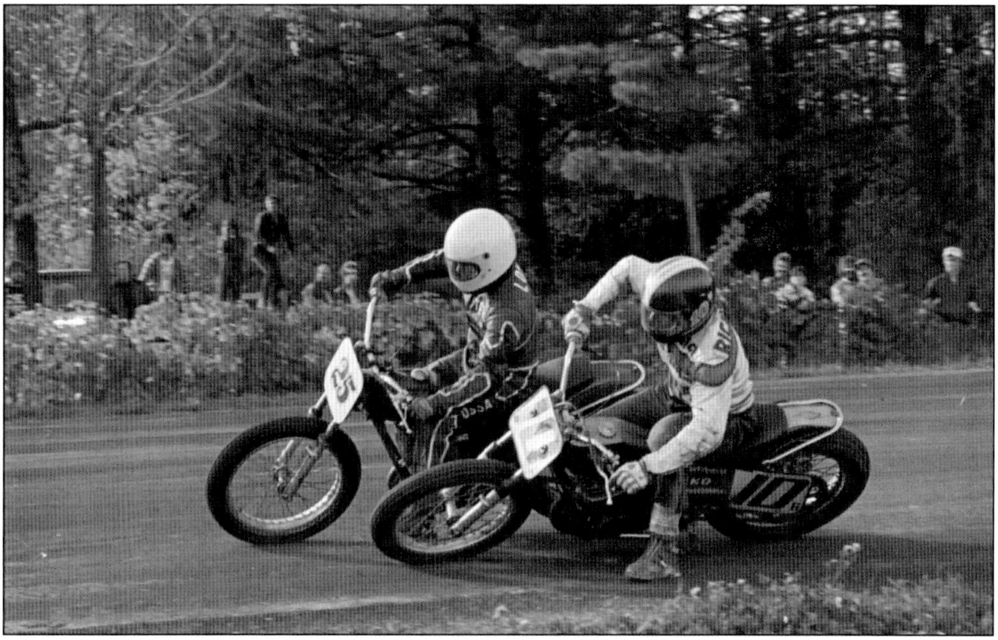

Steve Longo tries to hold the outside line as Ricky dives to the inside. Longo and Richtmeyer were good friends and put on many good races. They raced against each other for over 30 years. Longo still races today with his son Kyle. (Photograph by Joe Corbett.)

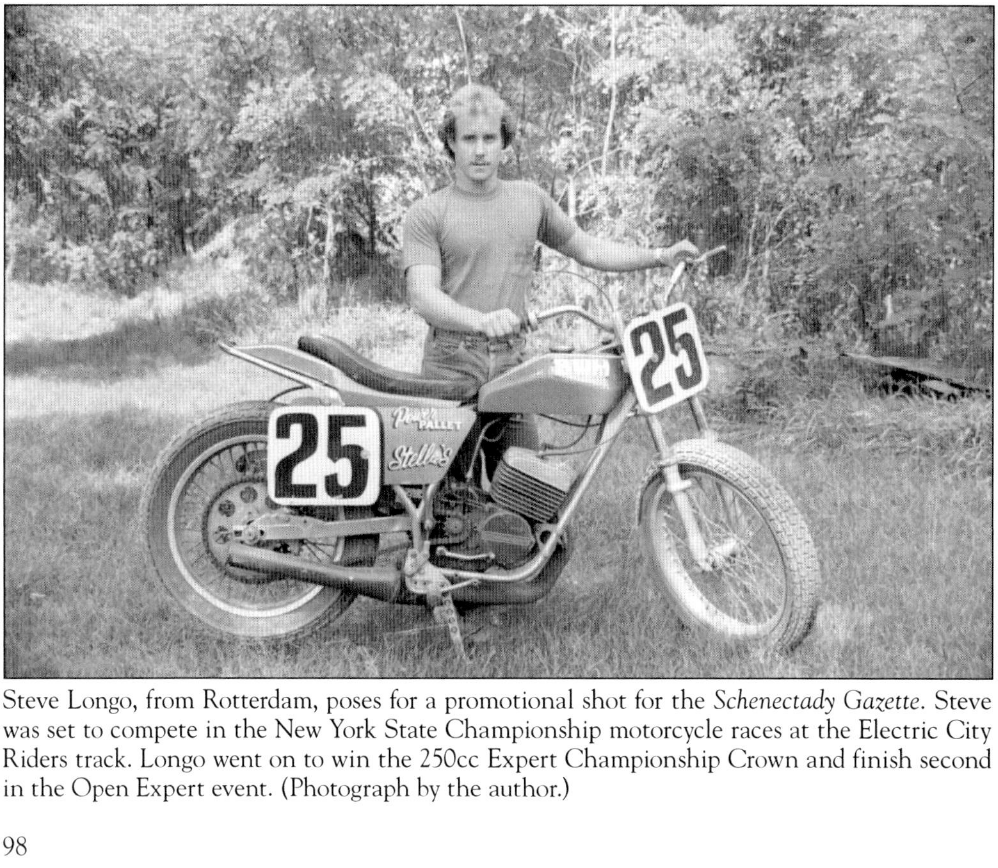

Steve Longo, from Rotterdam, poses for a promotional shot for the *Schenectady Gazette*. Steve was set to compete in the New York State Championship motorcycle races at the Electric City Riders track. Longo went on to win the 250cc Expert Championship Crown and finish second in the Open Expert event. (Photograph by the author.)

After taking the checkered flag, Ricky would do his trademark "Slide for Life." Those that were unaccustomed to seeing this thought that he had crashed. Richtmeyer was sponsored by many different brands of motorcycles during his career. He also road and ice raced and tried his hand at motocross. (Photograph by Joe Corbett.)

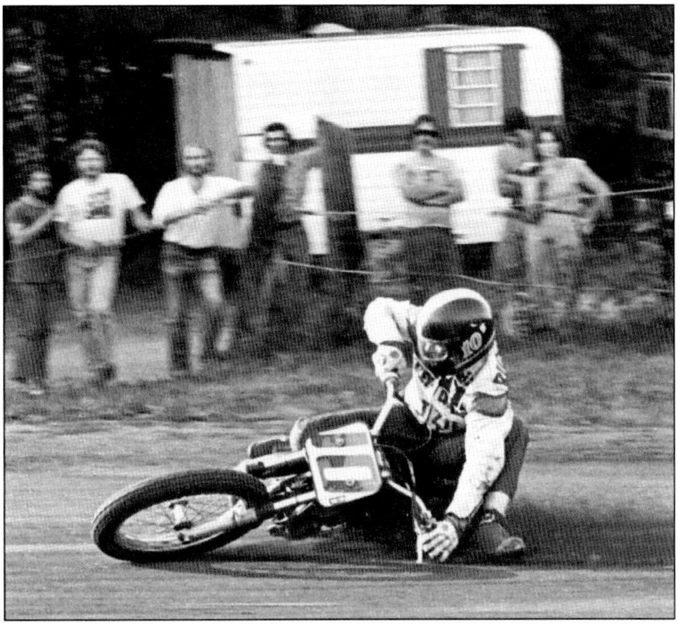

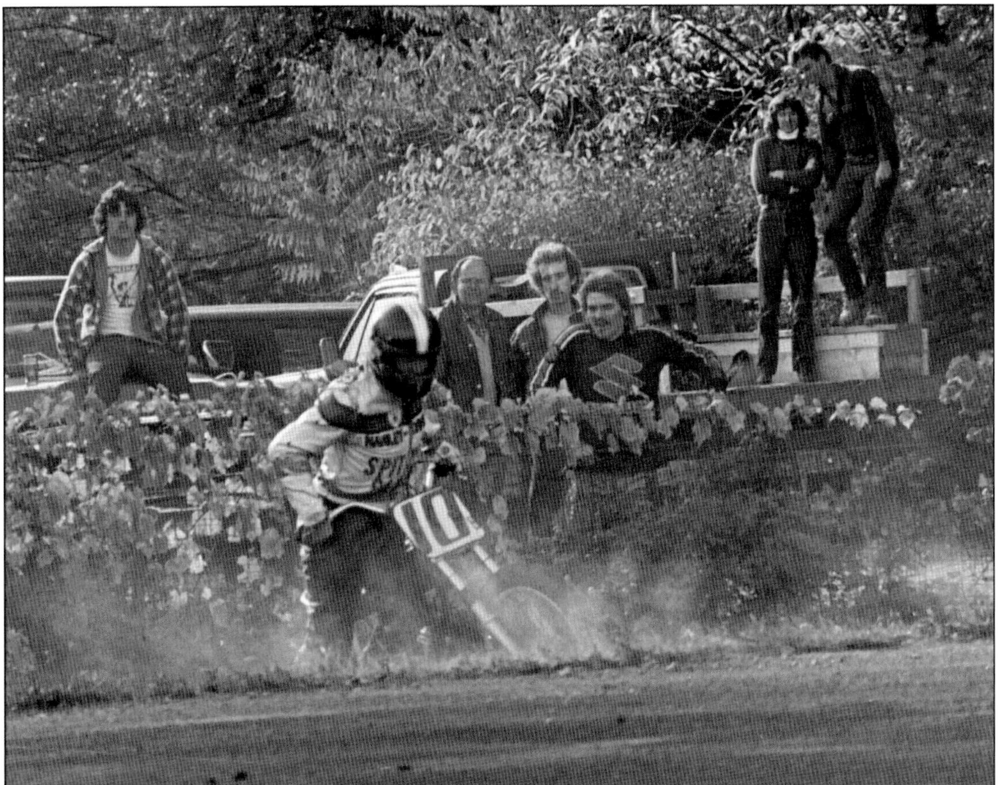

Sometimes the "slide" did not go as planned. Here, Ricky carried too much speed and went off the track, to the delight of the spectators. Through the years, he raced just about every brand of motorcycle, including Harley, Yamaha, Kawasaki, Suzuki, BSA, Triumph, and an Alouette. (Photograph by Joe Corbett.)

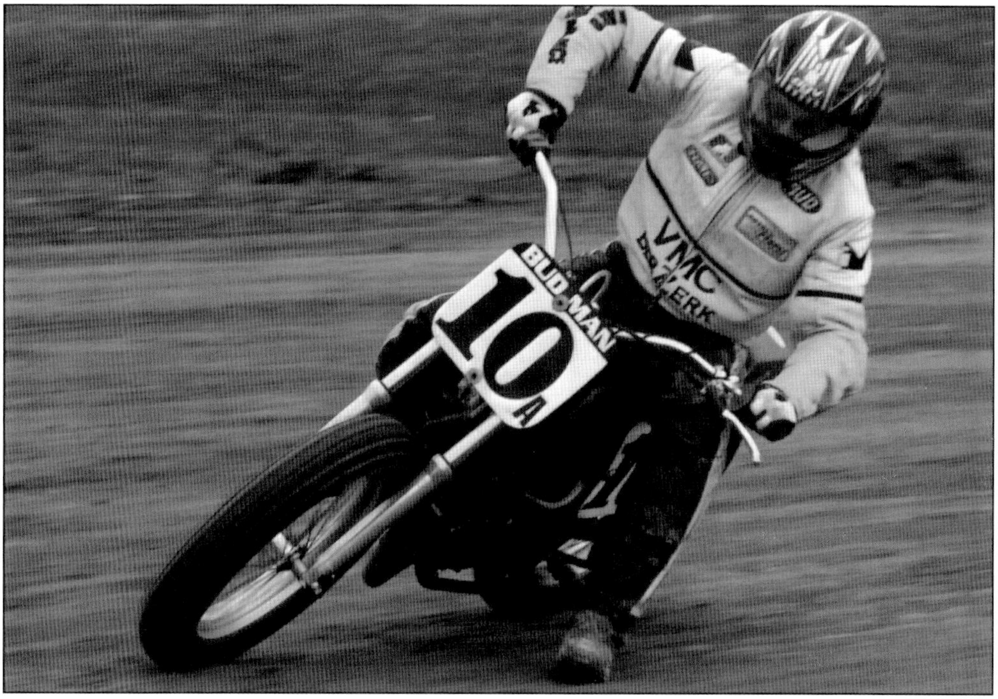

George's son, Aaron, continues the Richtmeyer legacy today. Known as the "Bud Man," he started racing in 1982 and continues to race in the Open Expert Class. (Photograph by Claire Richtmeyer.)

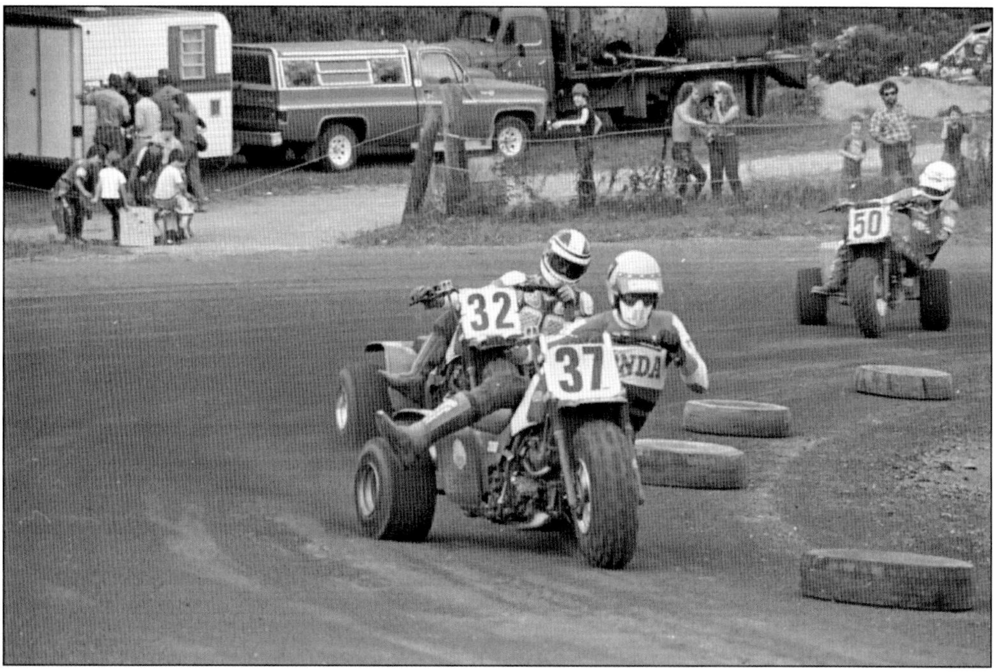

The all-terrain cycles got in on the action on the quarter-mile track. Special tires and handlebars were affixed to the machine to make them handle better. Mark Witthohn leads Jim Romeo in the ATC 250cc event. Rich Erickson, 50, gives chase. (Photograph by Joe Corbett.)

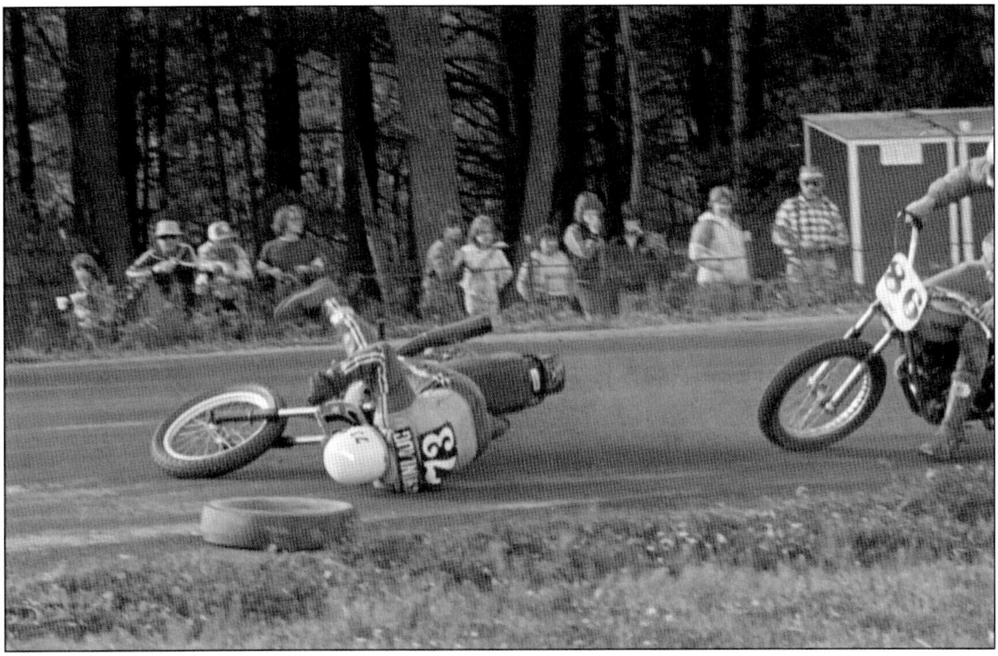

Jeff Kvinlaug tucks the front wheel and goes down, going into turn one, as Robert Rosa tries to slide by on the inside. (Photograph by Joe Corbett.)

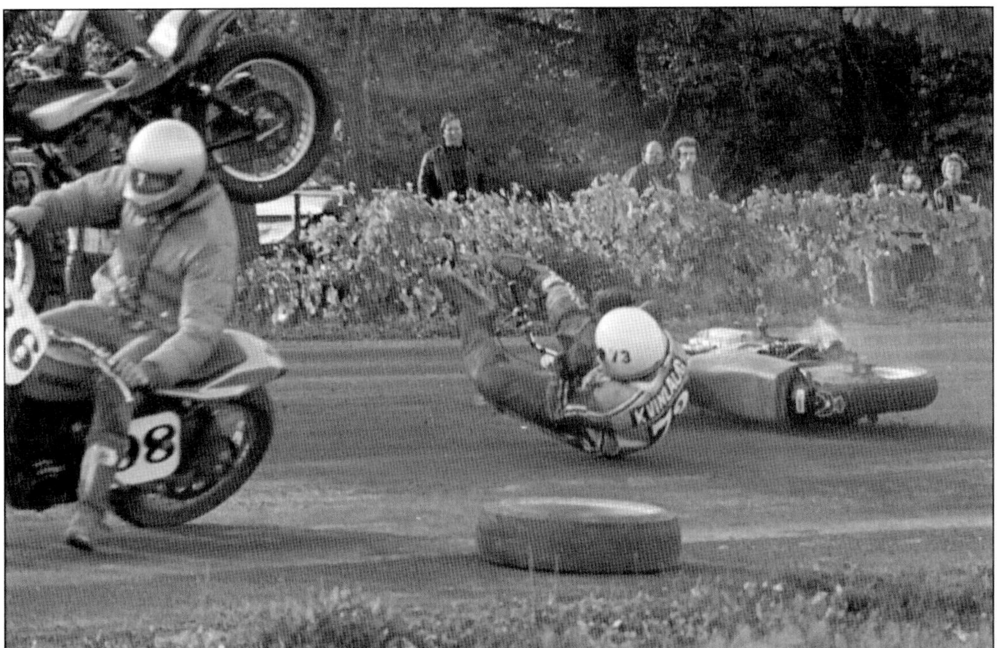

Robert Roosa clears Kvinlaug on the inside as Craig Estelle flies over the top. Neither rider was injured in the crash. (Photograph by Joe Corbett.)

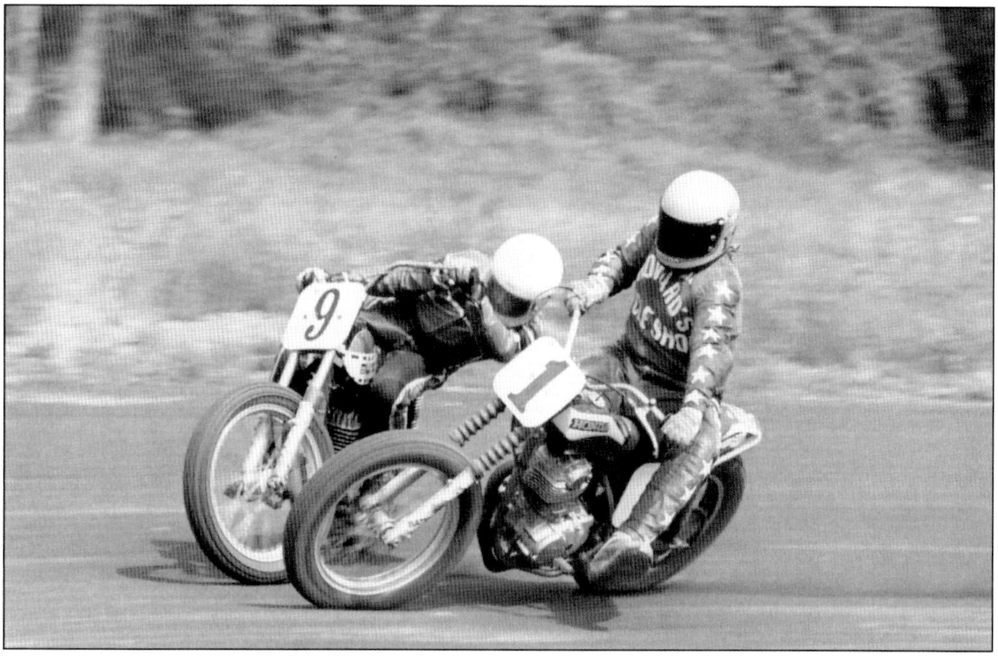

Matt Rozowicz tries to power his way around Bill Newell in the 360 Expert Class. Matt went on to become an American Motorcycle Association Grand National rider, the motorcycle equivalent to a NASCAR Cup racer. He was also the younger brother of racers Mike and Mark Rozowicz. (Photograph by Joe Corbett.)

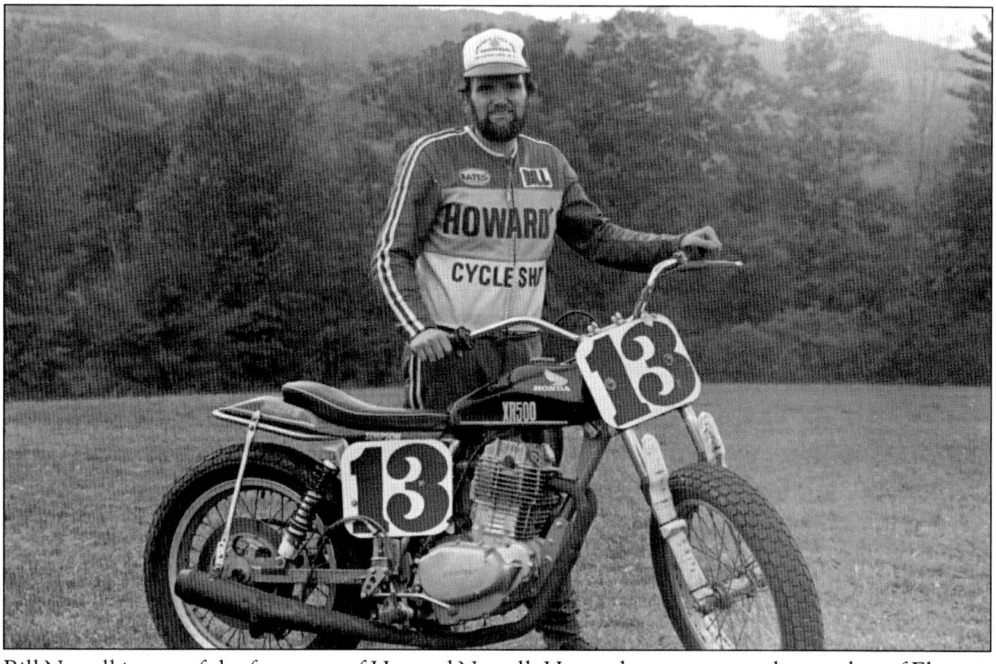

Bill Newell is one of the four sons of Howard Newell. Howard was a very early member of Electric City Riders who competed in polo, scrambles, and ice racing. Bill raced for 40 years, winning many championships, including one in sidecar ice racing. He ran Howard's Trail Sports in Burnt Hills, which sold Yamaha motorcycles until June 1991, when it closed. (Photograph by Joe Corbett.)

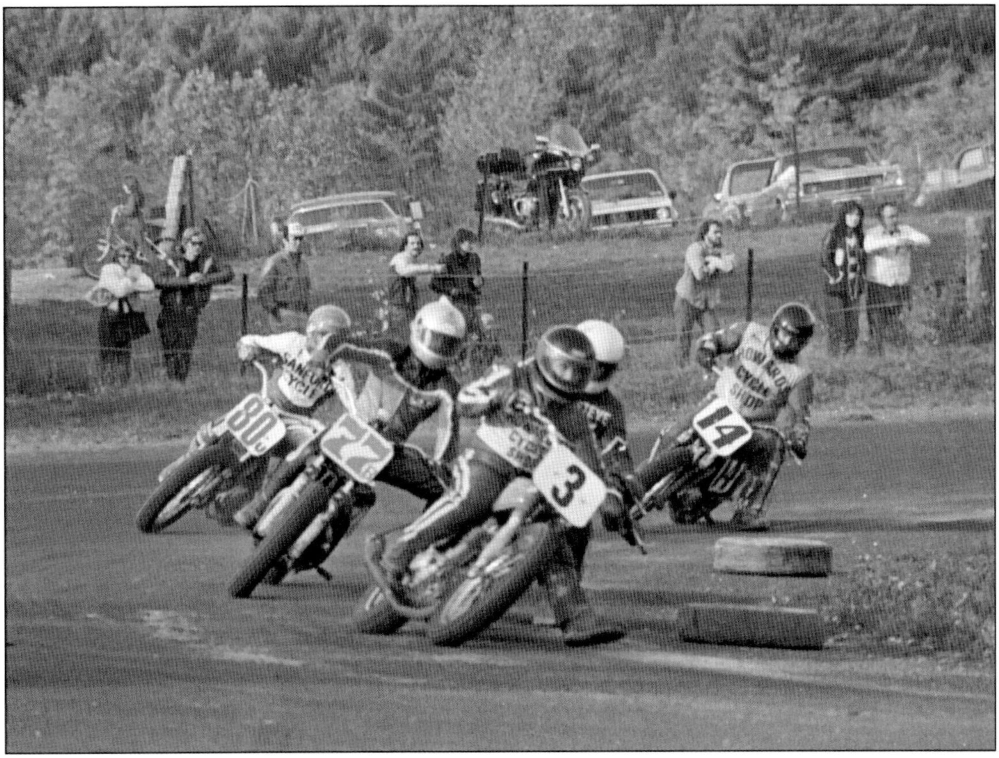

Tim Newell leads the 500cc Expert Class into the first turn, followed by Steve Longo, who is tucked behind in second place; Chuck Wager, 77; Gary Conklin, 80; and Jim Newell, 14, follow. This was a heat race to set the starting order for the feature event. (Photograph by Joe Corbett.)

Tim Newell was the oldest son of Howard Newell. Tim raced dirt and ice races and tried his skill at road racing. He poses here for the *Schenectady Gazette* in preparation for defending his 125cc Expert Class title for the upcoming New York State Championship race at the Electric City Riders track. He ran Howard's Cycle Shop in Ballston Lake, which sold Honda motorcycles until closing in December 1991. (Photograph by Joe Corbett.)

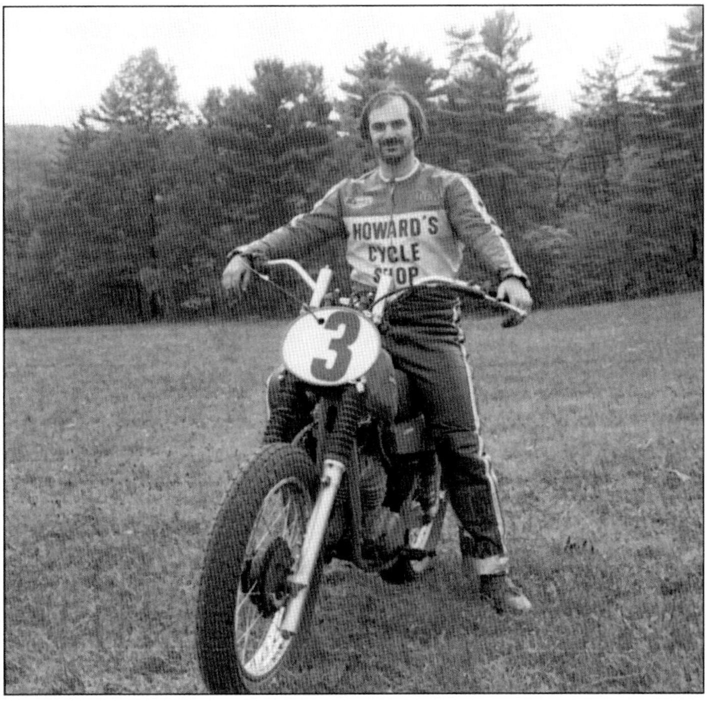

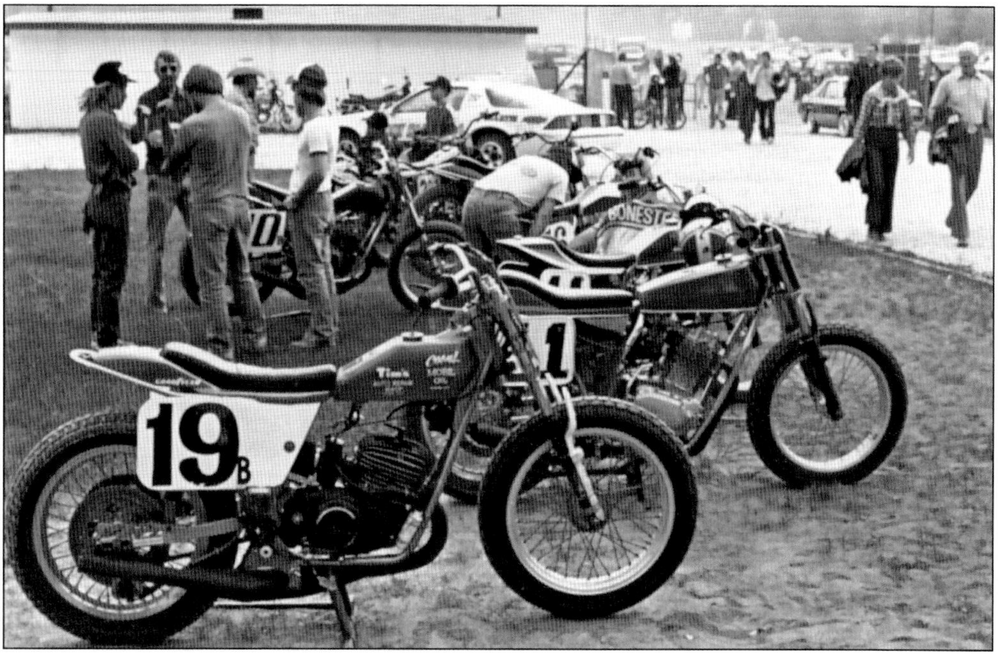

Race bikes are on display at the Albany Saratoga Speedway during a Friday night stockcar race. The riders put on a demonstration to promote an upcoming motorcycle race on the three-eighths–mile track. Many stockcar fans enjoyed watching the bike riders' daring moves on the track. (Photograph by Joe Corbett.)

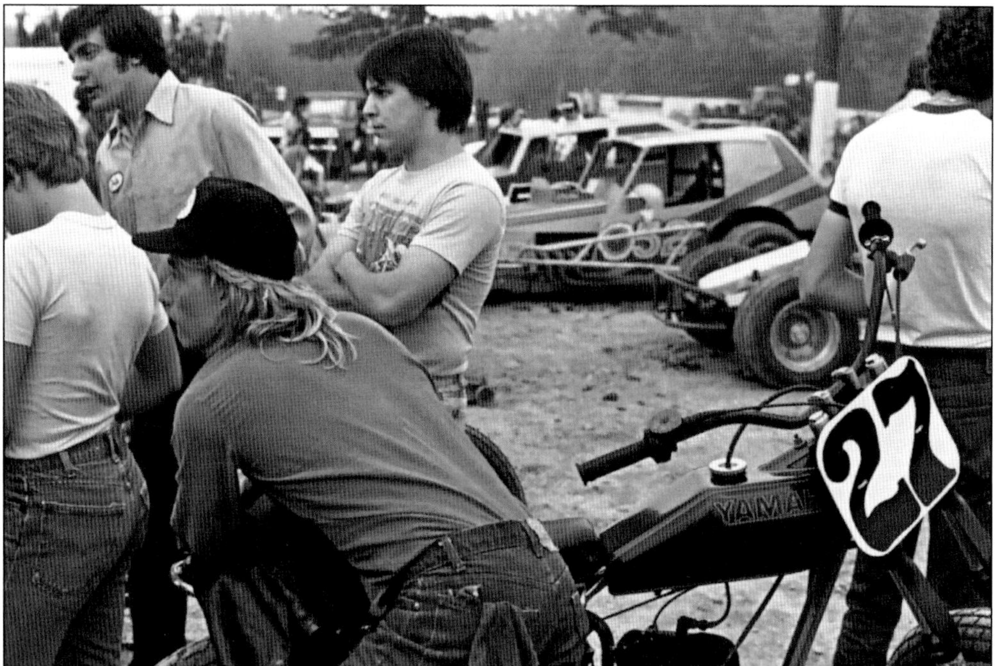

As the riders' meeting takes place in the Albany Saratoga Speedway pit area, from left to right, racers Brian Bonesteel, Pete Kissinger, Duane Veeder, and Greg "the Butcher" Scholz listen to the rules. Scholz was a meat cutter at his family's market in Schenectady. (Photograph by Joe Corbett.)

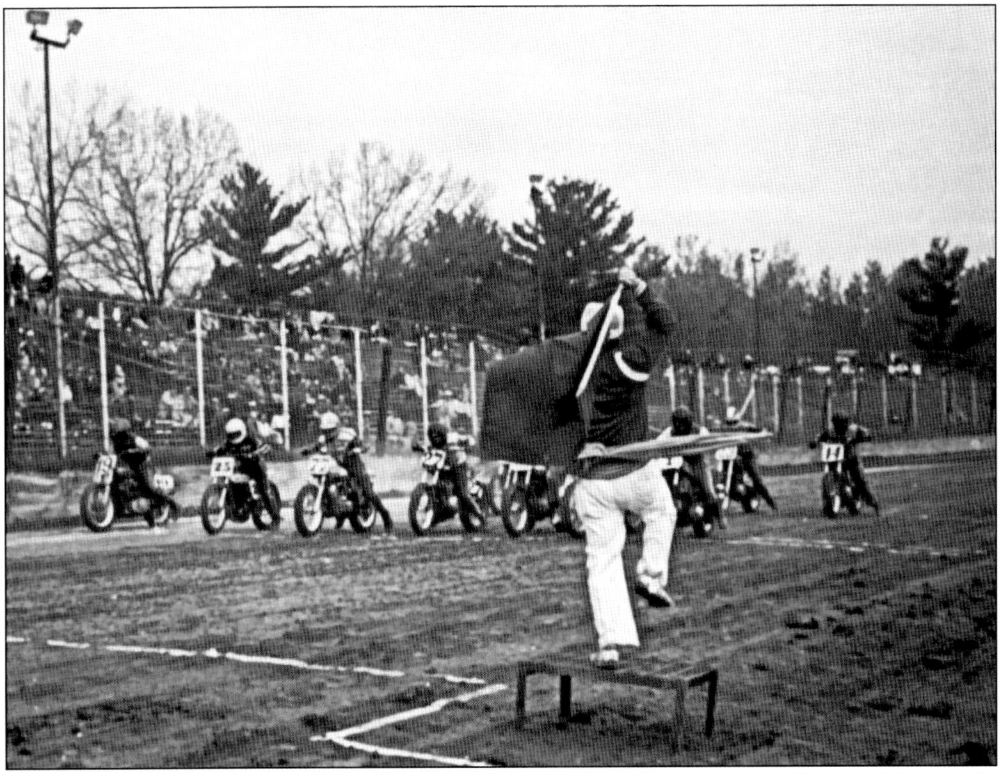

As Harold "Pee Wee" North waves the green flag, the Open Experts take off. From left to right are Duane Veeder, 19; Steve Longo, 25; Chuck Wager, 77; Chris Eberle, 27; Stephen Flach, 1; Steve Myrick, 23; and Jim Newell, 14. (Photograph by Joe Corbett.)

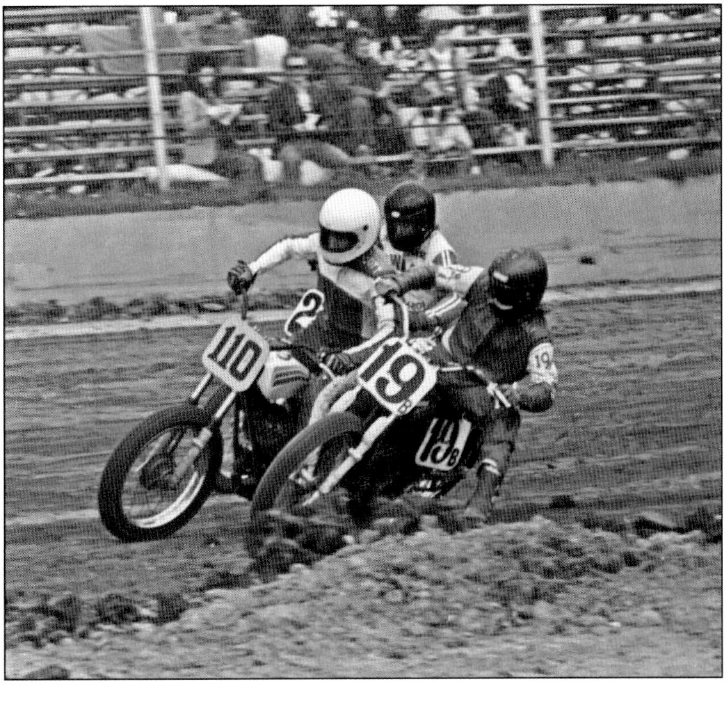

Duane Veeder dives underneath Scott Mitchell and Chris Eberle. Veeder, from Fultonville, was one of the top short track racers to come out of the northeast area. He went on to race a Harley-Davidson XR750 in regional and grand national events. (Photograph by Joe Corbett.)

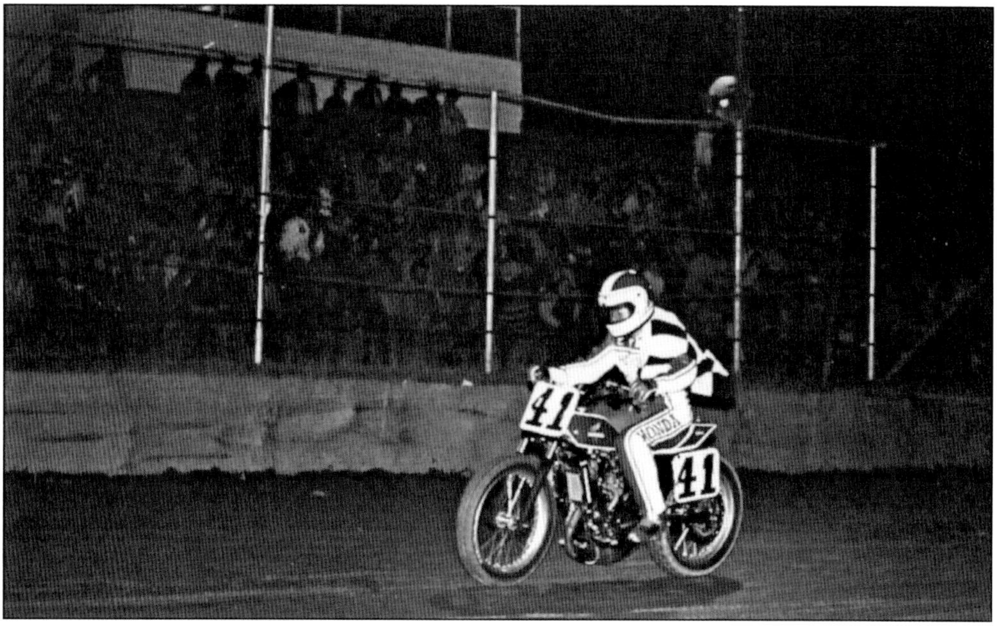

Brian Bonesteel takes a victory lap at the Albany Saratoga Speedway. The track has held stockcar races at its facility since 1965. The racing surface has switched from asphalt to dirt a few times since it was built. Recently, the future of the track has been in doubt. Lyle Devore has taken over the track's operation with great success. Motorcycle racing is back on the schedule after a long absence. (Photograph by Joe Corbett.)

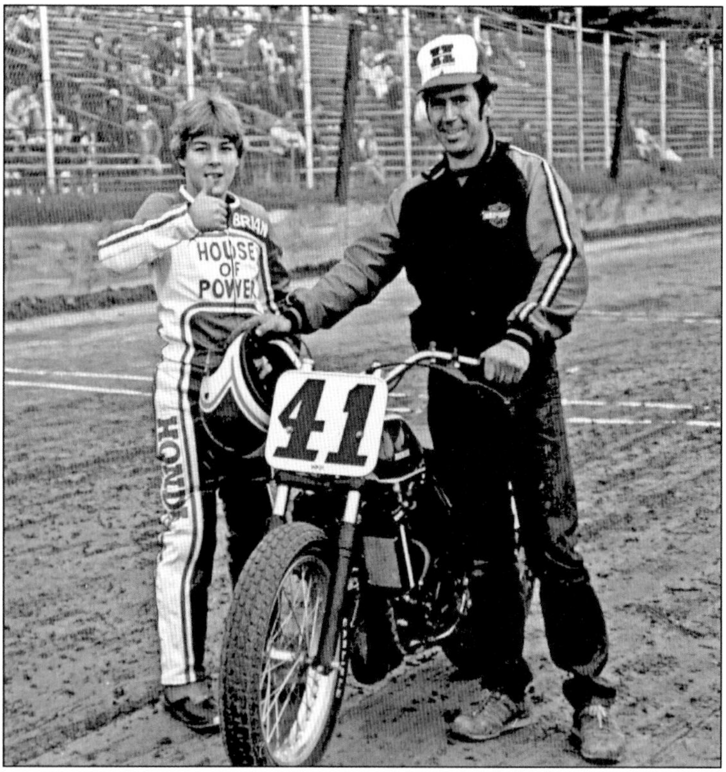

Brian Bonesteel, sponsored by House of Power Honda, had the Albany Saratoga Speedway figured out. He won five feature events on June 18–19, 1983. Bonesteel, who had now won a dozen features on his Honda at Albany Saratoga Speedway that season, won the 250cc Expert, Open Expert, and Combined Open features on Saturday and came back with wins in the 250cc Expert and Combined divisions in Sunday's racing card. His father, Wayne, looks on appreciatively. (Photograph by Joe Corbett.)

Eight

Various Motorcycle Events

Through the years, a variety of events have been promoted around the area, including hill climbs, road runs, motocross, trials, enduros, and sand drags.

Well-known events such as the Americade, which caters to the motorcycle touring crowd, and the Harley Rendezvous, a party celebrating American motorcycles, are still held every year.

Custom motorcycle shows have been held in the local armories and on the streets of Schenectady at different times throughout the years.

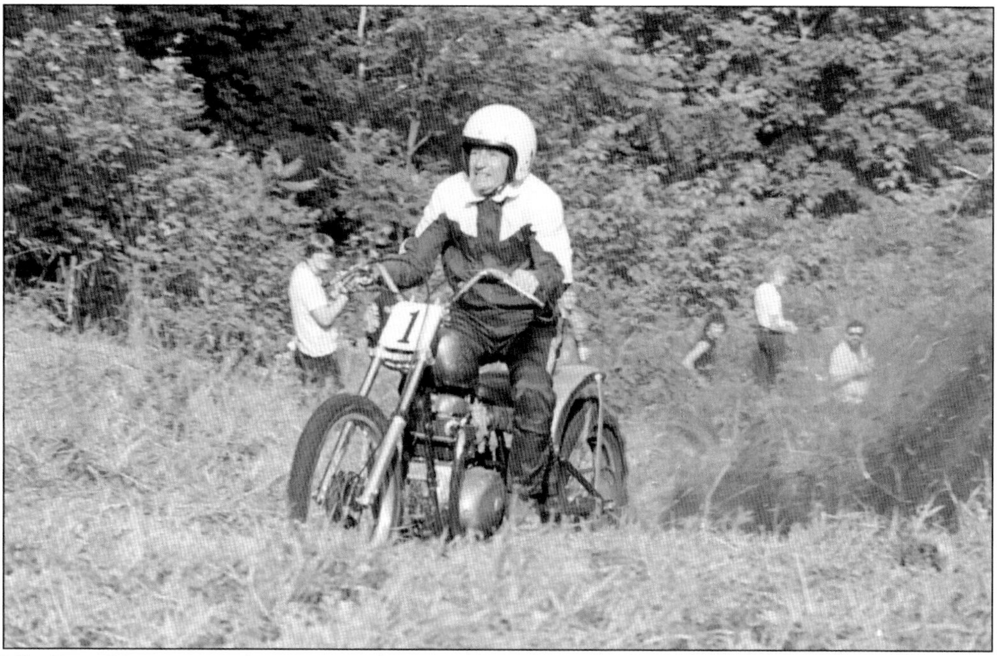

The Royal Mountain ski area, run by Jim Blaise, brought back motorcycle hill climbs after a long absence. In the 1980s, the AMA professional hill climbers made a stop at Royal. In this photograph, Earl Bowlby, a 10-time hill climb champion, makes a run at the hill on his 750cc BSA. (Photograph by Joe Corbett.)

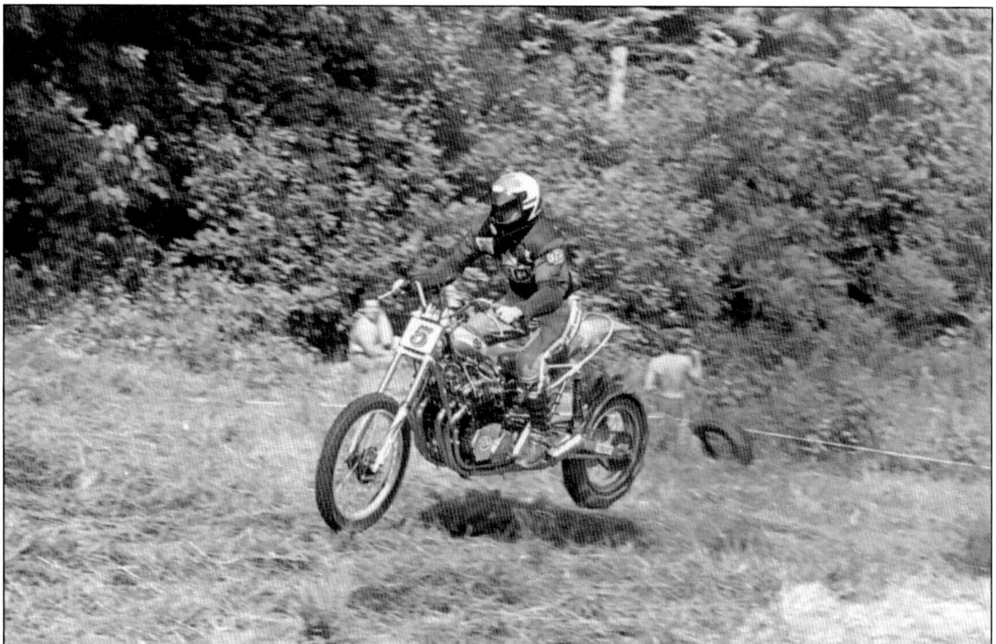

John Williams, a five-time 500cc champion from Ontario, Canada, takes his STP-sponsored Honda up the hill. John's machines were beautifully prepared. (Photograph by Joe Corbett.)

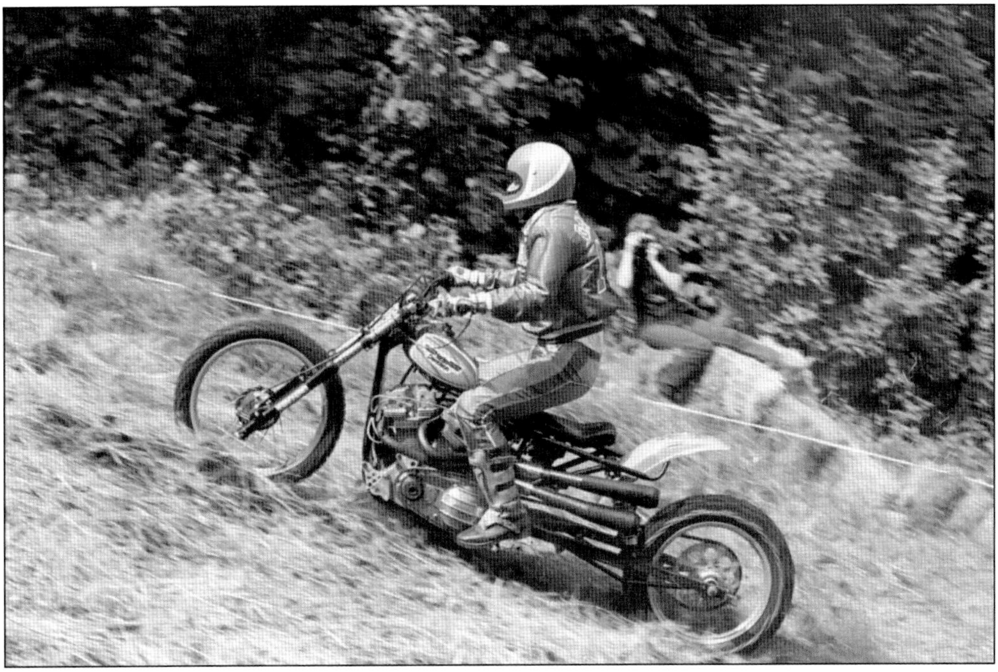

Lou Gerencer attacks the hill on a 750cc Harley-Davidson. Lou was from Elkhart, Indiana, and was a hill climb champion. Hill climbs are still held once a year at Royal Mountain, hosted by the New England Hill Climb Association. (Photograph by Joe Corbett.)

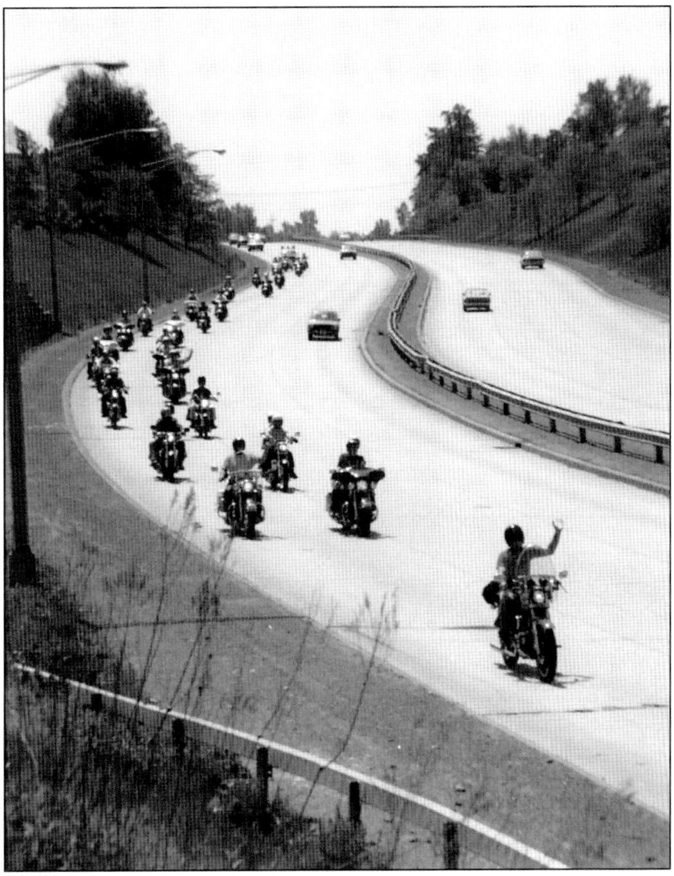

Dean Splittgerber leads a group of riders on Interstate 890 on the way to the 75th anniversary of Harley-Davidson in Milwaukee, Wisconsin. Dean runs Spitzies Harley-Davidson in Colonie and was a former drag, ice sidecar, and scramble racer. (Dean Splittgerber collection.)

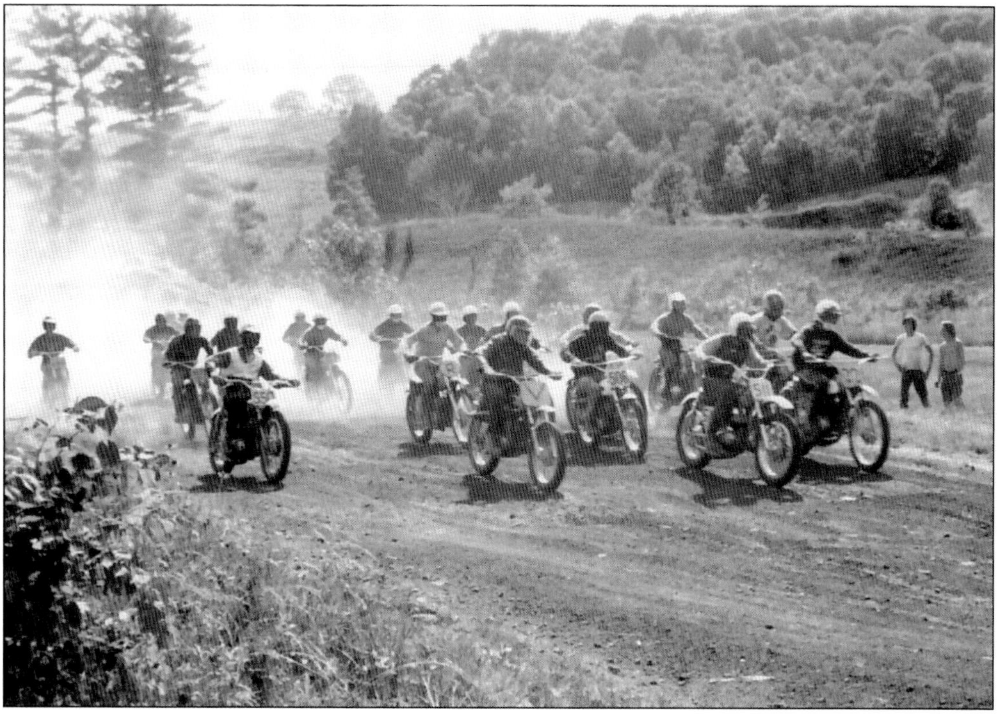

Motocross competitions really started to take off in America in the early 1970s. Some of the early tracks were in Clarksville, Claverack, and Millerton. The Clarksville track, built in 1962 by the Knickerbocker Motorcycle Club, only ran one event due to complaints from the neighbors. (Photograph by Greg Rickes.)

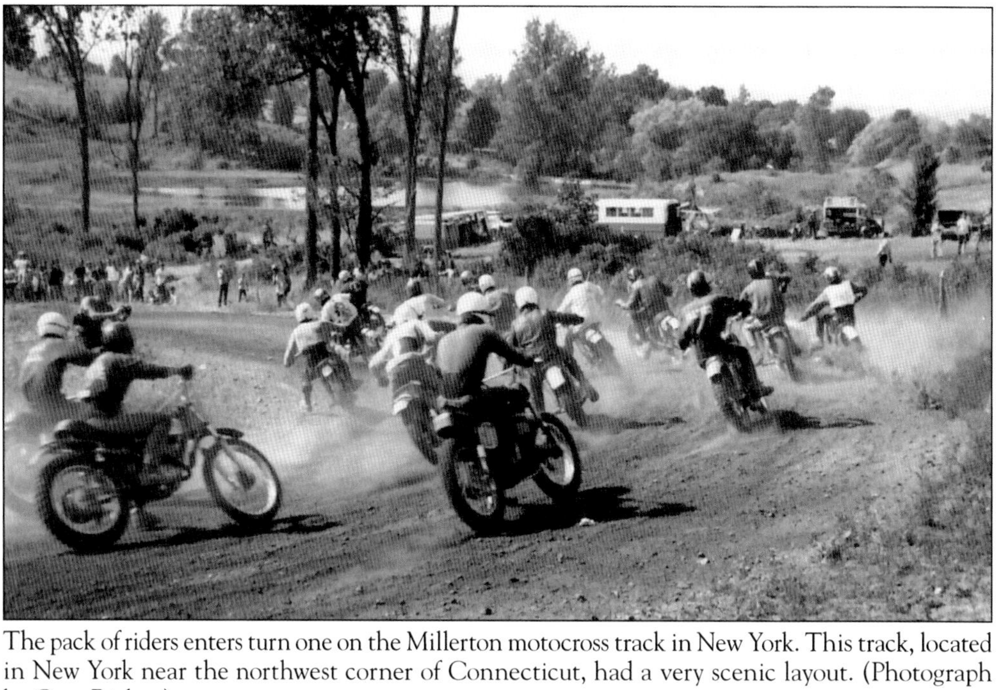

The pack of riders enters turn one on the Millerton motocross track in New York. This track, located in New York near the northwest corner of Connecticut, had a very scenic layout. (Photograph by Greg Rickes.)

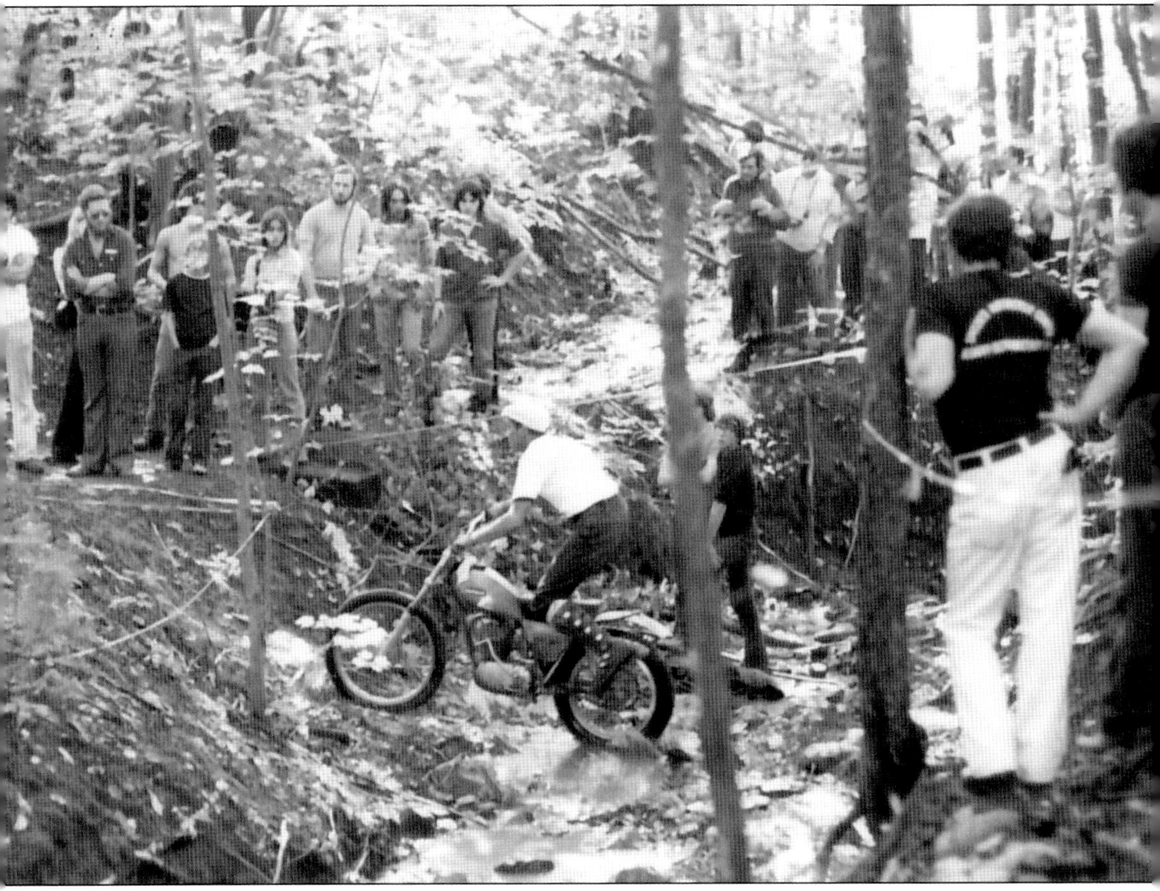

Mike Hickok rides the trials course on his Ossa. The object of a trials event is for riders to ride a section of a marked course and not put their feet down. Each time a rider touches the ground, he or she loses a point. The rider who loses the least amount of points is the winner. (Photograph by Larry Dagostino.)

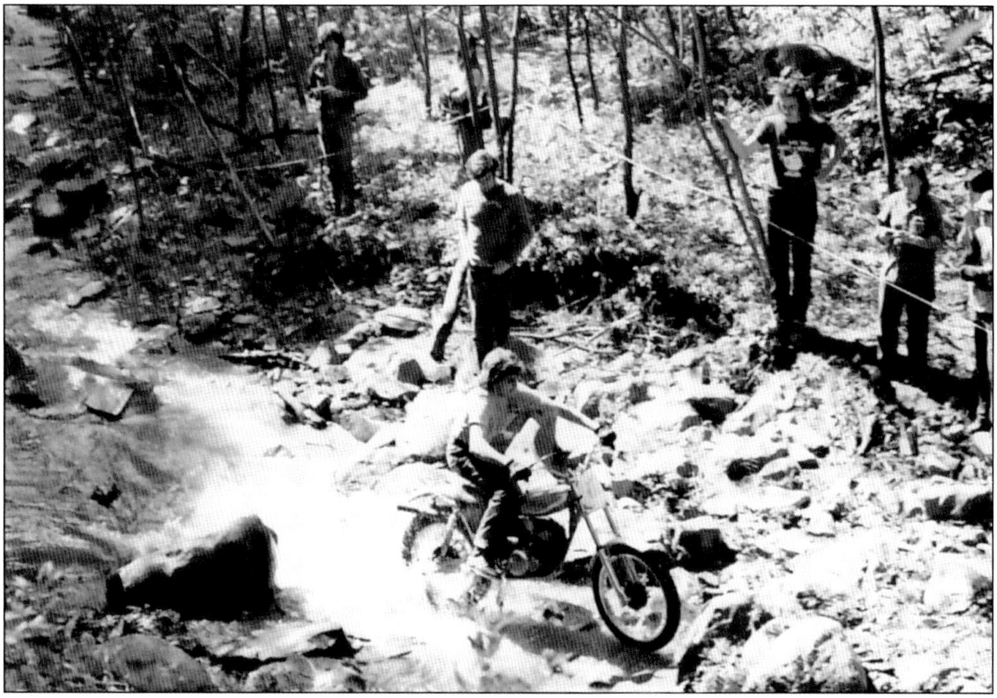

This unidentified rider prepares to exit the creek on his Suzuki RL250 as the judges look on. This event was held near the entrance of the Electric City Riders scrambles track. The New York State Championship trials event was held there in 1998; complaints from new neighbors put an end to the trials events at this location. (Photograph by Larry Dagostino.)

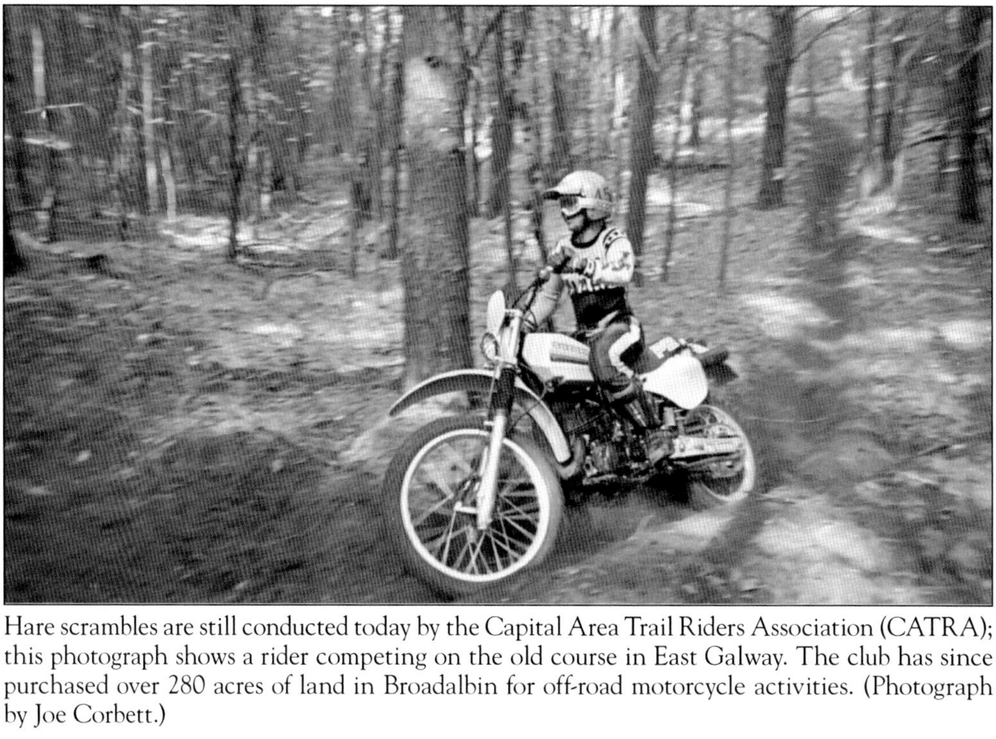

Hare scrambles are still conducted today by the Capital Area Trail Riders Association (CATRA); this photograph shows a rider competing on the old course in East Galway. The club has since purchased over 280 acres of land in Broadalbin for off-road motorcycle activities. (Photograph by Joe Corbett.)

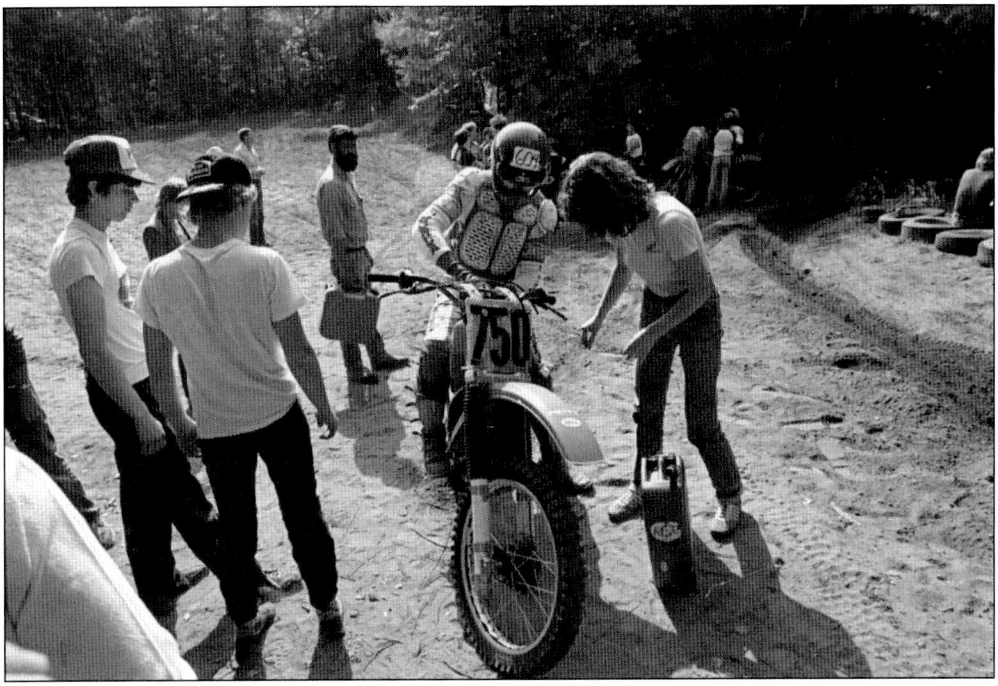

A hare scramble event consists of multiple laps of up to eight miles per lap. The rider with the quickest time wins. Here, Brad Young and his wife, Mary, make a pit stop to refuel his Honda CR480 during the event. (Photograph by Joe Corbett.)

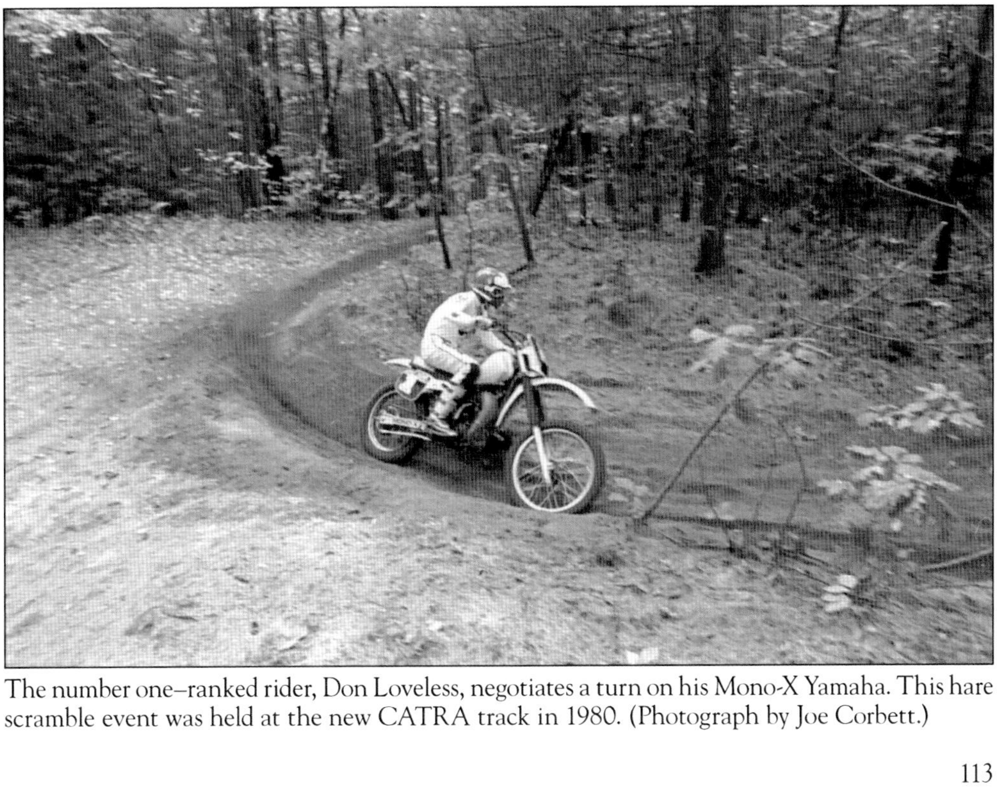

The number one–ranked rider, Don Loveless, negotiates a turn on his Mono-X Yamaha. This hare scramble event was held at the new CATRA track in 1980. (Photograph by Joe Corbett.)

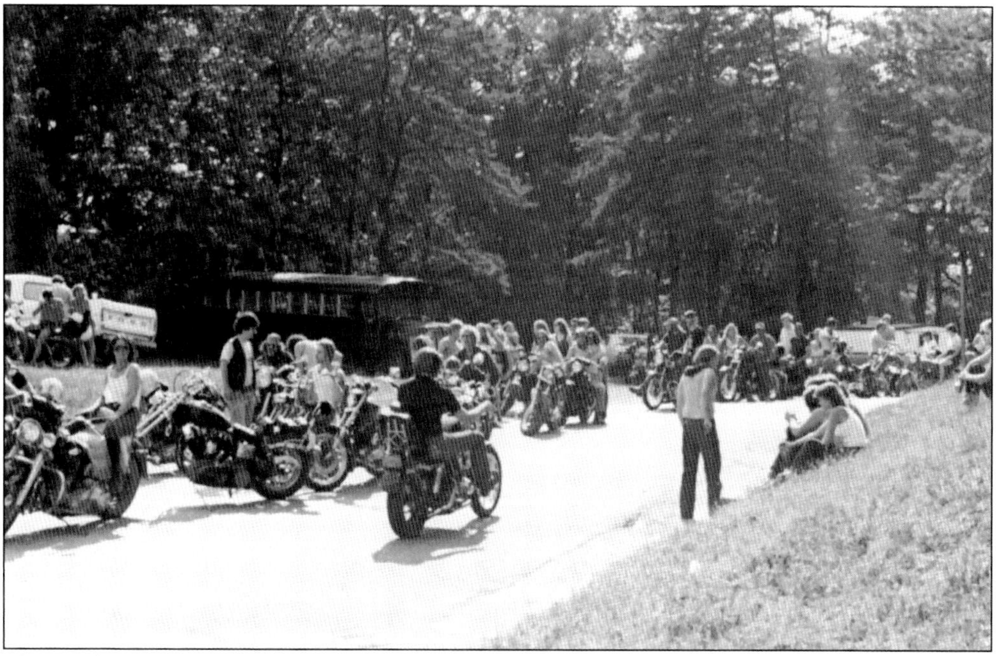

The Brotherhood Against Totalitarian Enactments (ABATE), which has since changed its name to American Bikers Aimed Towards Education, holds an annual helmet protest at the state capital in Albany. Bikes line up at the Six Mile Waterworks on Fuller Road, getting ready to descend on the capital to try and persuade the government to repeal the helmet law. (Photograph by the author.)

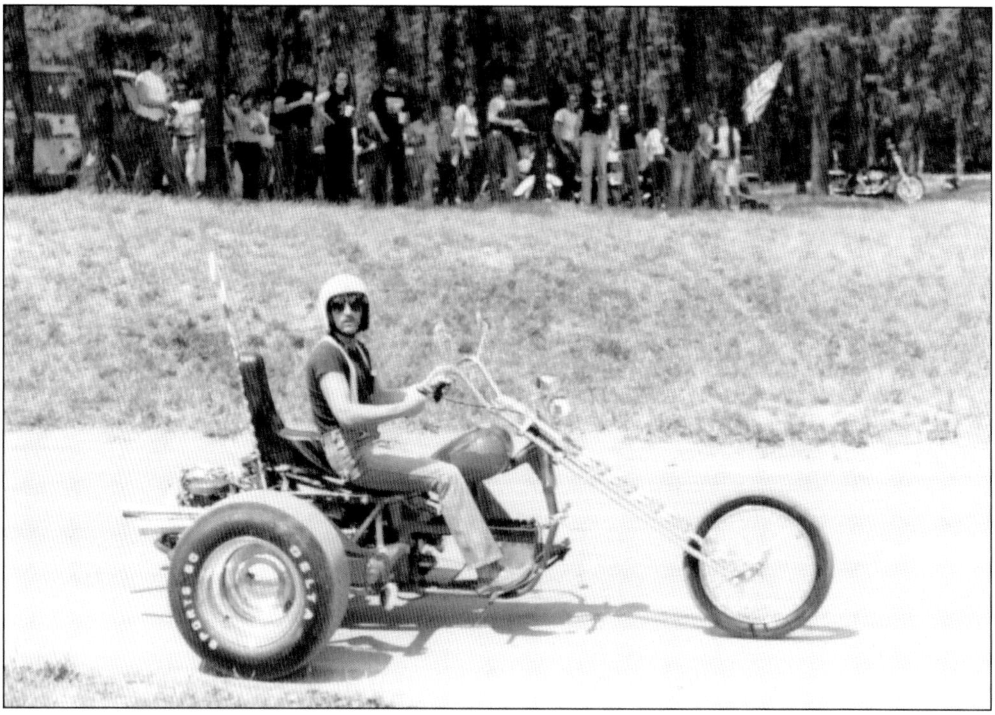

A Volkswagen-powered three-wheeler leaves to ride in the helmet protest. After the run, big parties are held at the Six Mile Waterworks Park. (Photograph by the author.)

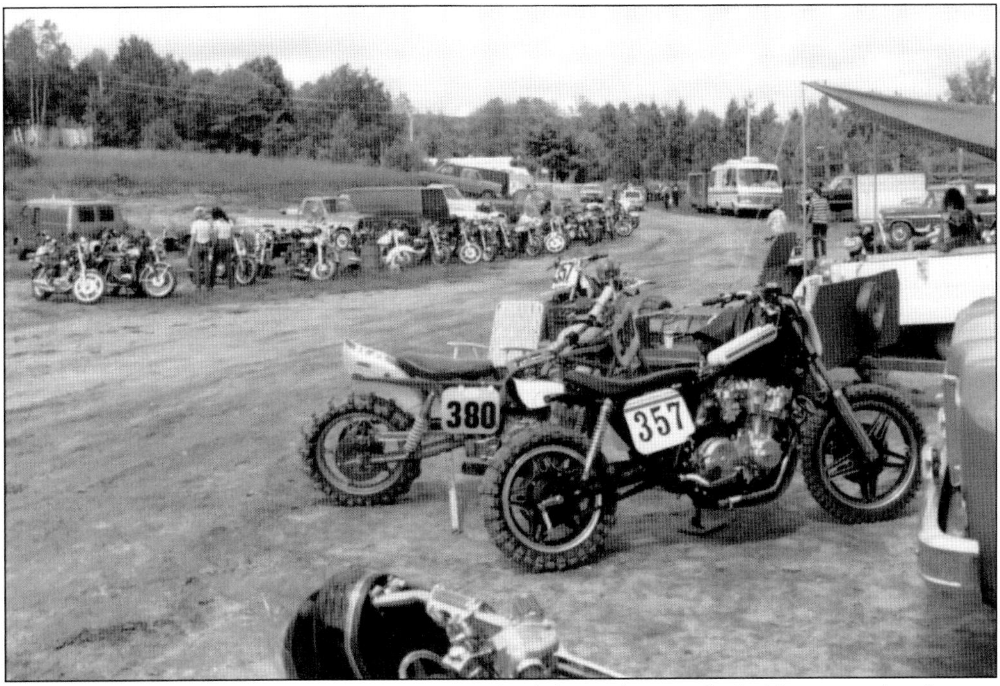

The AM-JAM (American Jamboree) motorcycle club was known for holding a weekend event in Cobleskill. The club also held sand drag races at the Glad Rags sand drag track in Corinth. The pits are lined with both street and race bikes getting ready to compete in different classes. (Photograph by the author.)

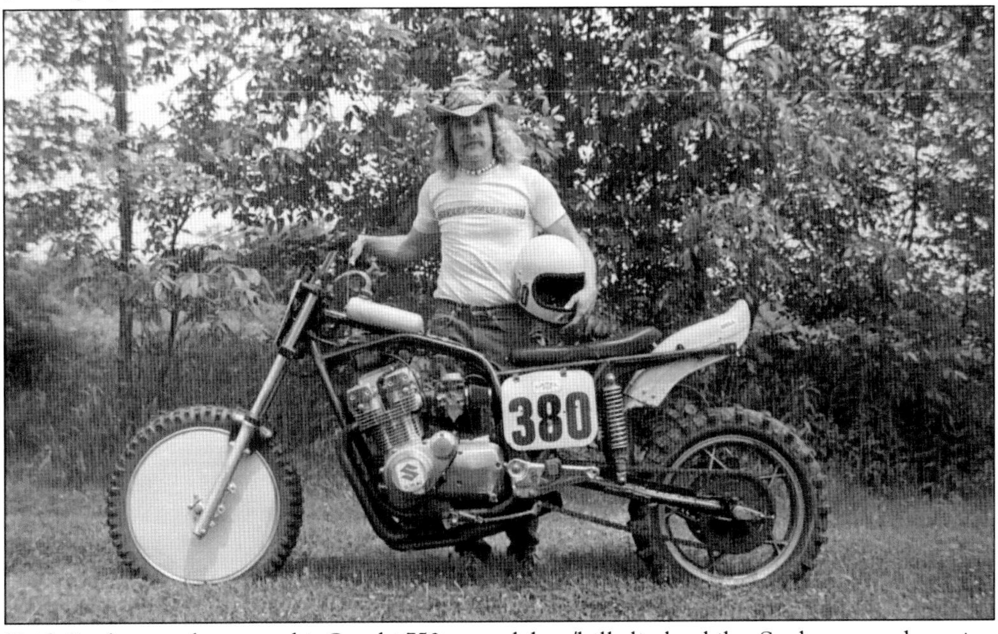

Keith Supley stands next to his Suzuki 750cc sand drag/hill climber bike. Supley was a champion snowmobile racer, racing in Booneville, Greenville, Cobleskill, and Schroon Lake. He was sponsored by All Season Arctic Cat during the winter and competed in short track, sand drags, and hill climbing in the summer. (Photograph by Joe Corbett.)

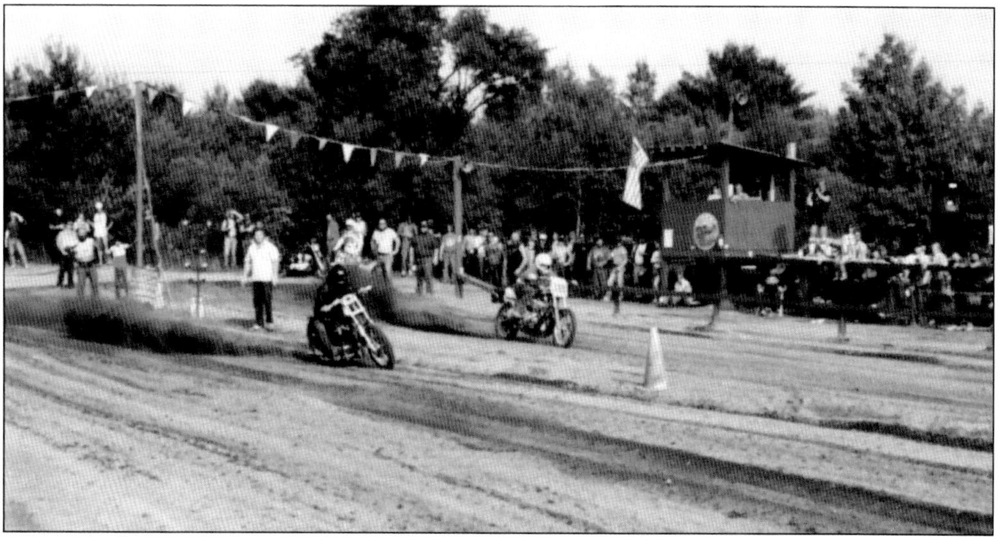

Tony Mattioli and Keith Supley compete for the Top Eliminator Trophy at the Glad Rags event. To the delight of the pro-Harley crowd, Mattioli went on to win on his Harley-Davidson. Supley was on a Suzuki. Tony went on to race Top Fuel drag bikes until being injured in a crash. (Photograph by the author.)

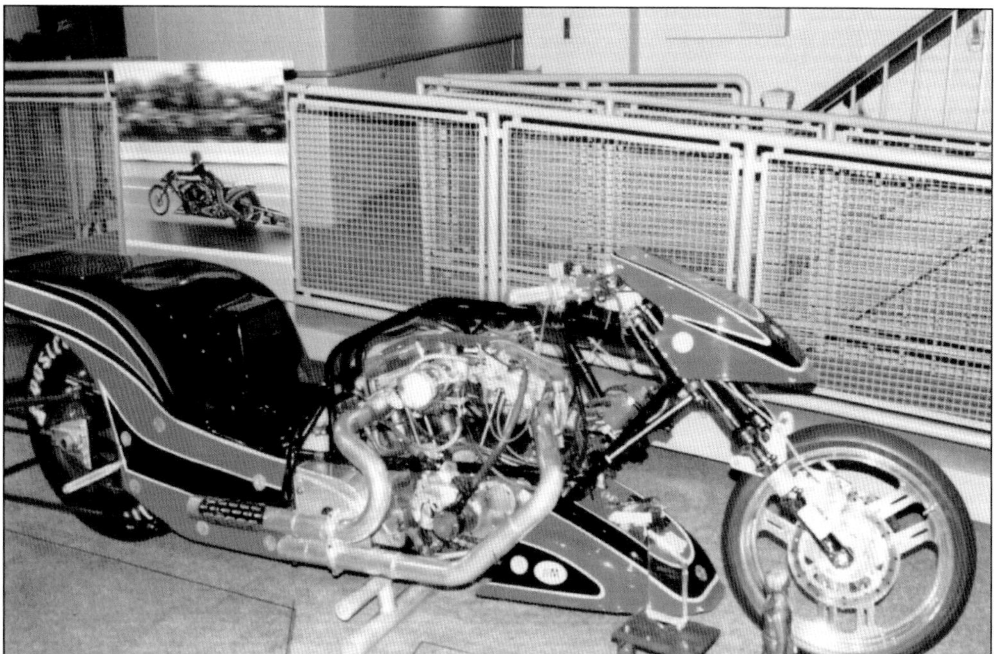

Tony's Harley-Davidson dragster was on display at the Saratoga Auto Museum. It was part of a show called "From Asphalt to Ice," which featured motorcycles from all forms of the sport. Tony raced in the International Hot Rod Association and the All Harley Drag Racing Association. (Photograph by the author.)

Nine

Ice Racing

With the freezing weather that is experienced in the northern regions of the country, it would seem only natural to extend the motorcycling season. In the early days, different methods were tried to adapt a motorcycle to work on the ice. The tires were removed and screws were bolted to the rim or chains were wrapped around the tire, though neither attempt had much success.

The Ice Spike, developed in Sweden, made its way to the States by the 1950s. Ice racing with spiked tires never caught on here, as they were costly and dangerous. Development of a better alternative began soon after. Tires with sheet metal screws screwed into the tire became the way to go. This set up provided racing action similar to riding on a dirt track.

Ice races have been held at numerous area lakes, including Saratoga, Mariaville, Warners, Thompson, Ballston, Sacandaga, Lake Desolation, Lake George, Iroquois Lake in Central Park, and the pond at the old Trout Out Inn.

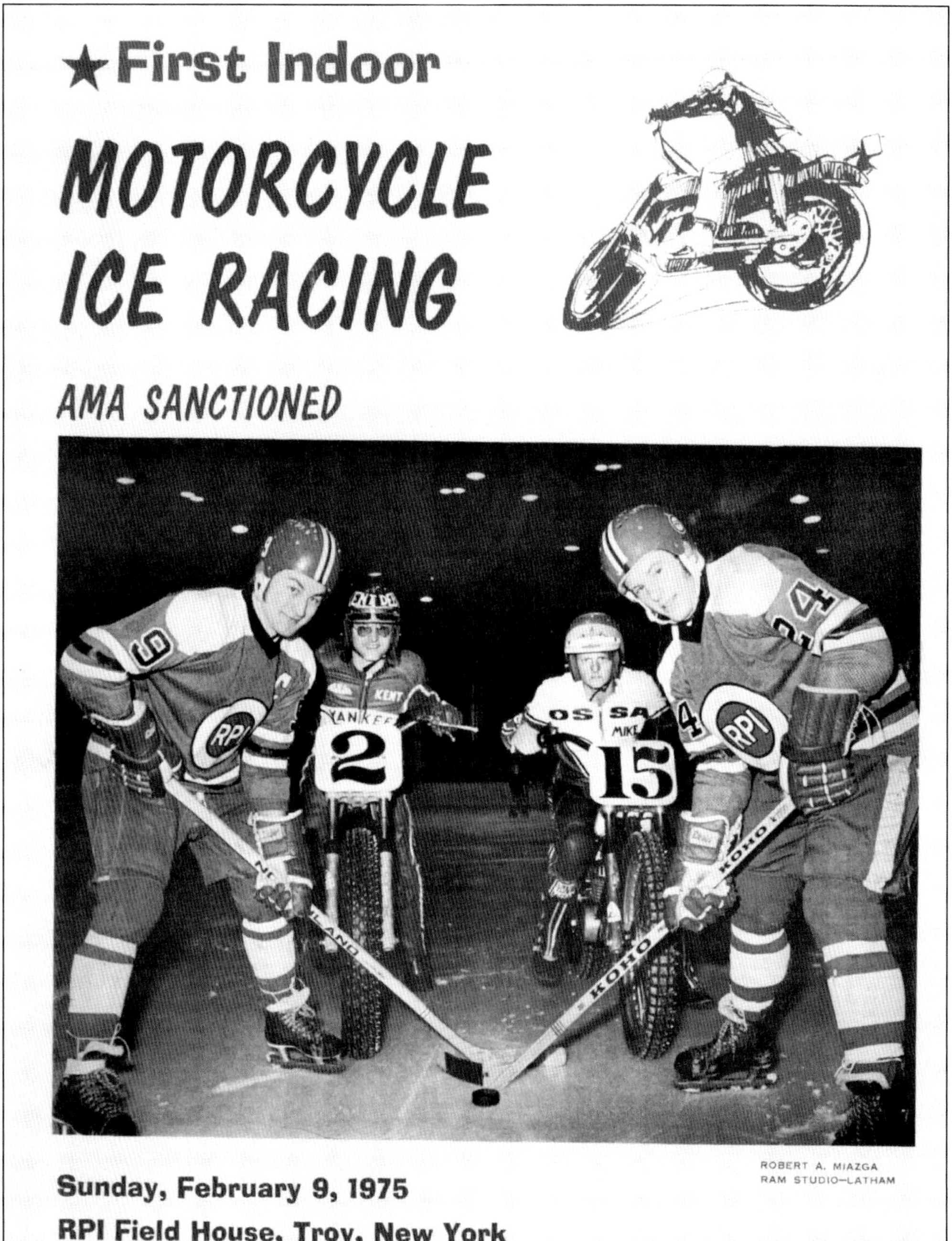

The first AMA-sanctioned indoor motorcycle ice race was held at the RPI Field House in Troy in 1975. The races were held within the walls of a hockey rink. Here, Kent Debie (number 2) and Mike Hickok (number 15) pose on the cover of the program with two of the RPI engineer hockey players. (Author's collection.)

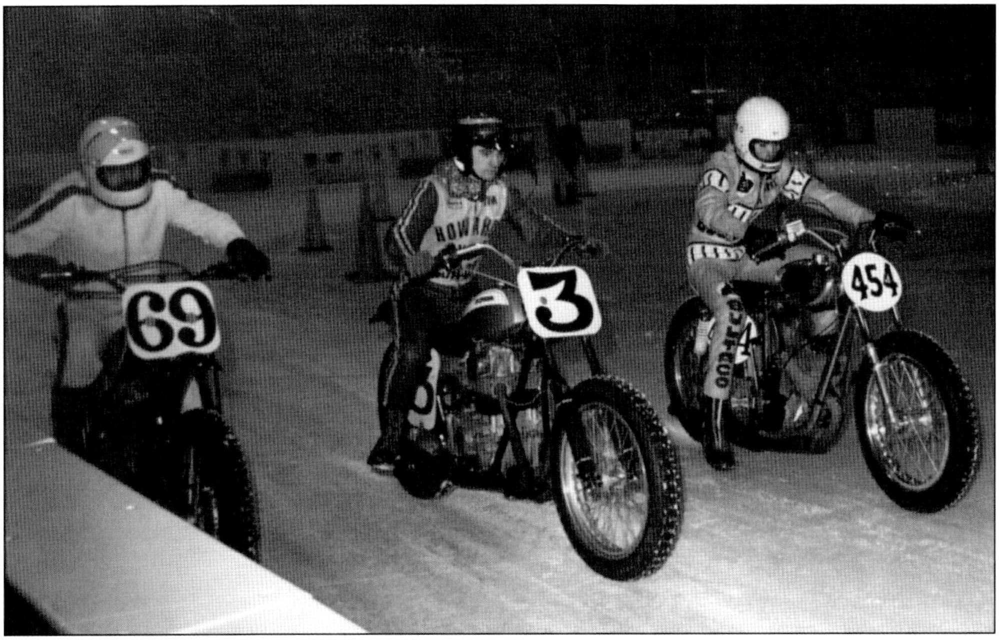

From left to right, Bobby Newell, Tim Newell, and Barney Waldron prepare to face off on the RPI hockey rink in the 350cc Class. Bikes of all sizes, from mini cycles to sidecars, competed at the event. Riders were able to compete by invitation only. (Larry Dagostino Jr. collection.)

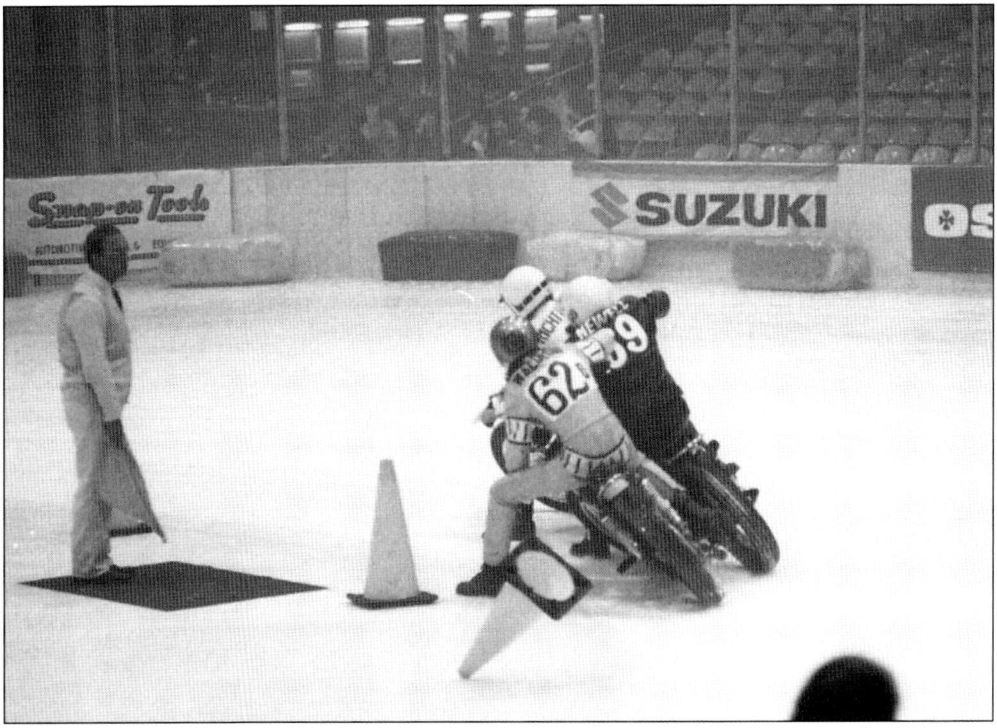

Racing action is tight on the indoor track as George Richtmeyer leads Bobby Newell and Barney Waldron into turn one. The action could be compared to roller derby, with elbows out and a little hip checking used to improve position. (Photograph by Greg Rickes.)

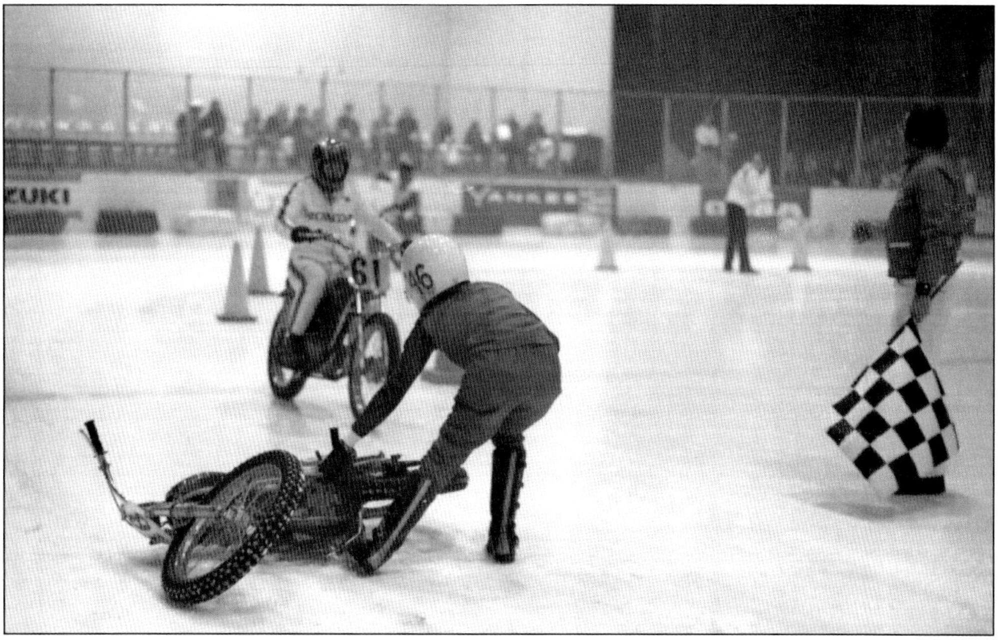

Jeff Clark looks to see if he is able to safely pick up his bike after losing control while coming out of the fourth turn. Tim O'Neil, 61, safely goes by on the inside as the flagger, Bob Supley, looks on. (Photograph by Greg Rickes.)

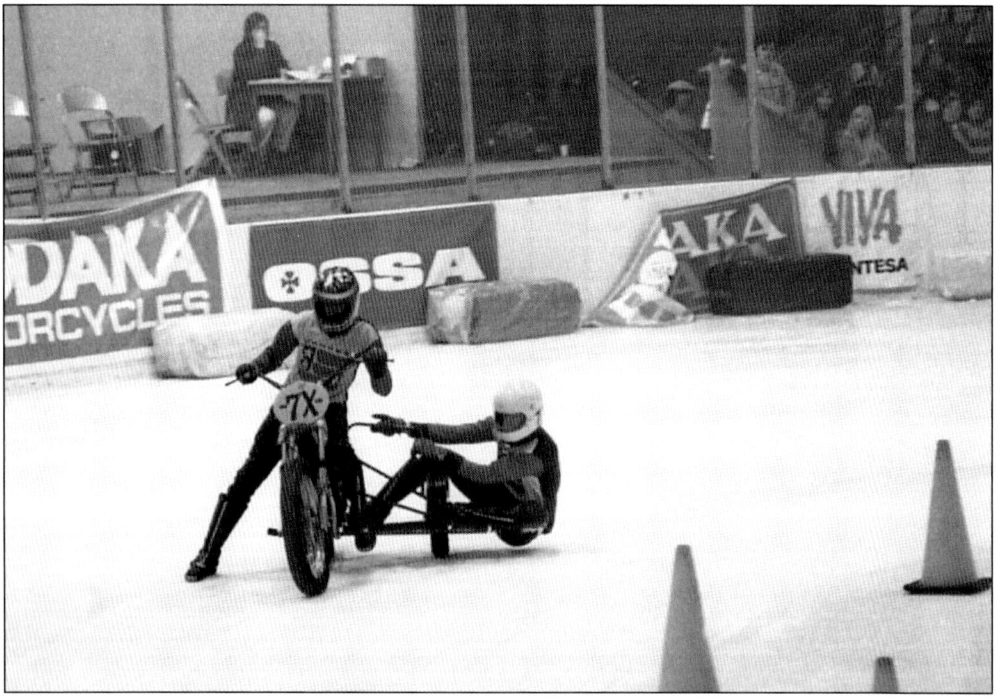

Brian Jueckstock and his passenger, Tom Vincent, put on a sidecar exhibition for the crowd. Rider participation was good, and the crowds were enthusiastic. The next race, held indoors in March 1975, was the last. The studded tires dug through the ice, and the RPI management was afraid that the refrigerated floor would be damaged. (Photograph by Greg Rickes.)

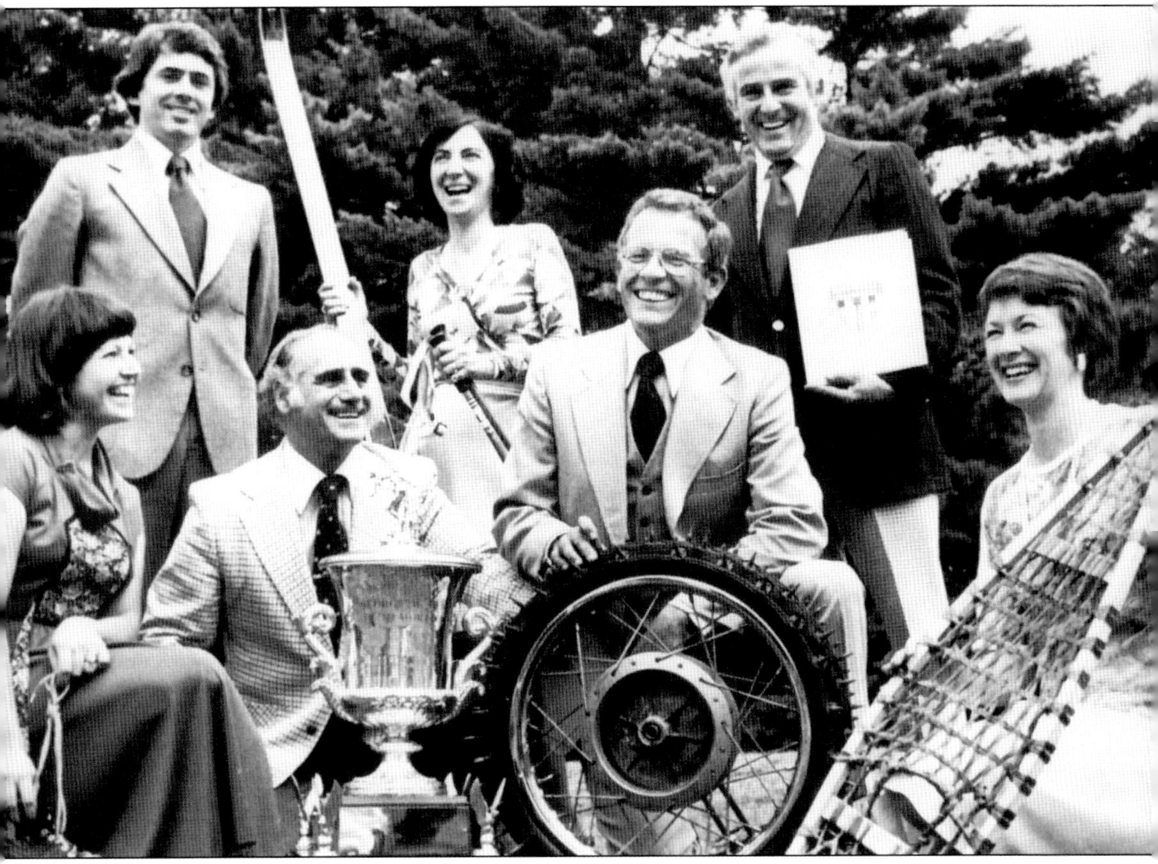

The first Saratoga Winter Sports Festival was held in the winter of 1977–1978. The festival included skiing, skating, snowshoeing, snowmobile racing, and stockcar and motorcycle ice pacing. Pictured here from left to right are (first row) Theresa Goodwin, Larry Dagostino, Robert Schock, and Bernie McAvinney; (second row) Roger Shearer, Johanna Farra, and Jerry Moreau. Notice the spiked tire used for display; these tires were no longer used at this time, but they looked good in the photograph. (Larry Dagostino Jr. collection.)

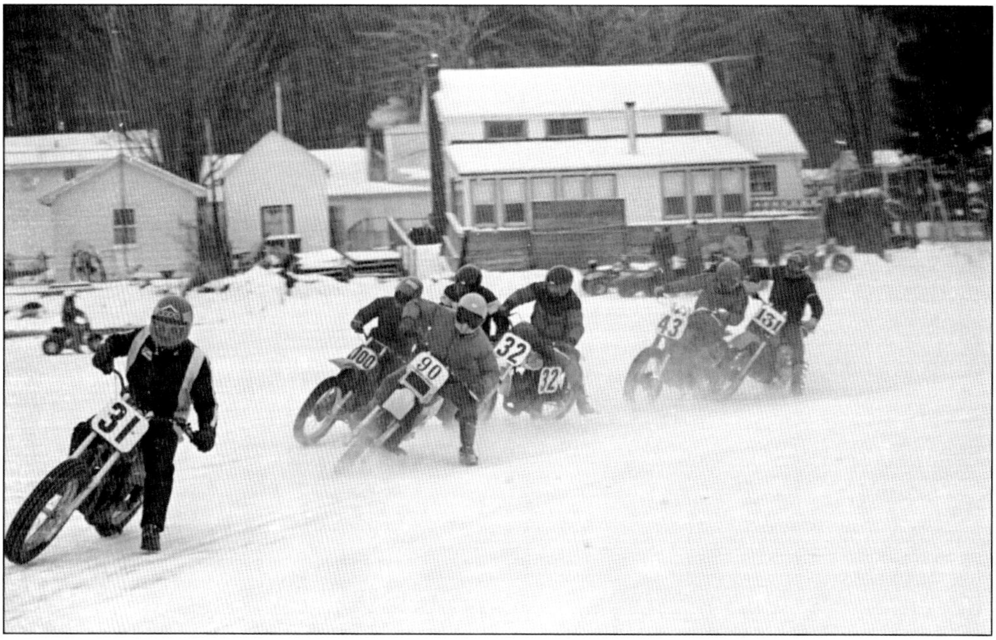

Racing on Saratoga Lake was part of the Saratoga Winter Sports Festival. Because of the long winters in the northeast, ice racing is the only motorcycle sport available. Riders from all disciplines—such as motocross, enduro and short track—would compete. Here, Dave Pahl leads the 125cc Expert Class and is followed by Don Rajczi (no. 98), Jay Skidmore (no. 100), Greg Scholz (no. 32), Bryan Burnham (no. 43), and Tom Daniels (131). (Photograph by Joe Corbett.)

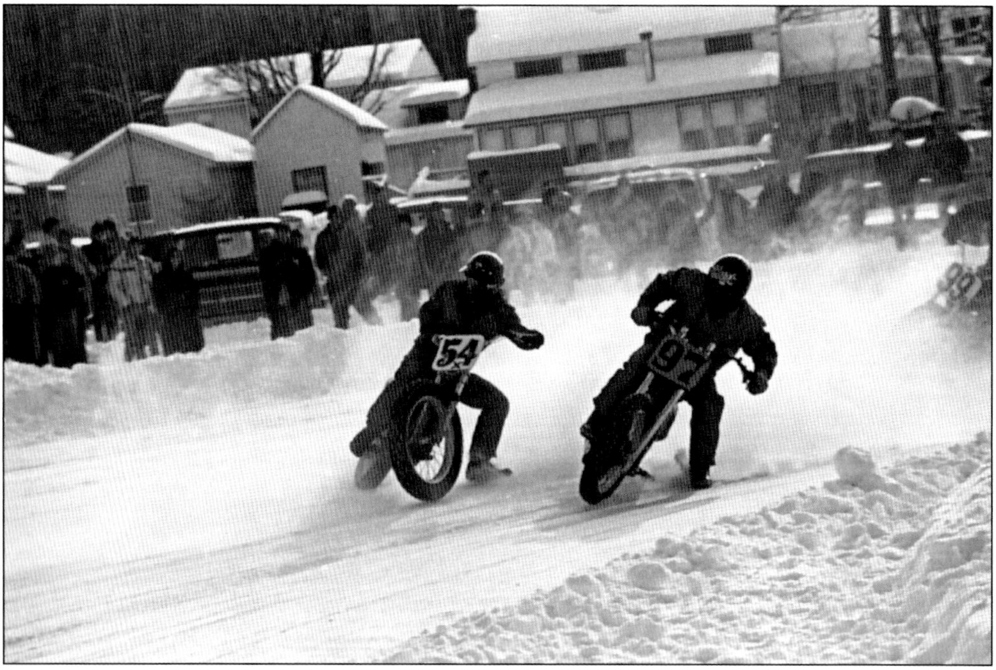

A good-sized crowd watches as Kurt Spoonagle dives inside the completely sideways Barney Waldron. Spoonagle went on to excel in short track and observed trials riding. Waldron races vintage stockcars today with the North East Stock Car Old Timers Club (NESCOT). (Photograph by Joe Corbett.)

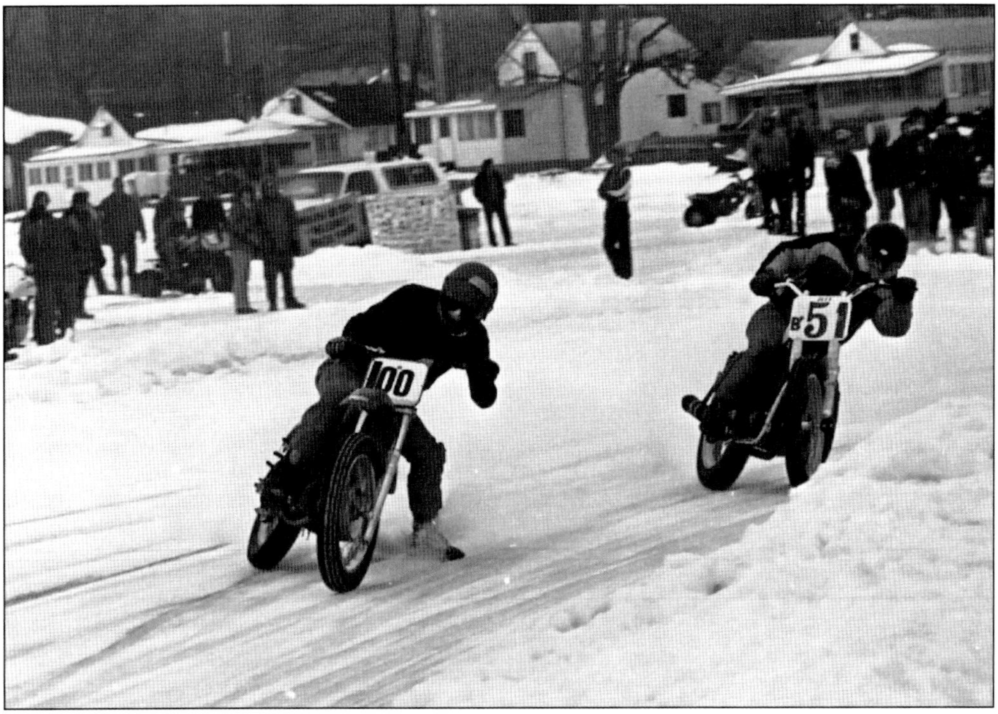

Jay Skidmore, from Millbrook, and Jeff Jenkins, from Lake George, were two of the men to beat in the sport of ice racing. Jay has a slim lead over Jeff in this photograph. Skidmore still races today and assembles ice-racing tires to sell to other racers. (Photograph by Joe Corbett.)

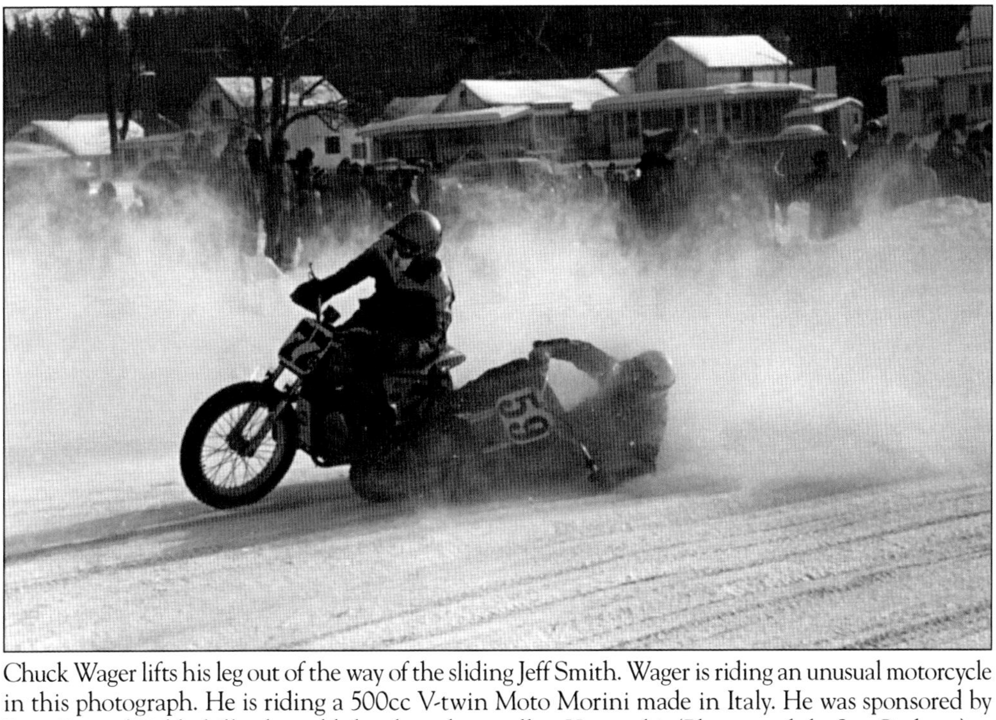

Chuck Wager lifts his leg out of the way of the sliding Jeff Smith. Wager is riding an unusual motorcycle in this photograph. He is riding a 500cc V-twin Moto Morini made in Italy. He was sponsored by Stan Fain of Cobleskill, who sold that brand, as well as Kawasaki. (Photograph by Joe Corbett.)

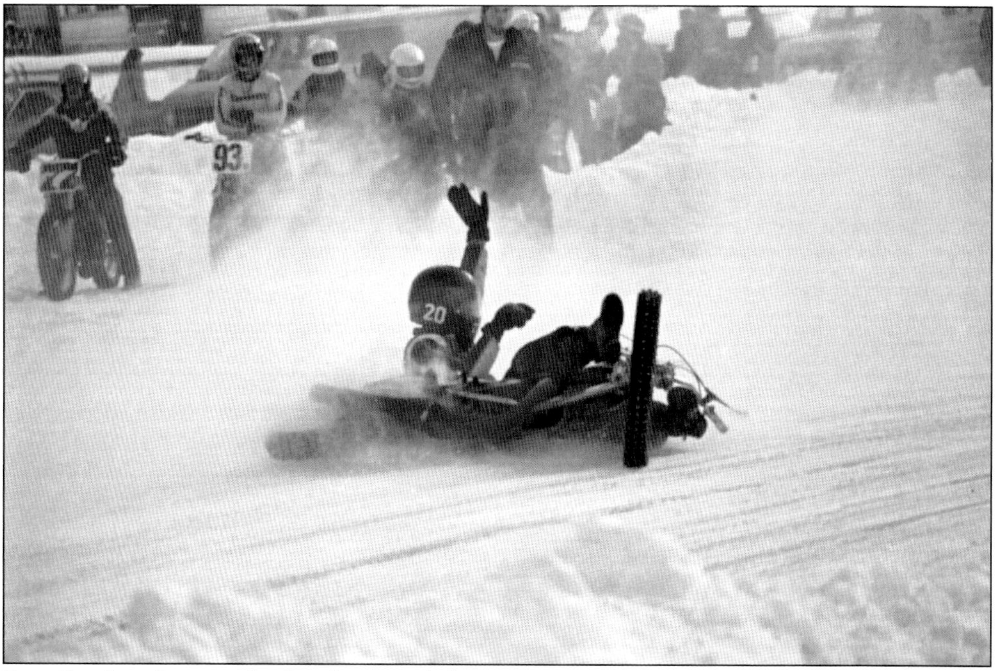

Dave Bartkowski waves his hand to signal the oncoming riders of his position. Getting run over by a studded motorcycle can have unpleasant results. Corner workers will wave a caution flag and help free him from his machine. (Photograph by Joe Corbett.)

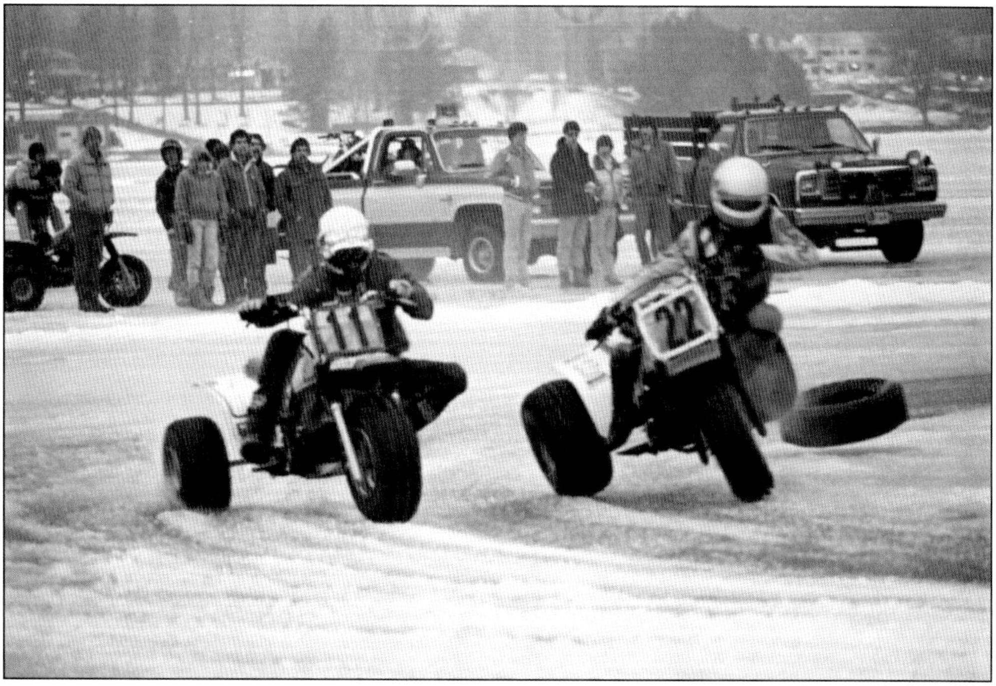

All-terrain cycle riders provide some excitement as the inside rider hits the tire on the inside of the course and goes up on two wheels. Riding an ATC takes a lot of agility to keep the machine under control. (Photograph by Joe Corbett.)

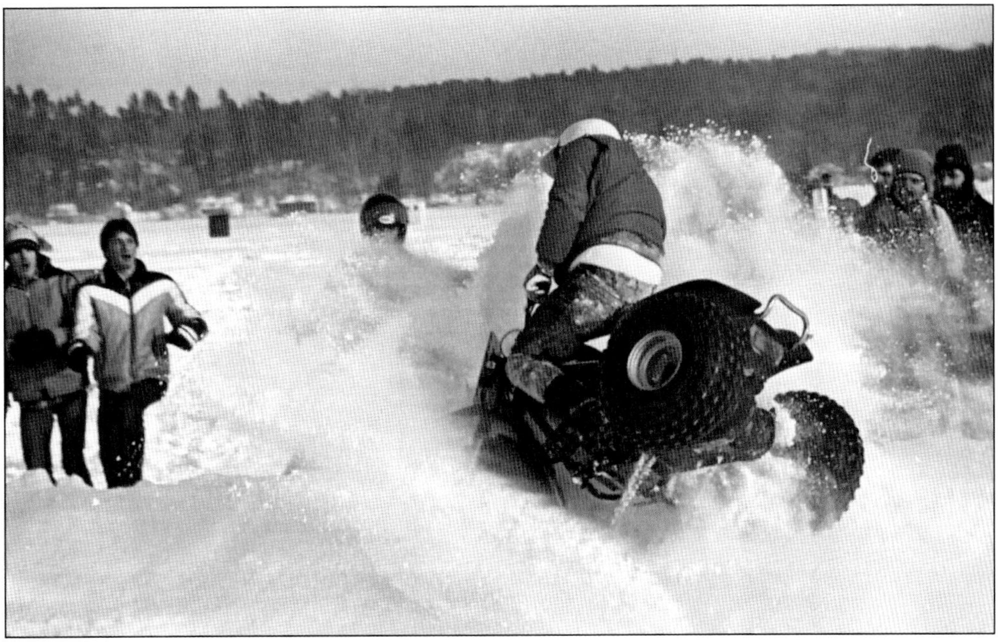

This ATC rider, competing in the class that does not use studs, loses control and hits the snow bank. The spectators are trying to decide which way to go to avoid the out-of-control rider. AMA insurance regulations eliminated the ATC classes shortly after. (Photograph by Joe Corbett.)

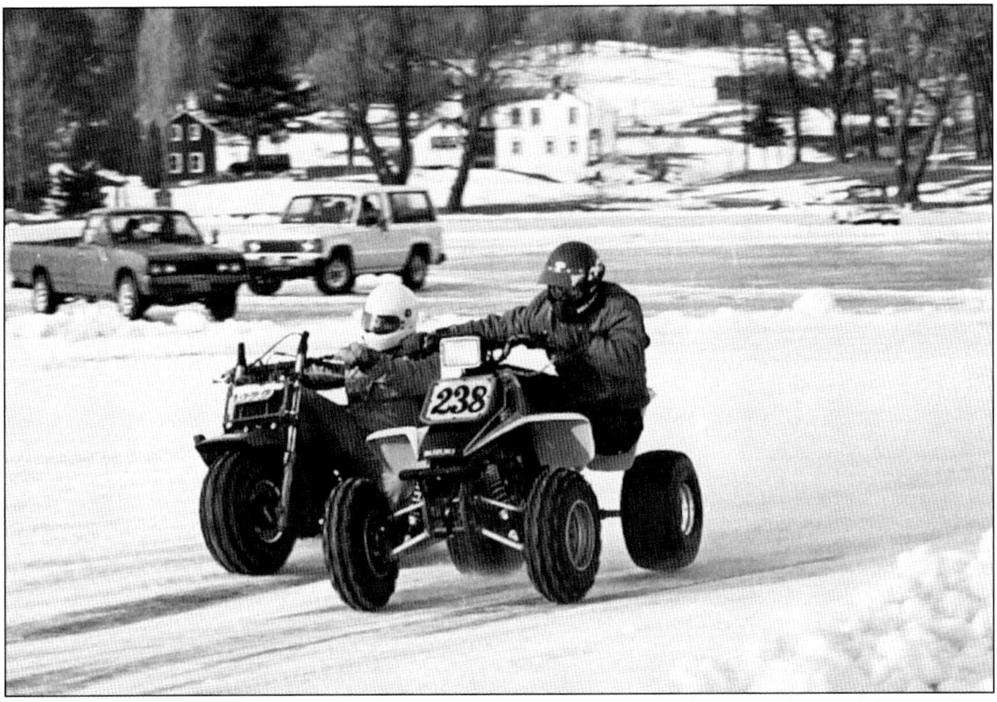

By the mid-1980s, the ATC was losing favor with the racers. Dealers were banned from selling them in 1984 as they were considered to be unsafe. Quads gradually took their place and are now a common site, both on the racetrack and on the trails. In this photograph, taken on Warner's Lake, the two machines compete together in the same class. (Photograph by Joe Corbett.)

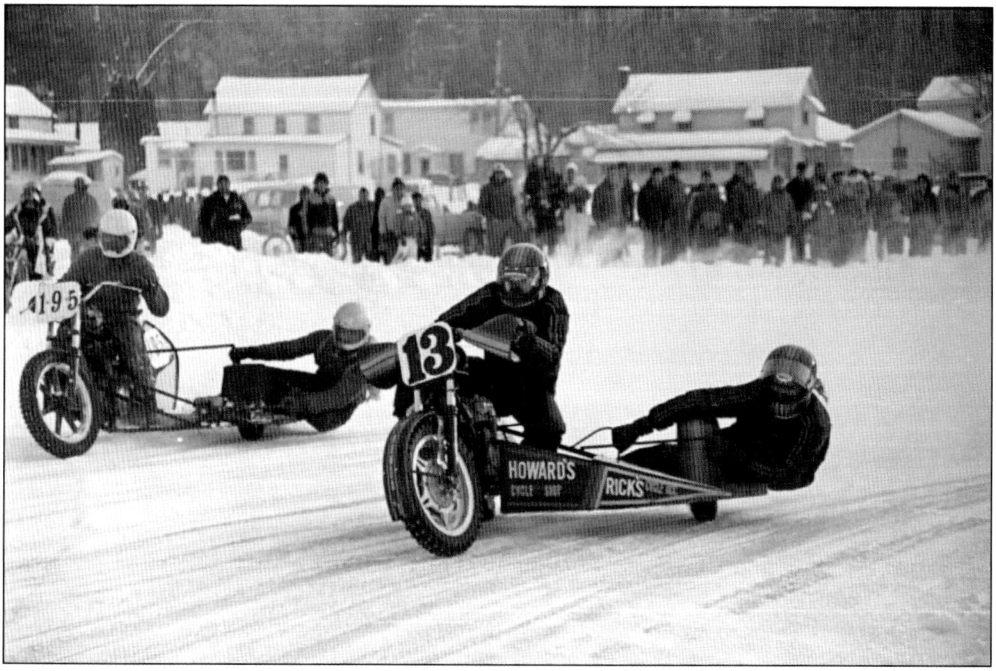

Sidecar ice racing became popular in the 1980s. All of the sidecars were homemade, leading to many different styles used to achieve the same goal. Two sidecar classes competed: the Lightweight Class of 500cc or less and the Heavyweight Class of 501cc and larger. Bill Newell and his passenger, Rick Baldwin, slide inside of Steve Ritzko and Jim Percaro in the Heavyweight Class. They had many close races throughout the years. (Photograph by Joe Corbett.)

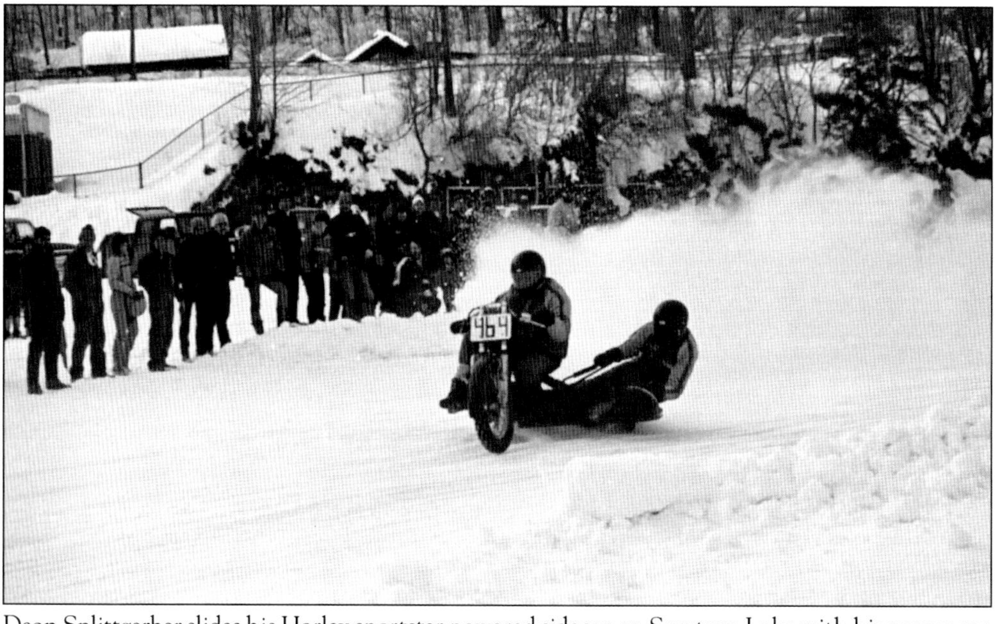

Dean Splittgerber slides his Harley sportster-powered sidecar on Saratoga Lake with his passenger, Rick Franklin, hanging on. The sidecar was built by Jack Bartkowski, who also helped the team hook it up. Franklin raced in the Lightweight Sidecar Class as well. He was a motorcycle officer in Albany for many years. (Photograph by Joe Corbett.)

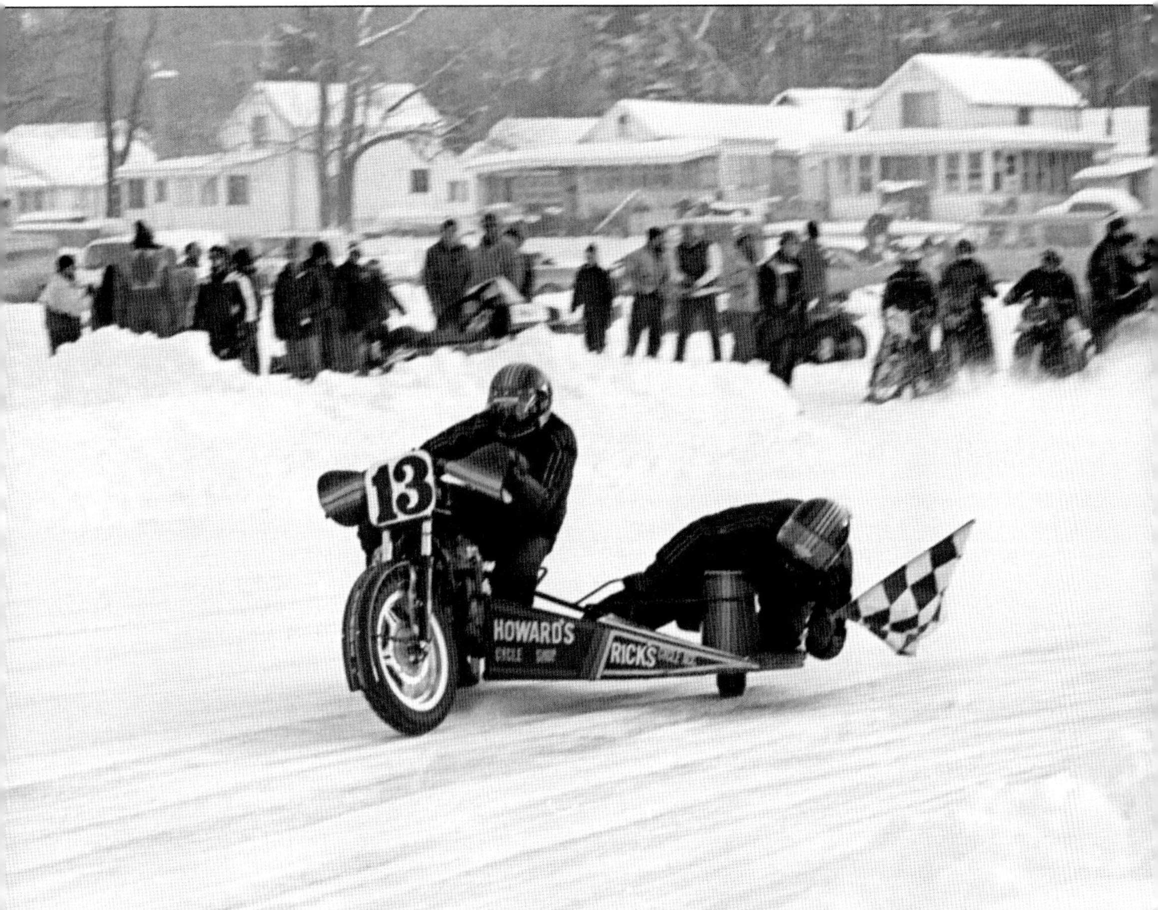

Bill Newell and Rick Baldwin slide their Honda 750cc-powered sidecar for a victory lap. This Howards Cycle Shop sidecar team was the team to beat, winning most of the races that they entered. Winning is what racers dream of. Steve McQueen said it best: "Racing is life. Anything before or after is just waiting." (Photograph by Joe Corbett.)